Techniques and Problems of Theory Construction in Sociology

Techniques and Problems of Theory Construction in Sociology

JERALD HAGE
University of Wisconsin

A Wiley-Interscience Publication

JOHN WILEY & SONS, NEW YORK · LONDON · SYDNEY · TORONTO

Library of Congress Cataloging in Publication Data

Hage, Jerald, 1932–
    Techniques and problems of theory construction in sociology.

    Bibliography: p.
    1. Sociology—Methodology. I. Title. [DNLM:
1. Sociology. 2. Sociometric technics. HM 24 H141t
1972]

HM24.H33   301'.01   72-6447
ISBN 0-471-33860-5

Printed in the United States of America

10-9 8 7 6 5 4 3 2 1

This book is dedicated to the many students in my sociology courses who have helped both with thoughtful questions and puzzled faces to stimulate the development of a number of these techniques and their criteria of utilization.

Preface

The origin of this book occurred in a failure and a desire not to make the same mistake again. In the fall of 1964, Bob Alford and I attempted to teach students how to think by using some basic classics and teaching as a team. The course left most students confused but us convinced that perhaps a better modus operandi might be found. Gradually, over the years, through a number of experiments, various techniques have been found and explicated, until it seemed justifiable to have a special course on theory construction. At each step in this development, it became increasingly clear that guidelines needed to be made explicit. What also became clear were various stumbling blocks that students had in their thinking. Thus, this present effort is an attempt to indicate what these blocks might be as well as to provide techniques for developing various aspects of a theory.

In addition to the aid of many classes in the past seven years, this book has profited from the probing critiques of two other Columbia students, who were also influenced by Hans Zetterberg, namely, Kurt Finsterbusch and James Price. Both of these men have spent much time criticizing two successive drafts. They helped identify a number of weaknesses and have made many suggestions that have found their way into these pages. There are some points about which we disagreed and therefore they are not responsible for the errors that I continue to have.

The typing has been done by a variety of people. The first draft was done by Ms. Butler in Birmingham, England, the second by Ms. Owens, and the third by Ms. Peckett, both of Madison, Wisconsin. I appreciate their patience in working with my manuscripts.

However, the biggest debt I owe is to the many students, both graduate and undergraduate, who have literally suffered through my courses as these techniques were developed. Continuously, I discovered that what seemed clear to me was not clear to them. More critical was trying to learn the many stumbling blocks that they had in thinking about problems. Finally, I particularly appreciated the fact that a number of students, especially in the beginning, took a chance on an experiment that seemed to have little opportunity for success. I hope that they find the present effort a justification for their time, energy, and hope.

JERALD HAGE

Arrigas, France
June 1972

Contents

Techniques and Problems
of Theory Construction
in Sociology

INTRODUCTION

The purpose of this book is to suggest methods for constructing theories and to specify some of the problems involved in metatheory. Techniques for finding theoretical concepts and statements, for specifying their definitions and linkages, and for ordering them into some coherent framework are discussed in the first part of the book. The second part considers several complementary issues in the area of metatheory, or the points at which sociological theory and the philosophy of science intersect.

During the past decade there has been an acceleration in the number of attempts to organize sociological facts into some coherent theoretical statements or theory (e.g., Homans, 1961; Davis, 1963; Blau, 1964; Thompson, 1967; Caplow, 1964; Hage, 1965; Mott, 1966; Berger, Zelditch, and Anderson, 1966; Price, 1967; Marsh, 1967; Etzioni, 1968). Since we have been gathering facts and speculating in sociology for some seventy years, if one counts the beginning of the *American Journal of Sociology* as a bench mark, this is indeed a promising trend. Parallel with this development has come a renewed interest in the problems of theory construction (Zetterberg, 1963; Galtung, 1967; Glaser and Strauss, 1967; Willer, 1967; Strinchcombe, 1968; Blalock, 1969), an interest that has remained largely dormant since the pioneering work of Weber (1949 in English), and Durkheim (1938 in English).

It is not strange that these two events should be occurring side by side. As hypotheses or postulates and axioms are formulated and organized into theories, some attention must be paid to how the hypotheses are stipulated and integrated theoretically. As we move closer to sets of mathematical equations, as has economics, it becomes important to consider a variety of operational issues. This is, of course, exactly why Weber and Durkheim were concerned with problems of theory construction, and exactly why they developed more elegant and advanced theories than their contemporaries (Nisbet, 1967; Kuhn, 1962).

Most of the new works on theory construction are exegeses of many of the important ideas in the philosophy of science, such as the nature of explanation, the difference between inductive and deductive reasoning, and the problem of causality (Dubin, 1969; Willer, 1967; Stinchcombe, 1968). They also provide examples, sometimes even brilliant ones, of either concepts (Stinchcombe, 1968), or hypotheses (Zetterberg, 1963; Blalock, 1969). Unfortunately, very few provide techniques as such for constructing theories, irrespective of their titles. There are two exceptions. Glaser and Strauss (1967) report their own experiences in developing concepts and suggest the importance of the comparative method with empirical data for doing so. Blalock (1969) provides some rules for axiomatic theory construction and considers some problems of constructing operational linkages, particularly the problems involved with machine solutions. But even these two exceptions concentrate on some parts of a theory to the exclusion of others. Indeed, when comparing the two books, one would hardly recognize that they are discussing the same discipline, and yet they are equally relevant. Similarly, while all of the books on theory construction have in various ways touched on metatheory, they have not attempted to delineate precisely what importance this has and how it articulates with the philosophy of science.

This present book attempts to build upon these previous efforts in two ways. The tasks of theory construction are broken into a series of steps, and each step contains a number of techniques. Rules are suggested as to when a particular technique should be used. Some attention is also given to the general strategies which are relevant to a particular part of a theory—for example, the general strategy of searching for general variables. Occasionally, there is a discussion of how particular techniques can be misused, and of the dangers of a mechanical approach to theory construction.

There are a number of different metatheoretical problems. This monograph only focuses on three or four, those that appear most relevant to the task of theory construction: the problem of the most appropriate definition of a sociological theory, the criteria for evaluating theories, the relationship between theory and knowledge, and the specification of three major theoretical orientations in sociology. How these meta-theoretical problems articulate with theory construction—that is, why are they important for this book—is also indicated.

THE TASKS OF THEORY CONSTRUCTION

Where in the world do we begin to construct a sociological theory? The most important starting point is with an interest in some problem, whether intellectual or practical. It may be a vague and ill-defined interest, but it is something that we at least like to talk about. My own interests, for example, have centered around the problem of social change. This problem, however, covers too much territory—the first stumbling block in constructing a theory. We need to sharpen the focus of our interest by selecting a more manageable part, more specifically, a single variable. It might be the degree of resistance to social change or the rate of social conflict or the amount of affection in a relationship. Whatever it is, once we have refined our interest this far, we have taken a major step towards facilitating our thinking about a theory involving this variable. This does not mean that we have abandoned our interest in the larger problem. It remains our ultimate objective. But we can reach this goal much more easily if we start small. If we do not, our interests will remain too diffuse.

Once we have sharpened our focus, we are ready to begin. Just as we have suggested that our interests can be subdivided into smaller problems, so too we can subdivide a theory into a number of more manageable parts, or separate tasks, in the process of constructing a theory. Chapters 1 through 6 discuss those tasks.

At the beginning of each chapter, there is a discussion of general strategy. This is critical for several reasons. I believe that the lack of development of sociological knowledge is due less to the inherent difficulties of our object of study (think of what econometricians have dealt with) than to the wrong choice of strategies. In any case, particular strategies would seem to be helpful to our thought processes, at least as guidelines for action. In contrast, other strategies seem to hinder these processes.

Once the strategy is suggested, the particular tactics of implementation are discussed. There are usually between three and six techniques in each chapter. Some of the techniques require a knowledge of the literature, perhaps it might be better to say a particular approach to reading. Some of the techniques involve a certain way of conceptualizing the task at hand. Examples of such techniques are comparing several diverse contents for the discovery of new variables (Chapter 1), comparing diverse case studies in the search for causes and consequences (Chapter 2), asking why and how (Chapter 4), and the suppose-if technique (Chapter 6). These examples might be thought of as systematic ways of extending one's imagination. A number of techniques involve the capacity to change levels of abstraction. They are difficult to use, and yet if one can master them, they pay rich rewards.

The techniques provide pathways that are likely to lead to a successful conclusion, that is, to a theory. They may be likened to the role of the trainer in sports. He points out "dos" and "don'ts," but the athlete still must practice and perform—with a considerable amount of effort. Or, for those who think that constructing theories is an art, this book is like a class in making pottery. Almost everyone can be shown how to throw a pot, but this does not mean that everyone will make a beautiful vase—there are considerable differences in creative ability. But at least, there is hope that most can make a serviceable pitcher, and that is all that this book aims to accomplish.

An attempt has been made to provide a variety of techniques because there are many kinds of individuals. Likewise, while the techniques are discussed as separate and isolated acts, in fact they are not. One blends into the next. The unfolding of a complete theory is a unique event. For this reason, the ordering of the chapters is somewhat arbitrary. The particular sequence seems to work the best with most students, but it is not the best for everyone. In this sense, the reader is advised to use the chapters in the order in which his own needs emerge.

A large number of illustrations are given, at least one for each technique and frequently several. Some attempt has been given to choose areas that would have wide appeal, such as the writings of Marx, Durkheim, Simmel, Weber, Merton, and Homans, and the problems of stratification, conflict, centralization, deviance, and survival. Most of the examples are, however, either about societies, organizations, or role-relationships. These are the areas that I know best and therefore the book is inherently limited by this. Some of the same examples are discussed in more than one context. And, several extended examples from my own work are given in Chapters 5 and 6. This is particularly important since highly formalized theories are rare in sociology. It also represents an illustration of what can be accomplished with some of the techniques discussed.

In the final analysis, regardless of the number of illustrations, the reader is most likely to understand only with practice in using these techniques. Again, our analogy of training for sports is instructive. The procedures are not automatic and require sustained mental effort. But this is what makes theory construction fun and personally rewarding. As we achieve some progress—discovering some new concepts or theoretical statements—our patience is rewarded with a new vision of our social world. Theory construction is exactly like being an explorer and it contains all the fun of adventure as well as the hard work.

PROBLEMS OF METATHEORY

A book on theory construction has to consider more than just the strategies and tactics of how to construct various parts of a theory and then piecing these together into some coherent whole. There are a number of related problems, which might be called, as Merton has suggested, problems in metatheory.

The relationship between theory construction and metatheory is somewhat akin to the association between techniques of doing a survey and the general issue of when to use a survey. Problems of metatheory raise more general issues, they provide criteria of choice or standards. The consideration of strategies at the beginning of each chapter in Part One is an example of a metatheoretical problem and quite separate from the specific techniques.

There are other issues as well. These have been placed in Part Two to indicate that while they articulate with theory construction and must be included in a discussion about it, they concern different kinds of ideas. In Chapter 7, a definition of theory is given and reasons are suggested as to why this definition should be preferred over several others that one might want to consider. Once this is done, we have a standard by which we can evaluate whether something is a theory or a fragment of a theory, and more specifically, we know what is missing. The rest of the chapter considers standards for evaluating a theory and how theory, as defined, relates to the development of knowledge.

Another set of metatheoretical problems revolves around the specification of theoretical orientations. These might be called ways of looking at problems in sociology. They are not theories in themselves, but the start of a major theory. Chapter 8 defines theoretical orientations, con-

siders several alternatives, and specifies three major orientations in sociology: structural-functionalism, value analysis, and system analysis.
These particular orientations have been selected because they represent
such diverse ways of thinking and because they can be applied to a
variety of social collectives, from groups to societies. Again, their relationship to theory construction is apparent. In many ways they inform the
kind of theory that is built.

Although there is an exploration of some basic problems in metatheory, there are hardly satisfactory solutions for all of them. Readers will
disagree with some that are offered, but at least the issues are raised in a
general context. This encourages conversation and stimulates awareness,
which is all that one can hope for. In this sense, this book is very much
in the spirit of Lazarsfeld and Rosenberg's *The Language of Social
Research* (1955), which appeared at the time of the development of
empirical tools and methods in sociology. This book arrives at a time
when theory construction is more and more becoming a topic and a
subject for courses. Hopefully, this work can aid the present development.

PART ONE

The Tasks
of Theory
Construction

CHAPTER ONE

Theoretical Concepts

Theories can be started in many ways. The simplest way to begin is to search for some theoretical concepts to describe the social phenomena that interest us. If we want to examine specific aspects of our daily routine, we first have to have concepts to point to what we are examining. Labels like role set, gemeinschaft, the degree of stratification, and the level of education are intellectual pointers, highlighting what previously had been dim and obscure.

Even before we begin our search for new theoretical concepts or labels of social phenomena, we need to recognize that there are two major kinds. There are concepts like role set and gemeinschaft that label *categories* or classes of phenomena. There are concepts like the degree of stratification and the level of education that label *dimensions* of phenomena. Although both are needed, we are more interested in the latter kind of theoretical concept.

GENERAL VARIABLE CONCEPTS AND SPECIFIC
NONVARIABLE CONCEPTS

Since Weber's famous work on ideal types (1949), many sociologists have looked for typologies of nonvariable concepts, or at least sets of categorical concepts (Etzioni, 1961a and 1968; Blau and Scott, 1962; see review of organizational literature in Pugh et al., 1963; Nisbet, 1967 and 1970). An examination of the index of any sociological introductory text provides a good list of them. Sociologists, following the example of biologists, have felt that until we can classify, we do not have any hope of analysis. There is, however, more than one way to describe social phenomena. We can use general variables, that is, culture-free and timeless continua, or we can use specific nonvariables, that is, historically bounded categories. Naturally, there are various shades between these two extremes: some variables are more variable than others!

The list of general variables and nonvariables in Table 1.1 indicates

Table 1.1   Examples of Nonvariable and General Variable Concepts

Nonvariables	General Variables
Democracy	Degree of centralization
Capitalism	Degree of stratification
Revolution	Conflict rate
Urban	Population density
Bureaucracy	Proportion of administrative staff
Professional occupations	Level of professional training
Organic organizations	Amount of program change
Protestant	Degree of religious attendance
Blue-collar worker	Prestige rank or occupational income
Young	Years of age

some of the dependence upon categories in sociology. Democracy is an either-or phenomenon, a specific nonvariable or categorical concept, whereas the degree of centralization, a general variable, has as many cutting points as our operationalization allows. (See Ch. 3 on the problem of how to operationalize.) This is not true of democracy. Regardless of the number of indicators we might have, the concept categorizes a society or political system as being democratic or not democratic.

Perhaps what is most important is that democracy only applies to some societies (Athens, Weimar Republic of Germany, Third Republic of France, for example), and at some points of time. To make matters worse, democracy like many categorical concepts takes on different meanings in the same society. Democracy in the United States has meant something different in 1789 and in 1889, and will mean something else in 1989. In contrast, all societies can be placed along the continuum of centralization. Imperial Rome, the Massachusetts Bay Colony, and the People's Republic of China each has some degree of centralization. In other words, centralization is a dimension that they have in common. This is not to say that democracy and centralization are necessarily equivalent ideas. There are many things implied by the former that are not included in the latter. They are similar enough, however, to make their descriptive differences more striking. (For a slightly different comparison, see Meadows, 1967, p. 83.)

Bureaucracy is a popular concept in the study of organizations (Hall, 1963). But it means different things to different people. It is a time-bound idea as Weber himself argued (1947, pp. 337–338) that only admits of a presence or absence coding. General variables such as the proportion of administrative staff or the degree of formalization, or even again the degree of centralization, allow for a wide variety of scores, so that all organizations are placed on the same dimension. The reader might immediately ask, is not bureaucracy measurable, and are not some organizations more bureaucratic than others? A yes answer is true but somewhat misleading. What is frequently measured is not bureaucracy but a series of dimensions such as size, formalization, or proportion of administrative staff; an organization that scores high on one or more of these is then labeled bureaucratic. Despite the use of general dimensions, the idea of categorizing something as bureaucratic or not still remains even though the scaling is more subtle. The point to remember is that there are differences between this statement and the statement that 90 percent of the organizations are bureaucratic, the typical usage of the nonvariable concept.

The issue of whether the theoretical concepts are general in the sense of applying to all social phenomenon irrespective of time and place is important, but even more important is that the concepts represent continua, that is, they vary. Sociological ideas, such as norm, culture, and value are timeless entities, but the concepts do not have dimension or variation. We need to specify the properties of norms or culture or values, such as their degree of specificity or the extensiveness or their popularity (Morris, 1966). Once we have some variation, once we have a continuum as opposed to a class concept, then we have reached the first step towards the development of verbal statements about that variation.

Here it might be noted that the key issue is how one thinks about the concepts at hand. Sometimes a person will use a variable as though it were a class. The way in which one employs theoretical concepts, whether as classes or as continua, is the critical issue.

In terms of scaling theory, we might make the following distinction. Classes are nominal scales. Continua are ordinal, interval, and ratio scales. Furthermore, as we move toward a ratio scale, we obtain more and more variation in our variable. In addition, to be a general variable the scale must be culture-free and timeless. Interestingly enough, most but not all interval and ratio scales have this characteristic.

The Advantages of General Variables

There are several reasons why we are concentrating our search for theoretical concepts on general variables. *General variables, by being applicable to all cultures and historical epochs, allow us the possibility of finding a universal law.* If we utilize Protestantism as a theoretical concept in our hypothesis as did Weber (1930), we are limited to the Western world since the fifteenth century. There are some nonvariables such as revolution that appear to be general. But to find a revolution prior to seventeenth-century England is not easy. This may be a problem of semantics since unsuccessful slave revolts are not called revolutions. In any event, revolutions have not occurred in England since the seventeenth century. What has occurred is the increase or decrease in the degree of conflict. If one or more of our theoretical concepts in our hypothesis is a specific nonvariable, then our hypothesis is only as general as the most specific category in the hypothesis. For example, the statement that industrialization causes revolutions is limited by the lack of generality in the concepts of revolution and of industrialization. If we change the concepts and thus the statement to read something like sudden increases in the degree of complexity produce increases in the conflict rate, we have concepts and a theoretical statement that is much more general.

General variables also make classification more subtle. To use even several nonvariables, such as wealthy, old, or professional, in describing a person as a social being is not as informative as saying he has a million dollars, he is 65 years of age, and has had 16 years of education. This shift seems trivial and yet this is precisely the difference in subtlety between, in these instances, general nonvariables, either-or categories, type concepts, and general variables, continua, such as income, education, or age.

Even if our only objective is to classify and not to construct a theory, general variables permit a wide variety of scores, whereas concepts like Protestant or white-collar worker do not. They deny the many shades of grey that exist. This is true for all ideal types, nominal scales, and categories, whether general or specific.

Although it is harder to demonstrate, general variables make thinking much easier. Usually the nonvariable category has a wide variety of connotations and, as a consequence, it becomes difficult to formulate a hypothesis that would be true for all of the various meanings. Take the concept of profession (Goss, 1959; Goode, 1960; Wilensky, 1964; Hall, 1968 and 1969). For some, profession means the service ideal, for others expertise, for others a certain kind of training, for still others licensing. Hypotheses that are likely to be true for one of these meanings may not be true for others, and therefore, impossible to formulate. In contrast, general variables such as the level of professional training usually have one meaning or definition which makes them easier to handle. Compare population density with the concept of urbanism, or the degree of stratification with the concept of capitalism. Even the variable amount of program change, as difficult as it is to define and measure, is simpler than the concept of an organic organization (Burns and Stalker, 1961; Aiken and Hage, 1971).

What evidence is there that the search for general variables is likely to be a better approach in theory construction than the search for nonvariables? Cassirer (1953, Ch. 1) notes that in each of the major scientific disciplines, including biology, little intellectual progress was made until the field shifted from nonvariable to general variable concepts. In attempting to understand why this is so, he suggests several consequences of nonvariable concepts for perceiving reality and thinking about these perceptions. With a nonvariable concept, we classify an object. In so doing, there is the presumption that all of the reality has been captured with the label. The label "socialist society" totally describes the reality of a particular nation, or so it seems to the researcher who uses this descriptive tag. In contrast, general variable concepts do not carry this presumption. Once a society is scored on one dimension, such as the amount of regulation of the economy, along with the other societies in the sample, the researcher is encouraged to locate scores on other dimensions because he recognizes that he has only one continuum among many, perhaps an infinite number of them. Nonvariable concepts, describing all with one label, deny the complexity of reality, whereas variable concepts recognize this epistemological fact. In other words, it is easier to agree about a shade of grey than whether something is black or white.

Cassirer (1953) observes that with nonvariable concepts the process of generalizing or thinking as outlined by Aristotle is a steady movement away from complexity and subtlety in description to simplicity and crudity. To illustrate this, he uses the example of moving from the more specific category or substance of man to mammal to animal to living organism, and finally to all matter. Yet, at each more general level, less and less is known because the thinking and generalizing process with nonvariable concepts consists of eliminating properties. We know less and less about more and more. In contrast, general variable concepts eliminate qualifying adjectives or else substitute more complex ideas as they are made more general. To move from the frequency of *group political interaction* to *political interaction* to *interaction* in no way results in less information. Instead of reducing the number of adjectives defining the category, the thought process is to eliminate adjectives modifying the noun; we know the same piece of information about many more units of analysis. If the hypothesis involving the variable remains true at each level we have considerably expanded the range of our knowledge, while at the same time codifying it. This is less likely with nonvariable concepts, especially those that are specific to time and place.

There are other reasons besides those mentioned by Cassirer (1953) why nonvariable concepts have retarded the development of theory in each of the disciplines. One of the most important reasons is a lack of agreement upon what we mean by the concept. Primarily because there is an attempt to capture many ideas, and this is especially true with ideal types, a variety of connotations are included at the same time. The concept becomes complicated and thus difficult to work with. Attention becomes deflected from how it relates to other concepts to what is its best definition. How many arguments and discussions have there been over the meaning of Weber's concept of rational-legal authority? Or how many terminological pitfalls are there to a concept like capitalism, or worse yet, democracy? Variables like degree of centralization or amount of religious attendance are much easier to handle in this regard.

Many sociologists have not used variable concepts because they appear to capture so little. The degree of centralization is not a complete translation of democracy. A general variable does not include all that one wants for an adequate description. But again, here lies a paradox. By taking more simple concepts such as general variables as opposed to ideal types, we move toward what Cassirer suggests, finding a number of continua—and thus a much more complex description than is possible with any ideal type. The category of Protestantism, which excludes all individuals who belong to other religions, can be replaced by five or six variables that are applicable not only to Protestants but to other religions as well. The frequency of attendance, behavioral acceptance of doctrine, attitudinal acceptance of doctrine, and frequency of interaction with those of the same beliefs are helpful not only with adherents of Protestantism, but Judaism, Catholicism, Buddhism, and any other kind of group or organization, whether religious or not. If the researcher wants to, he can still restrict his analysis to the amount of Protestant attendance. But the point remains: we replace one nonvariable concept with a large number of general variables. In this way, the complaint that the real meaning of the concept has been destroyed is likely to be forestalled; everyone's favorite definition becomes another dimension. Probably in the process of this conversion, much more of the subtlety of the original nonvariable concept will become apparent.

Empirically, nonvariable concepts create difficulties as well. Precisely because they are so crude at the same time that they give the illusion of being so subtle, it becomes difficult to test hypotheses with them, even if some should be developed. In practice, we find that only a certain proportion of Negroes are uneducated, or that only a percentage of all workers vote for the Democratic Party, or that only some capitalist societies are democratic. While there can be many reasons why these theoretical statements are partially true or only true in a certain proportion of cases, it is important to observe that one reason is that the categories Negro, worker, Democratic Party, capitalist, are so crude that much is included that should be excluded, and vice versa. For example, instead of Negro, we may really want the general variable, the level of income. In the United States in 1976, some blacks but not all may be at the low end of the poverty scale. In this sense the level of income is a much more precise description because it excludes rich blacks and includes poor whites. If our hypothesis is the lower the level of income, the lower the level of education, then we have a theoretical statement that has some possibility of being universal. It can apply not only to blacks but to whites, not only to the United States but to the aborigines of Australia, the Serbs in the Austria-Hungarian Empire, or the crones in Astrolax, and not only in 1976 but in 1796 and 1697.

It is easy to demonstrate that as we reduce error—that is, exclude what should be excluded and include what should be included—we increase the size of the correlation between two variables. A most happy consequence!

The Strategy of Searching for General Variables

General variables help us find universal laws, they are more subtle in description and classification, and they make thinking easier. We should, therefore, concentrate most of our intellectual energy in searching for general variables and not specific nonvariables. This is to recommend a strategy somewhat at odds with current practice. The preference for nonvariable concepts, whether general or specific, is quite understandable.

There is an intuitive appeal to Weber's many specific nonvariable types. In short, who wants to argue with Aristotle?

The advantages of general variables have not gone unnoticed. If one compares the journal articles of the last few years with those of ten years ago, one sees that the incidence of general variables has increased. We find occupations being ranked in terms of status, religions being interpreted in terms of their relative emphasis on aceticism, and various ethnic groups being described as having minority status. All of these are attempts to find more general concepts of description and classification. This fact, the movement of the discipline towards general variables is perhaps the most powerful argument why the strategy of searching for general variables should be selected. Most sociologists have been forced, as were the biologists, the chemists, and the physicists before them, to find general variables to develop the theories that they need.

This is not to say that all sociological theories should be constructed of general variables and nothing else. We need general nonvariables to label our units of analysis, such as group, organization, and society, and to help us order our concepts into primitive and derived terms. (For a discussion of primitive and derived terms, see Chapter 5.) We also need nonvariables to delineate critical qualities along some dimension. For instance, although conflict rate is an important dimension, there is a just, noticeable difference between revolution and protest marches, between high and moderate conflict rates. For this reason, techniques are given for searching for nonvariables as well as variables in the third section of this chapter. *But our main concern and strategy is to search for the many dimensions describing a unit of analysis and not new units of analysis.*

In summary, we need to search primarily for general variables. They are a surer pathway for the construction of sociological theories because they are universal, simpler to work with, and perhaps most importantly, they help us to recognize that we need many of them. A sociological phenomenon is incredibly complex, and therefore, any intellectual strategy that helps us to recognize this fact is preferable.

SEARCHING FOR GENERAL VARIABLES

There are five techniques which are useful in the search for new theoretical concepts in the form of general variables. Not all of them are of equal importance or utility. The best techniques for both the facility and applicability with which they can be employed are the last two. The first three are more limited. Criteria of appropriateness are suggested, followed by one or more illustrations. With several of the techniques, warnings are given about how they can be misapplied as well as misused.

Converting Nonvariables Into General Variables

One situation many researchers find themselves in is the problem of finding some new concepts in an area that has been popular. In this situation the technique of converting nonvariables into variables can be a helpful one. Despite our criticism of the strategy of ideal types or kinds, previous efforts in their direction have not been entirely in vain. Frequently, they provide a springboard for our search of general variables. These previous efforts are most likely to be fruitful under the following conditions: when the nonvariables are relatively general or specific; when there has been an attempt to be more than just descriptive; and when the nonvariables have endured for some time. In particular, the writings of Weber (1947 and 1963), Durkheim (1933 and 1951), Simmel (1955), and Marx and Engels (1959), are fruitful sources of general variables because these writers were interested in moving beyond classification to some form of analysis. As a consequence, their works contain a number of general continua. The examples of Weber's kinds of social action and Durkheim's kinds of solidarity are discussed below to illustrate how one can convert nonvariables into variables.

We do not have to rely only upon the ancients and their wisdom. Contemporary work can also be a fruitful source of general variables. Again, the same criteria apply. If we find many sociologists using the same nonvariable concept, then we can suspect that there are one or more general variables involved. The discussion of democracy, capitalism, and kindred theoretical concepts suggests this. Below, the concept of sex, another similarly permanent general nonvariable and one that occupies contemporary minds as much, if not more, than the thought of our wise forefathers, is discussed.

The Case of Converting Sets of Categories. Even when the nonvariable concepts are male or female, presumably the most natural dichotomy in the social science literature (Tittle, 1969; and Phillips and Segal, 1969), there are implicit dimensions that authors use as the basis of their analysis of why there are differences between the sexes. For example, when Durkheim (1951, pp. 210–215) discusses the difference between the suicide rates of men and women, he suggests intelligence is the clue. In other words, because women are less intelligent, they have lower suicide rates!

We do not have to agree with Durkheim and his male chauvinism to notice that there is a lesson to be learned. As soon as the author attempts to explain differences between the proportion of men and women who do something—anything—the author is forced to find a variable. Frequently but not always he slips the general variable into a single sentence. But once written, it is easy for us to find.

The procedures for converting any pair, triplet, or any number of categories like male-female is a simple one. We read rapidly. We look for some general variable, culturally and temporally free, that helps explain why there are differences.

Of course, sometimes we will not find it in the author's discussion. There may even be no discussion at all. Statistical yearbooks are filled with general and specific nonvariables. Every page contains a possible thesis. When there is no explication, then the fifth technique, discussed below, is recommended.

To give an example from my own work, I encountered differences between two nominal categories, surgeon and internist (Hage, 1963). The question was why? A search of the existing literature on physicians led to the recognition of the basic dimensions of the relative reliance on consultations in diagnosis and the relative reliance on reading as a method of learning. Note that these same general variables can be used for differentiating a large number of occupations, not just interns in medicine and surgery, and allow for the development of hypotheses regarding resistance to change.

Another and more interesting example is Durkheim's suggestion (1951, p. 148) that the real reason for the differences between the suicide rates of Protestants, Catholics, and Jews is the degree of regulation of life prescribed by the religion, or to use his terms, the number of dogmas, and not their content, whether for or against suicide. It should be noted that this variable—degree of regulation—is contained in only one sentence in his long discussion about the differences between the three religions. Once we discover in the discourse the implied dimension, we can reformulate his hypothesis (as others have done) as follows: the greater the degree of religious regulation, the lower the suicide rate among its adherents.

The Case of Converting Types. Sometimes the author has done some of the work for us by organizing the sets of categories into several types, that is, a typology. Frequently the use of the word "type" as opposed to "kind" is a clue that we are likely to find several general variables without much effort beyond reading rapidly and being aware of the characteristics of a general variable. Barton (1955) has called this procedure substructuring and his illustration with Fromm's kinds of familial relationships is informative.

The procedure consists largely in reading the original discussion closely, attempting to find the implicit dimensions that can derive the kinds or types in some property space, as Barton calls it. Since he has discussed this, we need not elaborate on his work. Instead we shall provide an example of it.

To illustrate Barton's technique, we might examine the key concepts of social action in Weber (1947, pp. 115–118). Some of them were primitive terms, that is, concepts useful for deriving other concepts (see Ch. 5). There are several dimensions in Weber's discussion of his types of social action. A major defining element is the degree of planning, another is the amount of self-interest, and a third is the number of goals or objectives (see Fig. 1.1). These dimensions were found by reading rapidly.

Degree of Planning[b]	Degree of Self-Interest[a]	
	Sake of self	Sake of others
Non-self-conscious	Habitual	Affectual
Self-conscious	Zweckrational	Wertrational[c]

[a] See Weber (1947, p. 115 and paragraph 3 of p. 116).

[b] See Weber (1947, p. 116, paragraph 3, and p. 117, paragraph 4).

[c] See Weber (1947, p. 117, paragraph 4). Note the consistent contrast between a single ultimate value and multiple self-interest ends that might be in conflict.

Figure 1.1 Converting Nonvariables into General Variables: Weber's Types of Social Action.

Variables can almost leap from the page once we have trained ourselves to look for them.

By reading the discussion of a typology or by finding an implicit one, as is the Weber example, we discover not only a few general variables but some implied hypotheses as well. Weber implies there was only a choice between multiple goals of self-interest and a single idealist goal, an unpleasant choice indeed. Also note how much better we can begin to understand Weber's concepts.

A similar case to the implied typology is the paired comparison, that is, the case when two nonvariables are explicitly employed as a dichotomy.

An illustration is Durkheim's (1933) famous mechanical and organic solidarity (Table 1.2). The procedures remain the same. We read rapidly, looking for dimensions. In the process of reading the division of labor, we can find many. Some are obvious and others are not. The division of labor, moral density, and social density are well known since they are specific hypotheses of Durkheim, but less familiar ones are also included, indicating how rich some of his writings are. The reader might skim *The Division of Labor in Society* and see how many general variables he discovers. There are many more than those in Table 1.2.

Table 1.2   Converting Nonvariables Into General Variables: Durkheim's Dichotomy of Mechanical and Organic Solidarity

Mechanical Solidarity		Organic Solidarity
Low	Numbers of social relationships (p. 257)	High
Low	Population density (social density) (pp. 257, 261–262)	High
Low	Frequency of interaction (moral density) (p. 257)	High
Low	Communication rates (p. 259)	High
Low	Transportation rates (p. 259)	High
Low	Population size (pp. 260–262)	High
Low	Frequency of conflict (pp. 266–270)	High
High	Intensity of conflict (p. 270)	Low
Low	Level of welfare (pp. 270–271)	High
Low	Level of production (p. 272)	High
Low	Quality of production (p. 272)	High
Low	Intellectual interests (p. 273)	High
Low	Sensibility (p. 273)	High

SOURCE: Durkheim, 1933; also see Burns and Stalker, 1961, for an attempt to apply some of these ideas to organizations. The differences are illuminating.

Gemeinschaft or gesellschaft, folk or urban, sacred or secular, capitalism or socialism, democracy or autocracy, and many other pairs represent fruitful places to begin a search for general variables (see Nisbet, 1967, for his discussion of five famous paired concepts in sociology). The test for the general variables is: does the dimension appear to be a timeless, culture-free continuum on which all the analytical units can be located without too many being at one end of the scale or the other. This is a very simple test to apply. If there is any doubt, one can think of several disparate units of analysis (this is defined in the third section of this chapter). For example, we might choose several kinds of social action and then ask ourselves if can we score each of them on the number of goals involved, one of the dimensions implied in Weber's discussion. If all the cases we think of can be scored, and, more significant, if we have chosen our cases to be representative of different times and places, then we have a general variable. For example, if we think of social actions, like talking about the weather, playing sports, studying for exams, and dating, we ask ourselves can we apply the number of goals as a dimension to these various kinds of acts. Interestingly enough, not only can we, but we discover that the same act can vary with the individual and his cultural context. The units of analysis, that is, studying for exams, sometimes involves one goal and sometimes more than one. This is the way in which we know that we have a general continuum.

Reducing Several Variables to a Basic Dimension

The technique of reducing several variables to a single basic dimension is also one of the procedures for finding primitive terms (see Ch. 5). It is most useful where there appear to be a number of variables with an underlying dimension. It is perhaps one of the hardest techniques to employ because it requires an ability to change levels of abstraction, moving from high specificity to high generality and back again.

The Case of Definitional Reduction. Zetterberg (1963) has provided several illustrations of this technique under the title of definition reduction; the title suggests the method. If the concepts have the same implicit theoretical definition then it is possible to substitute the common definition for each of the concepts to which it applies. Suppose we note that the implied definition in a number of concepts such as group, organization, and society is social collective. We can substitute the concept social collective for each of these other terms. In this way, we "discover" a variable that has been used in one area of sociology has not been used in another. Although stratification is a key sociological concept, it has not been employed much in the study of organizations. There are many other illustrations of variables used for one kind of social collective or in one institutional sector but not in another.

Perhaps the best illustration of the reduction of several general variables into one is the new variable rank. Implicit in the ideas of level of wealth, level of power, level of status, and level of education is a common theoretical definition: differential ranks. (See Galtung, 1966.) Therefore, the level of wealth, of power, of status, and of education can be replaced by the single more general variable, the level of rank, that is, high rank, medium rank, and low rank. If we have hypotheses about the association between the variables of wealth, power, status, and education, and variables describing group behavior and attitudes, these can now be replaced by a single hypothesis, *the variable containing level of rank*. Lynes (1950) applied stratification theory to the area of taste. His discussion of highbrows, middlebrows, and lowbrows, while in some respects a parody, has an element of truth in it. Parallel to the bourgeoisie, aristocracy, and proletariat are the classes of tastemakers in the arts and culture. The many ways in which individuals can be ranked have been explored in sociology (Zetterberg, 1962; Galtung, 1966).

How does one find the implicit definition? Chapter 3 provides several techniques, but, in general, reading rapidly and looking for synonyms is the simplest way of beginning. If the synonym is on a higher level of abstraction, then we know we have some opportunities to create a new general variable.

The Case of Analogy. Another source of more general variables is the fruitful comparison. The latter is successful as long as there is a general variable that describes both cases being compared equally well. The test of appropriateness is a simple one. If we find analogies compelling, then we probably have some general variable implicit if not explicit in the description.

For instance Goffman (1961) has made an interesting contrast between the mental patient and the convict. Implicit in his analysis is the degree of coercive control over the clients. Once this becomes the bridge between mental patients and convicts—they are both highly controlled, at least in the days when the book was written—practices in one institution are translatable into the context of the other. A more explicit use of this method is found in Elkins book, *Slavery* (1968), in which the consequences of servitude are surmised on the basis of what is known about the effects of concentration camps. Using analogies seems to be the source of much of Simmel's (1955) inspiration, even though he never made explicit the particular dimension that allowed the comparison. For example, much of the brilliant discussion of conflict hinges upon the variables of the intensity of subjective conflict, hate, and the intensity of objective conflict, damage or loss to the other party, and how direct or indirect the conflict is. With these links, Simmel is able to bring together quite disparate kinds of conflict. Perhaps the clearest example of this is found where Simmel lumps together socialism, children's games, price competition, etc., using the general variable, competition (1955, pp. 73–74). Unlike the previous illustration where the search is for the common definition, here the problem is to find the more abstract dimension that gives meaning to the juxtaposition.

Combining Scores to Create a New Variable

The technique of combining several variable scores to create a new variable, or general continuum, rests primarily on an existing empirical literature. It is the pattern of research findings that implies the need for a general variable. This technique is most useful when where are exceptions to a hypothesis, particularly if the correlations are usually as high as .5 or .6, or higher. Another case when this technique can successfully be used is when we have a rare phenomenon, such as a riot or revolution. In both these situations we can look for two variables that normally are not found together and which, for whatever causes, are now associated. This has been called deviant case analysis.

The Case of the Discrepancy. The best-known illustration of this is Lenski's new variable, status crystallization, which he calls status disequilibrium (1954, 1966, 1967; also see Smith, 1969). In general, we know that the level of education is correlated with the level of prestige or status. Although the correlations are high, they are not perfect. The exceptions, those with rank discrepancy, appear to have different attitudes and behavior than the majority who conform to the hypothesis about consistency in rank. (Admittedly, this point is still being debated in the literature.) For example, we might normally expect that the higher the rank, the more conservative the political attitudes are, which is generally true, but when there are discrepancies among wealth, education, and power, it appears not to be so. Hence, the birth of a new idea, rank disequilibrium, a variable created by adding a high score on education with a low score on income, or vice versa. It should be pointed out that the theoretical utility of the new variable is measured by the fact that it accounts for exceptions by indicating differential responses, and this is an important test because Blalock and others have noted that if the two original variables account for the variance, there is no need for a third.

This illustration provides one general rule for the creation of new variables by combining variable scores. Once we find an exception to our hypothesis, but with a pattern in the data, we would seem to have a need for a discrepancy variable. One place where this is done a great deal is where there are differences between attitudes and behavior. Here discrepancy variables—creed without deed—have become important problems in their own right.

The Case of the Rare Event. Another kind of empirical situation when the use of scores on two variables to create a third variable is indicated is a social phenomenon that seldom occurs. This may be a collective event such as a riot or a part of the distribution that represents a small proportion of the cases.

As an illustration, Svalastoga (1965) explains the basic distribution of rewards in society by suggesting that those at the top have several qualities not normally found together. Therefore, they earn a disproportionate share of the income or status of power as a result. Typically one expects two dimensions are either negatively associated or else have a small correlation. But if, for whatever reason, they are found together, there is multiplicative change in behavior, with a correspondingly different reaction from society, that is, much higher rewards. For example, the personal qualities may be creativity and intelligence. Again, the reasoning is much like that above; one finds a discrepancy to a hypothesis, an association between scores that is rare.

This same theme, one that has many implications for theory construction, runs through much of Weber's work, *Protestant Ethic and the Spirit of Capitalism* (1930). The hypothesis is that the three or more values that composed the ethic could not be maintained simultaneously for long because they produced considerable psychological tension in the religious adherents. For Weber, this tension was the source of the extra motivation or drive needed for the industrial revolution. The theoretical beauty of this reasoning is that the tension on a group level can be sustained for only short periods of time, even if its consequences remain long afterwards. This helps understand the possible causes of sudden and short bursts of group activity. Similarly, the problem of revolution may be the conjunction of several variables together that produce a multiple effect in the conflict rate.

This technique does not necessarily depend upon other writer's discussions. Instead we look for a certain pattern of findings, the exceptions to our rules or theoretical statements, and these become the stimulus for thought. Our thought or search is guided by the observation that frequently the explanation is to be found in two things occurring together that typically do not.

Comparing Diverse Contents to Discover New Variables

The three previous techniques for the discovery of variables largely depend upon the literature, theoretical and empirical, and are not appropriate for original units of analysis. We also need a technique that can be applied at any time, whether there is a literature or not. The technique of comparing diverse contents would appear to be a method that can be employed whenever we want.

The procedures are as follows. *First,* specify the unit of analysis, including some definition. If possible, it is desirable to make the definition clear and precise by limiting it to one of the several possible meanings. Then it will be easier to find examples. The *second step* is to write down diverse examples of the analytical unit, being sure to provide as much diversity as possible (Glaser and Strauss, 1967). Since sociologists consider the norm a fundamental general unit, we shall use it as an illustration. If we specify norms that come from different societies and from different institutional realms, we might choose:

Thou shalt not kill.
Do not sleep with your wife until after the child is weaned.
Wear safety goggles.
Do not smoke.
Walk on the right side of the ship when going forward during general quarters.
Bring flowers when invited to dinner.

Probably no more than five or six examples or cases are necessary, but what is critical is that they come from radically disparate settings or contexts. The crux of this method is the maximization of diversity in only a few examples. This is how we expand our consciousness!

Once this is done, the *third step,* the important one, is to search for inherent dimensions such that when each norm is scored, most norms are not placed at one end of the continuum or the other. This means that nonvariable concepts or labels such as ethics, mores, laws, customs, economic norms, or political norms cannot be selected because two or three would be scored zero or one. Besides, as we have already noted, the degree of economic norms is not a variable; adding "degree of" in front of it does not make it a variable. However, the severity of sanction is a dimension that allows considerable variation once it is operationalized. So can the specificity of the norm, the clarity of the norm, the severity of the consequences of deviance for others, the likelihood of these consequences occurring, the extent of norm conformity, the extent of norm enforcement, the periodicity of enforcement, the predictability of sanction, the visibility of deviance, and others. Some of these are mentioned by Morris (1966), who also uses nonvariable pairs.

An important assumption with this particular technique is that there must be some knowledge about the diverse contents being compared. Norms were deliberately selected because everyone has tacit knowledge gained from his life experiences. There are other sociological units of analysis that are more removed from our experience. Under these circumstances, one must read about several extreme examples. This can compensate for, or be a good substitute for, limited first-hand experience.

Perhaps the best evidence that this technique can work is the report of Glaser and Strauss' personal experiences (1967, Ch. 3). The authors called it the comparative method. They stressed the necessity of sampling different groups and getting as much diversity as possible. Like the author, they found it was not necessary to have many examples, that is, the rules of sampling for theory construction are quite different from those of collecting empirical data.

Combining Basic Elements to Generate New Variables

This is a relatively easy technique to use, provided that one does have some general elements and dimensions. The second discussed technique, b above, helps one to find the basic elements and dimensions. The combining method is most practical once one has discovered several variables and started the process of ordering them into more and less abstract concepts. It is best employed after this previous technique has helped us discover many general variables because it is an organizing device.

An example is in Table 1.3 where an earlier version of a typology of

Table 1.3   Using Basic Dimensions and Elements to Generate Variables: The Case of Variables for Role-Relationships

Dimensions	Persons	Activities	Places	Times
Quantity	Number of role partners	Number of activities	Number of locations	Frequency of interaction
Quality	Involvement	?	?	Duration

general variables for role relationships is to be found (Hage and Marwell, 1968). The cross-classification of the basic dimension or primitive term of quantity with the elements of person, activity, place, and time produces four derived variables, including several made famous by Homans (1950). (As a matter of fact, we discovered the basic dimension by using the second technique.) What is more interesting is the case where one has a basic dimension—in this instance, what we originally called quality—and some empty cells. This is how we found act effort and location compactness, two of the more interesting ideas.

The great advantage of employing an organization of variables such as this typology is that, as one adds more basic dimensions and elements, the number of variables increases exponentially through time. For example, a student suggested the idea of continuity as a basic dimension for describing role relationships. This is different from any of our other dimensions. When this is cross-classified with time (the continuity of times), it gives us the variable periodicity, that is, does the role relationship articulate always at the same time. The union of location and continuity creates orbity, that is, the same daily and weekly round of places. As far as the author knows, this concept has never been discussed in the role literature and yet it appears to be illuminating. The continuity of role partners is also a fundamental concept since most role relationships endure while role partners change. Indeed role partners vary considerably along this continuum, from the relatively stable spouse to the relatively nonstable nurse.

In the area of macrosociology, the author found the idea of the degree of normative equality by cross-classifying social structure with the basic dimension of rights (see Table 1.4). This can be defined as the distribu-

Table 1.4 Using Basic Dimensions and Elements to Generate Variables: The Case of Variables for Societies

Dimension	Social Structure (Distribution of)
Knowledges	Complexity
Powers	Centralization
Rewards	Stratification
Rights	?

tion of rights, such as the right to trial, the right to vote, the right to attend school, the right to own land, or the right to protest, among various social groups or categories in the society. Again, one might say that the idea has been implicit in various writings, especially on the subject of social justice. But the important point is that the concept came not from the literature, but from the method of combining or cross-classifying several more abstract concepts—social structure defined as distribution and the concept of rights.

Several observations can be made about this particular technique. In the process of developing new variables by the use of inherent elements and dimensions, the *ad hoc* nature of the previous technique is being systematically organized. This procedure also allows for the movement toward ever more general dimensions and concepts thus being similar to the second technique above. In the process of attempting to find parallel ideas, one may stumble against a major block: the lack of a label for a particular phenomenon. In this case, words or tags have to be invented.

SEARCHING FOR GENERAL NONVARIABLES

Although the descriptive heart of any theory is the general variables, it is still necessary to have general nonvariables. As has been suggested, there are three kinds of general nonvariables that are of particular importance. The first kind is most important for the classification of analytical units, i.e. the focus of the study, what is to be analyzed. These are our sociological flora and fauna, and, as in biology, we need names to point to them. We need nonvariables to locate the units that are being described by the general variables (Dubin, 1969). In sociology, we already have many analytical units: groups, role sets, organizations, norms, communities, values, societies, role relationships, positions (Johnson, 1960; Bredemeier and Stephenson, 1962; Lundberg, Schrag, and Larsen, 1963; Broom and Selznick, 1963; Wilson, 1966). But we want the label to be a general one, independent of historical time and place; we should avoid concepts like bureaucracy or peasant society, which are limited to particular times and places.

The second most important kind of nonvariable is the element, a primitive term that defines classes of phenomena. Elements become important in the organization of concepts. The third kind of general nonvariable is qualities, such as riots or revolutions or anomie. As Marx noted more than a century ago, quantitative differences can make qualitative changes. We want to label these and again we need general nonvariables.

General nonvariables are harder to find than general variables although sociology presently has more of the former. There are more nonvariables because we have spent so much time looking for them, one unfortunate legacy of Aristotilean thought and Weber's influence. The nonvariables are harder to find because each general nonvariable is a complex phenomenon with a large number of defining properties, each of which must be operationalized. The critical problem is to pick the correct score that divides white and black, the operational point at which a group is no longer a group, or a revolution is no longer a revolution. This is not an easy task. Our problem with general variables is just the reverse. It is to discover as many as we possibly can, multiplying dimensions ad infinitum. With nonvariables, we have to select a few decisive ones among a vast array of possibilities. Selection always seems harder than proliferating new concepts because it involves a more critical ability, a faculty for knowing what is most important, a sense of relevance.

Using Variables to Find Nonvariables

If indeed it is easier to find continua than to decide what is an organization, then one approach is to start with general variables and use these to order some nonvariables. This is helpful primarily with finding the qualities. The method consists of taking a general variable and then dividing it into quantitative zones, such as positive and negative, or high, medium, and low.

Suppose we take the degree of conflict and divide it into none, low, medium, and high. This suggests the qualities of consensus, competition, protestation, and revolution or rebellion. (See Fig. 1.2.) This leaves aside the precise definitions, a point to be discussed in Chapter 3. But the principle remains that one quantity can subsume a variety of qualities, which for various analytical purposes need to be specified. The analytical model is like a thermometer with special scales for gas, liquid, and solid.

Sometimes this technique is best handled by specifying a positive

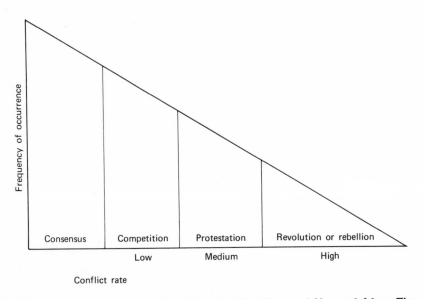

Figure 1.2.   Using General Variables to Find General Nonvariables: The Case of Conflict.

or negative zone, as has been done with the continuum frequency of interaction. Again, this raises important questions about what is positive and negative interaction, but the idea seems to be a useful one, at least for stimulating our imagination. A large number of attitudinal scales are constructed on this implicit idea, and it is perhaps here that this kind of zone specification is most helpful.

This technique does not assume that all of the qualities necessarily exist. The specification of high, medium, and low is a formal procedure that allows one to search for critical qualities. They may or may not exist. In general, however, we are concerned with delineating those terms that already have a basis in the literature, particularly if they have survived for some time. It suggests that we should at least think about them before we reject them. In this way, some of those more historically bound concepts, such as industrialized society—a range in the variable level of development—might be included.

Combining Elements to Create New Nonvariables

This technique is most appropriate when we have several basic elements such as those in Table 1.4. Essentially we ask ourselves if we can combine elements of a more general nature to create new analytical units.

As an illustration suppose we have person, activities, places, and times. We might simply combine them to create a classification scheme for different kinds of activities. We have person activities, place activities, and time activities. Another and more formal example is in Chapter 5.

Sometimes the juxtaposition of different sets of terms that are kindred in some way, the meaning of the idea of element nonvariables, can produce new layers of interpretation and complexity. Take the example of the basic social processes—socialization, institutionalization, social change, and social conflict. If we start to systematically combine these nouns in all their combinations—a simple exercise in logic—we create some interesting complexities: the socialization for social change, the institutionalization of social change, the conflict of social change, the institutionalization of socialization, the social change of socialization, the social conflict of socialization, etc. What we have done has called our attention to processes within processes. Some of these exist in the literature and others do not. The important point is that the combinations change our perception and thus ultimately our thinking about process analysis.

The rules for the technique of combining elements are quite simple. One takes general nonvariables that are found inside a larger unit of analysis and then cross-classifies each nonvariable with the larger unit.

Thus position, role, authority, and status are parts of social collectives. By cross-classifying, we can generate a number of new analytical units.

Decomposing One General Nonvariable Into Several

Another approach to the discovery of general nonvariables, and a useful one for generating units of analysis, is to take a general nonvariable which is itself an analytical unit, a concept that has a large number of different meanings. When we have a rich concept, then typically, although not always, there are several hidden analytical units. This can be an instance when we may need additional concepts.

A case in point is the concept of role. A review of the literature (Gross, Mason, and McEachern, 1958; Biddle and Thomas, 1966), indicates the wide variety of meanings. By substructuring the definitions, as is done in Table 1.5, we can delineate a number of different units. Here

Table 1.5   Decomposing a General Nonvariable to Create Several Nonvariables: The Case of Role

Level	Occupant Individual	Relationship
Person	Persona	Interpersonal
Part of person	Social types	relationship
Position	Position	Role-relationship
Part of position	Role	

the key is to find mutually exclusive and exhaustive definitions. Frequently, as in this instance, one definitional dimension involves the unit of analysis. Typically, general nonvariables shift levels of analysis, moving from one kind of unit to another. If this can be articulated, then we generate additional analytical units.

The concept of alienation is another excellent example of the creation of other analytical units by the process of determining different definitions. The article by Seeman (1959), and the book by Blauner (1964), illustrate how one can pay attention to the ways in which words are employed and discover implicit themes that then become the basis of new concepts or ideas.

One does not want to keep adding new concepts unless there is a need for them. The usual criterion is that these units have different dimensions, necessitating separation. An inspection of the distinctions made usually indicates how fruitful a particular application of this technique can be. If the basic distinctions do not seem important then perhaps we do not need the generated analytic units.

SUMMARY

Theoretical concepts are the foundation of any theory. The first task in constructing a theory, therefore, is to find some concepts to use in our theoretical statements. The most helpful kind of theoretical concept is the general variable, a continuum that applies to any culture and at any point of time—to societies that have ceased to exist, that presently exist, and that have yet to come into existence. These criteria, culture-free and timeless, are easy to apply and thus make our task of recognizing general variables a simple one.

We want general variables because they increase our chances of constructing some theory that will endure and because they make theory construction much easier. General and specific nonvariables are much harder to work with, although every theory has to have at least a few of them.

The five techniques for searching for general variables can be grouped into two pairs separated by a single technique. Converting nonvariables into variables and reducing several variables to a single variable depend upon an existing literature. We find them by reading rapidly, looking for general variables in the former technique and a common definition in the latter. The third technique is a combination of scanning the empirical literature and thinking about it. Discrepancy variables can be created by combining scores that are not normally associated. They help us to explain the rare events and the exceptions. Thus while not helpful on every occasion, the technique becomes very important under certain conditions.

Comparing several diverse contents and using basic elements and dimensions are two techniques than can be used with and without an existing literature. In particular, we are apt to find many variables by listing several diverse cases of a particular analytical unit and then searching for general dimensions upon which they can be scored. The only underlying requirement is at least some prior knowledge about the particular cases. It does not have to be first-hand experience; it can come from a variety of sources: books, movies, and conversations. The technique of combining elements and dimensions works well in conjunction with the comparison of several diverse contents. Once we have a number of variables we can create still more by organizing them. By cross-classifying the element with a very general dimension, we can discover still more variables.

There are fewer techniques for the discovery of nonvariables perhaps because they are harder to find. Three techniques are suggested; each of them is most appropriate for a particular kind of general nonvariable. General variables are most helpful in finding the general nonvariables of qualities, ranges that make a difference. The technique of combining elements creates new elements, and the technique of decomposing a general nonvariable helps us to discover more units of analysis.

These techniques are best used in combination rather than singly. We have separated them mainly for the purpose of identifying more clearly what procedures are appropriate for each of them.

CHAPTER TWO

Theoretical Statements

Once we have discovered some theoretical concepts, we want to connect two or more of them into some statement about social life. However much we can describe social phenomenon with a theoretical concept, we cannot use it to explain or predict. To explain or predict we need a theoretical statement, a connection between two or more concepts. As soon as we hypothesize that the greater the centralization of the organization, the greater its efficiency, as did Weber (1947, p. 337), or that increasing stratification leads to greater social conflict, as did Marx and Engels (1959, pp. 14–17), or that the greater the population density, the greater the division of labor, as did Durkheim (1933, pp. 256–282), or that increased conflict creates integration, as did Simmel (1955, pp. 87–109), we have moved from description to some form of prediction.

There is a confusing and bewildering number of names for a theoretical statement. Among them are hypothesis, proposition, axiom, postulate, assumption, premise, corollary, and theorem, each of which has some subtle nuance in meaning. Each one typically designates a kind of theoretical statement, but the kind is almost never made explicit. Zetterberg (1963) has suggested that a hypothesis is an unconfirmed theoretical statement whereas a proposition is one well substantiated by evidence. Axiom, postulate, theorem, and corollary involve the ordering of theoretical statements (see Ch. 6). Because there are so many names, it seems best to avoid using any of them and therefore the preference for the neutral term theoretical statement. However, hypothesis is used as a synonym from time to time because it has the most widespread usage in the sociological literature (for other distinctions, see Reynolds, 1971, Ch. 4).

EITHER-OR AND CONTINUOUS STATEMENTS

There are several ways in which our concepts can be connected in a theoretical statement, just as there are several kinds of theoretical concepts. Unfortunately, the differences that concern us in constructing a theory, have, as far as the author is aware, gone unnoticed. Terms like hypothesis, premise, or relational statement, while differentiating among theoretical statements either on the basis of the amount of evidence in support of the idea or else in the hierarchical order in the theory do not tell us if the connection is continuous or discrete. It is this distinction that is critical when one is searching for theoretical statements. Again, the choice is between either-or connections, the ideal-typical constructions of much of Weber's work, or continuous connections as implied in each of the statements listed in the first paragraph of this chapter. The former are best labeled logical statements, such as in the format of syllogistic reasoning (e.g., all men are animals). The latter might best be labeled mathematical statements because they may permit addition, subtraction, multiplication, as well as more advanced forms of mathematical reasoning found in algebra and calculus.

There are eight verbal statements in Table 2.1, four of which are connected noncontinuously and four of which are connected continuously. These illustrations indicate some of the differences between the ways in which concepts can be interrelated. Perhaps the simplest way of distinguishing between these two forms of theoretical statements is to note that concepts can be connected with constants, powers, and coefficients in a continuous formulation. This is not possible when the verbal theoretical statement contains some form of the verb to be.

Unfortunately, symbols have been rather imprecisely used. The logical notation $A = B$ may mean all developed societies are democratic societies (Schrag, 1967). The algebraic notation $A = B$ may mean as

Table 2.1   Examples of Different Formulations of Hypotheses

Either-Or Connections
1. The principal part of the learning of criminal behavior occurs within intimate personal groups (DeFleur and Quinney, 1967).
2. If Person dislikes Other and Other likes X, Person will tend to dislike X (Davis, 1963).
3. Organizations employing long-linked technologies seek to expand their domains through vertical integration (Thompson, 1967).
4. All revolutionary parties are ideological.

Continuous Connections
1. The greater the cross-pressuring for Person, the weaker his attitude toward X (Davis, 1963).
2. The more valuable to a man a unit of the activity another gives him, the more often he will limit activity rewarded by the activity of the other (Homans, 1961).
3. Increasing size generates structural differentiation in organizations along various dimensions at decelerating rates (Blau and Schoenherr, 1970).
4. As complexity increases, centralization decreases (Hage, 1965).

complexity increases, centralization decreases, and vice versa. (We will avoid the complications of group algebras where the law of association does not hold.) Although the symbolic representation is the same, the meanings are not, and herein lies a source of much confusion, as an inspection of Figure 2.1 makes clear. A = B means either-or in logic but not in algebra, and from this difference flows a number of differences about the way in which one thinks.

Logical reasoning can be a great help in ordering our concepts into primitive and derived terms, but it is not as much help in formulating a set of theoretical statements. Often a blessing in one area becomes a curse in another.

The Advantages of Continuous Statements

The continuous statement is much more precise. This is true even when we take the most primitive kind, namely, a verbal statement such as,

The greater the cross-pressuring for Person, the weaker his attitude toward X.

We might recast this statement with the verb to be as follows,

When Person is cross-pressured, his attitudes towards X are weak.

Either–or connection

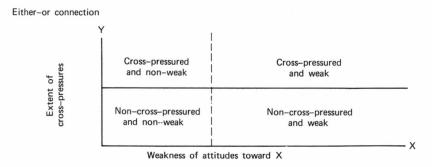

Continuous connection

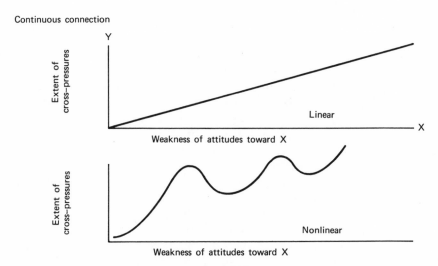

Figure 2.1   Graphic Presentations of Different Connections.

On the surface these appear to be exactly the same. Yet, if the two of them are graphed as they are in Figure 2.1, then one can see that this is not so. An either-or statement divides a graph into two parts, absence and presence. This remains true regardless of where the cutting points of cross-pressures and non-cross-pressures, weak and nonweak, are made. In this instance, general variables, and the same ones, have been used to emphasize the connection in the theoretical statement. We could recast the statement with relatively general nonvariables, thereby increasing the lack of precision even more. For example,

All middlemen have ambivalent attitudes.

It should be clear to the reader that different verbal statements lend themselves more or less to the addition of ranges, powers, coefficients, and constants, and increase the precision considerably. But using the simplest example, one without mathematical powers, limits, or other symbols, highlights differences in the slight change of format, that is, avoiding the verb to be.

Either-or statements can be phrased probablistically—for example, the principal part of the learning of criminal behavior occurs with intimate personal groups—but this does not change our argument. This is still a less precise statement when compared to the trace line stipulated by any statement that says the greater the X, the greater the Y.

The continuous statement contains more information. Suppose we have the hypothesis that the greater the degree of stratification, the greater the degree of centralization, a theoretical statement borrowed from Marx and Engels (1959, p. 16). We know from this statement that with each increase in the concentration of wealth we should obtain an increase in the concentration of power. We could modify the direct one-to-one ratio of this statement by adding coefficients, powers, or limits. Our hypothesis says much more than the statement that all stratified societies are centralized societies. The latter tells us that when we find one property, we find another—the essential thinking of inclusion or exclusion. The continuous connection tells us something about change in one variable or in two variables being associated with change in others and moves toward causality and control. This is a critical difference.

For the sociologist, it should be noted that continuous statements provide a simple solution to the study of change, including evolution. For example, one increment or increase in the degree of complexity of what Durkheim (Marsh, 1967) called the division of labor leads to or causes one decrement or decrease in the degree of centralization, that is the distribution of power in society. The first kind of change is considered so important in society that it has received a special name, structural differentiation (Parsons, 1966). Thus this one simple statement connects a major evolutionary process, the increasing complexity of societies, and tells us one of its consequences. Would we grasp the import and the sense of possible causality with the statement that all complex societies are decentralized societies? I suspect not. The continuous statement indicates where we are going, as well as where we have been, which is indeed most informative, assuming the statement is somewhat true. Each variable, of course, is a kind of change. When we connect two or more general variables in a continuous statement we are linking one kind of change with another.

Thus, we avoid getting into the difficulty confronting men such as Nisbet (1970), who wonders how one moves from one type to the next. To put it simply, the general remedy is the elimination of the verb "to be" in theoretical statements.

The continuous statement allows for some control or alteration in existing situations. We may need more or less of something, indicating that we correspondingly increase or decrease something else, depending upon the variables in the statement. If we want to increase decentralization, we need to increase complexity. Of course, it may not be easy to increase this variable from a practical point of view, but the statement does speak to the problem of what solutions might exist for particular problems.

Continuous statements are more complex. This is evident from the two examples provided in Figure 2.1. The trace line can have many curves and wiggles in it. It might approximate a sine or a tangent or some other transcendental function, curves that have proved to be very useful in engineering. On the other hand, the trace line might be a simple straight line, indicating what is called a linear relationship. The fact that we have these different levels of complexity allows us to move-closer to the real world in our theories for, again, even the straight-line or linear relationship does not have much empirical support. We do need complicated statements to analyze social reality. Nor do we lose any advantages that there might be with specifying a given area of a graph. With the ideas of limits and thresholds, we can have a particular specific statement if we need it. However, the reverse is not true. We cannot express mathematical powers, limits, and other symbols in either-or statements. Although we can express them verbally this does not mean that we have stated them syllogistically.

Admittedly the terms, either-or statements and continuous statements, are perhaps not the best labels for describing the differences discussed above. There are those readers who know the branch of mathematics called set theory, which is built upon logic. In various ways, it has become prominent in current attempts to build better sociological theory. The best illustration is the work of Galtung (1967). As a consequence, we are not attacking the use of logic or logical reasoning as much as arguing against either-or connections between concepts and suggesting that syllogistic reasoning with theoretical statements leaves much to be desired.

Either-or connections are too imprecise, contain too little information, and are too simple for dealing with the complexities of social phenomenon.

The Strategy of Searching for Continuous Statements

The reader might wonder how serious is this problem of theoretical statements cast in an either-or format. Here are some examples from the literature. In Davis' (1963) codification of balance theory we find the following example: friends tend to become similar in activities, friends tend to become similar in attitudes. At the same time and in the same article, we have: the more similar Person is to Other, the more Person will like Other. Thus, the differences between connections appear to be unnoticed. Although there are relatively few articles like Davis'—of which the author thinks quite highly—that explicitly formulate hypotheses, some of the recent ones illustrate the wide use of the verb to be in modern sociology (see Warren, 1968; Denzin, 1969; Peterson, 1969).

In fact, most of the current attempts at developing chains of hypotheses have included one or more either-or statements. In Thompson (1967), we have the following examples:

Organizations employing long-linked technologies seek to expand their domains through vertical integration.

Organizations employing mediating technologies seek to expand their domains by increasing the populations served.

In Price (1967), we have these hypotheses:

Except where Type A spatial mobility is coupled with a high degree of professionalization, organizations which have spatial mobility are more likely to have a high degree of effectiveness than organizations which do not have spatial mobility.

Organizations which have cooptation are more likely to have a high degree of effectiveness than organizations which do not have cooptation.

In both of these examples part of the problem comes from the use of non-variable concepts. This is especially true in Thompson's work. But either-or connections are used as well and it is therefore worth distinguishing between kinds of theoretical statements. In both of these authors there are hypotheses with general variables, indicating that the difference between these kinds of statements has probably gone unnoticed.

Our recommendation is to use the strategy of searching for continuous verbal statements. *Concepts should not be connected in either-or statements any more than the concepts themselves should be either-or descriptions.* Correspondingly, many of the objections to this kind of concept, the general nonvariable or type, apply to the either-or statement.

This does not mean that a theoretical statement must be symbolized. While it is certainly easier to perform mathematical operations and to think with symbols, it is not necessary to display them in symbolic form. A concern for effective communication dictates against too much symbolization. We can write our statements in verbal form even when we employ constants, coefficients, powers, and other paraphernalia from mathematics.

A simple illustration might make this point clearer. To say, as Blau and Schoenherr (1970) have, that increasing size generates structural differentiation in organizations along various dimensions at decelerating rates is to suggest a more complex idea than simple linear relationships, as in the greater the X, the greater the Y. When we want to integrate a number of statements like theirs into more comprehensive theories and derive all the implications of them, symbols can be helpful, easing manipulation, and thus thinking.

Some readers might interject a "but" at this point, raising the metatheoretical question about the appropriateness of mathematical equations at this stage of development in sociology. They might argue the many problems of measurement and the lack of agreement about definitions in the field. They might agree that equations have all the advantages cited above, but think it is impossible to implement them now because of the crudeness of our data and knowledge. There is perhaps much truth to this line of reasoning. We do have little consensus and much measurement error! At the same time, some of our difficulties connected with the lack of theoretical development in sociology might stem from our attempt to analyze a complex world with either-or hypotheses. Perhaps the opposite argument should be made, namely, that *we have waited too long and are preventing the development of sociological knowledge by avoiding the use of more complex statements, such as those found in mathematics.*

If we consider the simplest ideas in physics that have stood the test of time, equations like $P = V \div T$ or $I = E \div R$, we find that these are much more complicated than the typical sociological hypothesis. Yet, there is no *a priori* reason to assume that the social world is less complicated than the physical one. Most of us assume that the opposite is true. Therefore, it seems worthwhile to try the strategy of searching for more complicated theoretical statements now. Perhaps we will only begin to understand our measurement problems and definitional difficulties when we try more complicated statements, for only then shall we begin to make sense out of our chaos of data. Boyle and Galileo did a great deal with very crude instruments and little measurement precision. The same approach might also work in sociology. We might discover some knowledge, that is, well-substantiated hypotheses if we try mathematical formulations, even very complicated ones.

On the other hand, to say that all either-or connections are bad is not a true theoretical statement. There is a place in a theory where either-or statements are not only helpful but mandatory. In general, there are two situations in which they seem most appropriate: definitional premises and operational linkages involving thresholds. They might be considered the exceptions that prove our general rule, namely, as an intellectual strategy we should place more emphasis on continuous statements and less on either-or connections.

SEARCHING FOR CONTINUOUS THEORETICAL STATEMENTS

For the moment our immediate task is to find some verbal theoretical statements of the form: *the greater the X, the greater the Y*. We will not concern ourselves at this stage with the addition of coefficients, constants, powers, and other mathematical symbols. This is handled when we discuss operational linkages.

Converting Ideal-Type Constructs Into Simple Continuous Statements

The Case of Either-Or Statements. We have many more either-or concepts than we do connections between them in the literature. In general, the either-or concepts can be converted into continuous statements by changing the nonvariables into variables and then casting the verbal statement into the form: the greater the X, the greater the Y. Usually, however, we will find that one either-or statement that uses nonvariable concepts requires several continuous statements. Replacing one nonvariable concept with just one variable usually does an injustice to the original verbal statement. This can be illustrated with an example from Thompson's (1967) work. The statement that organizations employing long-linked technologies seek to expand their domains through vertical integration can be translated into the following idea:

the greater the capital investment, the greater the emphasis on the purchasing of suppliers and customers.

This may not be a fair translation of the idea of long-link technology, but it is an attempt to search for the causative factor that seems to lead to a policy of vertical integration, which is nothing more than an attempt to purchase suppliers and customers. Similarly, Thompson's hypothesis about mediating technology might be translated as follows:

> the greater the number of suppliers and of customers, the less the emphasis on the purchasing of suppliers and customers.

Again, many might argue with this recasting. Our main point is to say that most either-or statements, when they stand as isolated hypotheses, can be recast by changing the nonvariables into variables. This is done with the techniques described in the previous chapter. If there is some doubt as to whether the translation is a correct one, several different formations can be stipulated at the same time:

1a. The greater the processing time in manufacturing, the greater the emphasis on the purchasing of suppliers and customers.

1b. The greater the production volume, the greater the emphasis on the purchasing of suppliers and customers.

1c. The greater the standardization of the product, the greater the emphasis on the purchasing of suppliers and customers.

In other words, in doing research one can consider a variety of interpretations, thus making sure that the original insight is not likely to be lost in the translation.

As we add these alternative possibilities, we begin to get a more complex image of why organizations might pursue different policies vis-à-vis their environment. We also begin to see how a number of these variables might be interrelated—for example, greater large investments in machinery leads to more standardization, which in turn affects the volume of production by increasing it. Or, we can just treat each of these variables as separate causes of a policy of purchasing suppliers and customers, not attempting to organize some causal sequences or chain. Regardless, past efforts to formulate either-or statements are well worth scrutiny because they have much to offer.

The conversion of statements with variables is quite straight-forward and does not need to be illustrated. There is one problem and that is the decision to add "and vice versa." Implicit in the idea of the greater the X, the greater the Y is the notion that X is causing Y to change. Thus, we can change Price's (1967, p. 16) hypothesis from:

> Organizations which have a high degree of division of labor are more

likely to have a high degree of effectiveness than organizations with a low degree of division of labor

to

The greater the degree of the division of labor, the greater the degree of effectiveness.

We must raise the issue of whether we want one directional or two directional causality. This is difficult to decide and requires some knowledge about the reasons why the variables are connected in the first place. In practice, most of us tend to be a little imprecise on this point, for which Blalock (1969) has correctly criticized verbal statements. Also, this recasting makes us aware of the need for parameters such as limits and thresholds. The fact that our thinking changes with a different format is the best reason for using it.

The Case of Ideal-Types or Pairs of Constructs. A construct is a set of concepts, most of which are usually nonvariables. Weber's ideal-types are constructs as is Toennies' gemeinschaft vs. gesellschaft, Durkheim's organic vs. mechanical, and Redfield's folk vs. urban (Nisbet, 1967). Each of these ideas really contains many separate parts. Once one can stipulate the variables that define the parts of the constructs, then the formulation of simple continuous statements comes automatically. There are two kinds of constructs worth illustrating. The first is what might be called the ideal-types or pairs of constructs. Again, we shall use Durkheim and Weber's work because of their interest to most sociologists and because most readers are familiar with their writings. The second construct is the set of typologies, relatively organized sets of variables or nonvariables that are implicit theoretical statements. Here some of the contemporary work in organizational technology provides an interesting illustration. In Chapter 1 we listed a number of the different dimensions implicit in Durkheim's (1933) thesis on the division of labor (Table 1.2). Theoretical statements can be constructed between each of the polar ends of the variables upon the basis of the simple idea that if a unit of analysis has more than one continuum or dimension, then they must be interrelated. If not, then Durkheim's description is in error. For example, if organic solidarity is characterized by high population size, high transportation rates, and high communication rates then we can formulate this in statements as follows:

1. The higher the population size, the higher transportation rate and vice versa.

2. The higher the transportation rate, the higher the communication rate and vice versa.
3. The higher the communication rate, the higher the population size and vice versa.

Of course, these particular statements are perhaps not very exciting to contemporary readers because they appear to be common sense.

But if we continue to formulate the statements implied in Durkheim, some more exciting ideas become apparent. Among others are the following:

4. The greater the frequency of conflict, the less the intensity of conflict.
5. The greater the population size, the less the intensity of conflict.

These are perhaps more controversial and therefore interesting.

The important point is to recognize the simple steps in our procedure. *First,* list the general variables and their scores describing the two (or more) constructs as we did in Table 1.2. *Second,* connect the variables by statements of the form, the greater the X, the greater the Y, when one construct is scored high on both X and Y, and the greater the X, the less the Y when one construct is scored high on X and low on Y. *Third,* add vice versa if the author does not make clear what time ordering is appropriate or if this is not apparent in the variables themselves. The reader might continue this exercise with some of the other variables contained in Durkheim. As this is done a number of additional insights are gained.

Naturally we might not be willing to accept all of the theoretical statements derived in this way. One must still think about the value of the hypothesis derived by this method. But the procedure remains a simple and easy way of exposing the line of reasoning of other persons and casting it in a form that facilitates thought about it. These are essential first steps.

When the reader feels that the pieces of the construct do not fit together, as implied, there is probably a richer and more sophisticated analysis available. This can be shown in Weber's discussion of rational-legal authority. We find that Weber (1947, pp. 333–334), suggests the following concepts are part of his bureaucratic construct: hierarchy of authority, technical competence, offices, files, etc. We must first convert these into variables. Technical competency suggests level of education, while offices indicate the degree of complexity or specialization. Hierarchy of authority can be easily seen as the degree of centralization. We also know that Weber's main argument was that the rational-legal authority was more efficient than his two other ideal types. In other words, each of these components presumably contributes to efficiency. These can be stated as hypotheses. But then we want to ask ourselves whether each of these bureaucratic parts are themselves interrelated. Does the level of education correlate positively with the degree of centralization, or the degree of complexity with the degree of stratification? Upon thinking about this for a while, we can come to the conclusion that they do not, even though each of them might positively affect the degree of efficiency (as suggested in the famous footnote by Parsons, in Weber, 1947, p. 59). This chain of reasoning is illustrated in Figure 2.2. To simplify our analysis we have put the reasoning and statements in both graphic and verbal form. It should be noted that a two-directional arrow means "and vice versa," a one-directional arrow does not. Weber implies that structure determines efficiency but not necessarily the reverse. In contrast, in so far as bureaucratic structure has certain properties these are assumed to occur together, more or less. (Weber was somewhat cautious about this in his discussion of ideal-type methodology if not in his discussion of rational-legal authority.)

What we have now is an interesting middle-range set of hypotheses that indicates why an organization might never reach perfect efficiency. Or to put it in more Weberian terms, we can now explain why his models are ideal-types in the sense that they can never occur. The internal contradictions prevent continued evolution. (This theme of incompatible elements is a useful one when interpreting Weber because the latter uses this theoretical device over and over again.) Our theoretical statements in Figure 2.2 provide a dynamic conceptualization, suggesting how organizations can evolve along with their problems of moving equilibrium. The model of reasoning can be helpful in many theories. *Certainly, when reconstructing constructs, it is helpful to keep in mind the possibility of incompatible parts or continua.*

The guidelines are as follows: *First,* determine the components or concepts involved in the construct. They may be outlines, as they are in rational-legal authority, or they may be buried in isolated sentences, as most of them are in Durkheim's *Division of Labor in Society* (1933). If these components are nonvariables, then of course they must be converted. *Second,* explicate the major hypothesis, if there is one. *Third,* ask whether or not the major dimensions are interrelated. The search for incompatibilities may or may not be successful, but it is a worthwhile endeavor. If they exist, then an interesting set of theoretical statements is developed.

The Case of Typologies. Typologies are even more explicit statements, implied, that one type goes with another. As soon as an article or book lists more than one typology *for the same unit of analysis,* i.e. organizations or groups or individuals, then the author is really arguing

Weber's major premise: Rational-legal authority is more efficient.
His implicit hypotheses: Each component of bureaucracy increases or
contributes to efficiency.

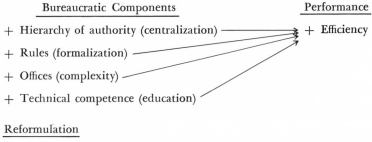

Bureaucratic Components   Performance

+ Hierarchy of authority (centralization) ———————→ + Efficiency

+ Rules (formalization) ———————

+ Offices (complexity) ———

+ Technical competence (education)

Reformulation

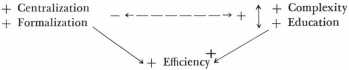

+ Centralization   + Complexity
+ Formalization — ←————————→ + ↑↓ + Education

+ Efficiency

The Hypotheses in Verbal Form
1. The greater the centralization, the greater the efficiency
2. The greater the formalization, the greater the efficiency
3. The greater the complexity, the greater the efficiency
4. The greater the education, the greater the efficiency
5. The greater the centralization, the greater the formalization and vice versa
6. The greater the complexity, the greater the education and vice versa
7. The greater the centralization, the less the complexity and vice versa
8. The greater the formalization, the less the education and vice versa
9. The greater the centralization, the less the education and vice versa
10. The greater the formalization, the less the complexity and vice versa

SOURCE: Weber, 1947, pp. 329–338.

**Figure 2.2   Converting Ideal-Types Into Sets of Continuous Statements:
The Case of Weber's Rational-Legal Authority.**

that each set of types is associated in some way. These should be cast
into theoretical statements.

An illustration of this is borrowed from the work of Perrow (1967).
In Table 2.2 are his original typologies relating technology to what he
calls task structure. While his article does not contain any hypotheses, a
number are clearly implied. What is especially interesting are the multivariate hypotheses created by the combination of particular scores on
certain general variables. Only some of these are given in Table 2.2.

Table 2.2 Converting Typologies Into Sets of Continuous Statements: The Case of Perrow's Framework

	Analyzability		Exceptions	
		Few	Many	
	Low	Craft (I)	Nonroutine (II)	
	High	Routine (III)	Engineering (IV)	

Task Structure

Type	Discretion	Power	Coordination	Group Interdependence
I Technicians	Low	Low	Plan	Low
Supervisors	High	High	Feed	
II Technicians	High	High	Feed	High
Supervisors	High	High	Feed	
III Technicians	Low	High	Plan	Low
Supervisors	Low	Low	Plan	
IV Technicians	High	High	Feed	Low
Supervisors	Low	Low	Plan	

Implicit Hypotheses

1. The lower the analyzability and the greater the number of exceptions, the higher the interdependence.
2. The greater the routine, the less the discretion of different levels.
3. The fewer the number of exceptions, the less the discretion and power of the technicians.
4. The lower the analyzability of problems, the higher the discretion and power of the supervisors.
5. The higher the discretion and the power, the more the emphasis on feedback as the mechanism of coordination.

SOURCE: Perrow, 1967.

There are many more, but those given indicate how the statements are formulated from the typologies.

The steps are as follows. *First,* check to be sure that the typologies apply to the same unit of analysis. In this case it is organizations. The typologies do not have to come from the same author. The more intriguing and comprehensive syntheses are obtained when different authors' typologies are juxtaposed. One is also more likely to discover more complicated relationships, which encourage more sophisticated mathematical techniques than simple two-variable linear equations. *Second,* if the typologies do not have general variables that define the types, then use the first technique of Chapter 1. In this case the variables are explicit in the diagrams included in Table 2.2. (But not in all those included in Perrow's original article. For example, he specifies four kinds of social structure: relationships based on social identity, relationships based on goal identification, instrumental security, and work or task identity.) *Third*, combine the variables thoughtfully. Perrow implies that only when two conditions are met is there going to be high group interdependence. The other hypotheses are created by noting what combination of scores produces which result. Thus, we find that routineness, the main diagonal in his typology, affects the discretion of different levels but that the number of exceptions has more effect on technicians, and analyzability has more effect on supervisors. The fifth hypothesis is included to indicate how different variables can be fitted together. It should be clear that these five do not specify all the hypotheses implied in these two rich typologies. The others are left to the reader as an exercise.

One of the more interesting aspects of this particular example of technology and its consequences for organizational structure is that we have discovered a theoretical statement that involves three variables, a much more complex statement than is typical with most of the techniques discussed in this chapter. We might recast it as follows:

(− analyzability) (+ number of exceptions) =
    group interdependence

Most of the classic writers in sociology are rich in implicit as well as explicit theoretical statements. This is especially true for the men of the Golden Age that Nisbet (1967) describes. If the ideas of these greats are to become hard currency as hypotheses, many of the constructs which Nisbet calls the great ideas of sociology need be looked upon as sets of theoretical statements and tested as such.

Reducing Continuous Statements to a General One

The technique of reducing several continuous statements to create a more general one is easily done once it is recognized how several definitions can be combined into a new one. The problem of definitional reduction has already been discussed and need not be elaborated upon. Zetterberg (1963, pp. 31–32) provides an interesting example of this technique, and we need not repeat it here.

This technique is an extremely difficult one because we are required to move to ever more general levels of abstraction, a thought process most people seem to find arduous. Regardless of the hard work involved, the effort is worth it. Discovering more general hypotheses, including basic premises or assumptions about the nature of our social world, can be the reward.

One way of proceeding is to recognize that we have a variety of social collectives. In particular, the author has found it useful to consider groups, organizations, institutional realms, and societies as a fourfold way of beginning the process of generalization. A theoretical statement for one of these levels may be true for another, or even all the others. Here we are calling attention to the simple fact that a part of a theoretical statement is never or seldom written: the part specifying the unit of analysis. For example, as complexity increases, centralization decreases, was written originally for organizations (Hage, 1965). Our next question is, is this true for groups, for societies, for institutional realms, and other kinds of social collectives? Again, this technique resembles the previous one. It largely requires our searching the separate literatures and then asking if the theoretical statement applies in contexts other than the one in which it is developed. If it does, then we have created a more general theoretical statement. If it does not, then we might consider why it does not. This can lead to the discovery of additional variables that were previously not part of the original statement and which should be added. We would then discover more complicated continuous statements involving three or more variables.

Combining Continuous Statements to Create New Ones

This technique is frequently called axiomatic reasoning (Zetterberg, 1963; Blalock, 1969; Hage, 1965), a most misleading label. This technique offers sociologists several advantages as a *heuristic*, that is, as a useful way of teasing out implications that might make worthwhile hypotheses. The essential reasoning involved is algebraic: if $A = B$ and $B = C$, then $A = C$ (Schrag, 1967). (Although this might look like a syllogism, it is not; the equal sign means that we can interchange the position of the letters, that is, $B = C$ and $C = B$ are the same theoretical statement. This point has not been understood by most critics because of the confusion between logic and algebra.) As the number of variable concepts and connections increase, this technique allows for the discovery of new theoretical statements.

Here, a word of caution is necessary. To say that $A = B$ is to imply that A causes B and vice versa. In practice, however, we seldom write our verbal statements in this way. We usually state only one direction. Frequently, when we think, we think about the theoretical verbal statement or an equation in one direction. But two-directional causality is possible and indeed probably common. Again, it is critical that we distinguish between what people normally imply and what is meant by the notion.

The manipulation of statements by combining them requires several assumptions. *First*, that one has some key variables involved in the unit of analysis, and preferably all of the major ones. The reason for this is that we want to reduce the probability of having some spurious result. Thus, the need to be sure that one has isolated the key variables. This does not imply that one has all the variables. Intervening and antecedent variables are not needed. *Second*, one must assume that the variables form some interdependent system so that the use of algebra is justified. In other words, does it seem reasonable to say that X causes Y and Y causes X. This advice is directly contrary to that provided by Costner and Leik (1971) and others who prefer to see asymmetrical statements, that is, only that X causes Y. This is the standard way in which many think about causality and there are certain advantages to this. However, from a theory construction viewpoint as opposed to one of theory verification, the assumption of interdependence or two-directional causality is a useful one.

How safe are such assumptions? Although no definitive answer can be given, there are several pieces of evidence that indicate they are not completely untenable. Most of the existing multiple correlation studies indicate that, after two variables are used, it is difficult to increase the size of the coefficient of determination, that is, indicating that all the variables are indeed present in a single system. On theoretical grounds, it seems wise to picture each unit of analysis, a general nonvariable concept, as consisting of some system of interdependent general variables or continua. This is implied in our first technique. Indeed it is what all of us implicitly assume in any case. While these systems of variables are relatively open, subject to influences from outside, this does not mean that the variables themselves describing the unit of analysis do not operate as if they were a closed system, because the influences are mediated via particular, if not all, variables (see Blalock, 1969, Ch. 2). For example, the variables forming the system of organizations affect the variables forming the system of the social position within the organization, but each of these can be analyzed separately as a system of interdependent variables or "blocks" (Blalock, 1969, p. 72). *The first assumption, that one has the key variables, is much less certain, and therefore suspect.* Usually some of the variables are missing; this creates difficulties in the theoretical conclusions derived from manipulation of theoretical statements derived by this technique.

The major advantage of this technique is gained when the theoretical statements of two authors are combined. When we study particular men, especially if their ideas have found wide currency, we can safely expect that each, no matter how insightful, sees only part of the totality of sociological reality. The combination of authors dealing with the same analytical unit allows us to synthetize their insights systematically, giving a much more complex analysis of social phenomenon. Simultaneously, we discover new theoretical statements not found in the works of either (see Zetterberg, 1963).

Several hypotheses could be combined to illustrate this (see Table 2.3):

The higher the centralization, the higher the production
The higher the centralization, the higher the formalization
The higher the production, the higher the formalization

This concept of systematic interrelations becomes clearer if the words "and vice versa" are added after each hypothesis, or if the following format is used:

Centralization = Production
Centralization = Formalization
Production   = Formalization

In this particular axiomatic theory of organization, there are eight variables. This requires seven major bivariate statements or propositions, which can then be used to derive 21 minor statements, or theorems or corollaries. The reader might try combining several of the other major propositions for himself to get a feeling for this technique. Here is an instance of where symbolizing makes life much easier and reasoning much quicker. If we have C(entralization) = P(roduction), F(ormaliza-tion) = E(fficiency), S(tratification) = J(ob satisfaction), S = P, S = A(daptiveness), and CO(mplexity) = −C, we quickly grasp how they can be interrelated into the 28 two-variable theoretical statements. Symbols make us less conscious of the words and more aware of the operations involved. It might be noted that this technique becomes quite awkward when there are more than ten variables. Then a very different procedure, discussed below, is advisable.

But the reader might well ask, isn't this technique merely a formula, which can be done better and faster by the machine? True, we could easily have a computer print out all the two-variable or even three-vari-able combinations. However, as always, we must make judgments about the efficacy of the theoretical statements that are discovered. Is it common sense or uncommon nonsense? Are these "Aha" experiences, new insights, or are they we've-seen-them-before statements?

Table 2.3   The Technique of Combining Several Continuous Statements to Create New Ones: The Case of Hage's Axiomatic Theory of Organizations

Major Propositions
  A. The higher the centralization, the higher the production (Weber).
  B. The higher the formalization, the higher the efficiency (Weber).
  C. The higher the centralization, the higher the formalization (Weber).
  D. The higher the stratification, the lower the job satisfaction (Barnard).
  E. The higher the stratification, the higher the production (Barnard).
  F. The higher the stratification, the lower the adaptiveness (Barnard).
  G. The higher the complexity, the lower the centralization (Thompson).

Derived Corollaries
   1. The higher the formalization, the higher the production.
   2. The higher the centralization, the higher the efficiency.
   3. The lower the job satisfaction, the higher the production.
   4. The lower the job satisfaction, the lower the adaptiveness.
   5. The higher the production, the lower the adaptiveness.
   6. The higher the complexity, the lower the production.
   7. The higher the complexity, the lower the formalization.
   8. The higher the production, the higher the efficiency.
   9. The higher the stratification, the higher the formalization.
  10. The higher the efficiency, the lower the complexity.
  11. The higher the centralization, the lower the job satisfaction.
  12. The higher the centralization, the lower the adaptiveness.
  13. The higher the stratification, the lower the complexity.
  14. The higher the complexity, the higher the job satisfaction.
  15. The lower the complexity, the lower the adaptiveness.
  16. The higher the stratification, the higher the efficiency.
  17. The higher the efficiency, the lower the job satisfaction.
  18. The higher the efficiency, the lower the adaptiveness.
  19. The higher the centralization, the higher the stratification.
  20. The higher the formalization, the lower the job satisfaction.
  21. The higher the formalization, the lower the adaptiveness.

Limits Proposition
  H. Production imposes limits on complexity, centralization, formalization, stratification, adaptiveness, efficiency, and job satisfaction.

SOURCE: Hage, 1965.

The newly found statements have to be considered carefully. There are several standards that can be applied. One test is to see whether some of the minor hypotheses or corollaries that are derived exist in the writings of other authors. Another test is to see whether there is empirical evidence for some of the new statements. In this particular instance, the alienation literature, Michel's iron law of oligarchy, and other hypotheses were "discovered" from the combination of the writings of Weber, Barnard, and Thompson even though their original works have little to do with some of these theoretical problems. This provided greater confidence in the technique and what it was creating. Again, our key point is that this is not a mechanical procedure like factor analysis. Instead, it is a guideline that can be helpful but, as always, critical judgment is essential. If the above standards, theoretical and empirical, are applied, then the technique is less likely to lead one astray.

Theoretically, there is an obvious difficulty with this method for creating verbal statements. Even if all the variables are interrelated as has been done in the seven main propositions and 21 corollaries that when one variable increases, everything else keeps increasing until infinity (Blalock, 1969, Ch. 2). Empirically, except in a few very special cases, this is most unlikely. This defect has to be corrected, which can be done in several ways. *First,* by creating other statements interrelating the variables in a different way. In Table 2.3 this is achieved by stipulating a limits proposition. *Second,* by creating some unidirection or nonreversible hypotheses. This is illustrated in Figure 2.2. It could also be done by adding one or more exogenous variables, those which are not part of the system but which affect it, such as Perrow's routine technology. We might take variables describing the environment or describing the resources available to the unit of analysis such as size, budget, or autonomy. This illustrates how to create Blalock's block discursive design. Both of these procedures prevent the increases in centralization, which lead to increases in production, and which in turn lead to increases in centralization, ad infinitum. They are best applied once one has stipulated all of the theoretical statements. Once we see all the connections, we can easily recognize places where either limits need to be stipulated or additional variables added with only one-directional causality.

Some sociologists have argued against the use of this technique (Costner and Leik, 1971). Their argument is that correlations between variables must be .8 or .9 before one can safely derive statements. They are right on this point but they are missing an essential idea, namely that this technique is not intended to prove statements as true, the purpose of empirical research, but to discover statements worth researching. Combining statements of different authors is most desirable, precisely in the early stages of theory construction when not much empirical evidence exists.

This technique is largely a heuristic device for searching for simpler verbal statements. Its major limitation is the simple bivariate and linear equations that one obtains. And even with eight variables, the technique is quite clumsy. But when little is known, theoretically or empirically, the technique can help us exploit what we have.

Comparing Diverse Case Studies

When we connect two or more concepts in some theoretical statement, we usually are implying more than mere association. It is helpful to ask two basic questions: (1) *What are the causes of the variable?* (2) *What are the consequences of the variable?* To help answer these questions requires several diverse case studies about the same variable or set of theoretical concepts. As we immerse ourselves in them, keeping these questions foremost in our minds, then continuous statements will suggest themselves.

Suppose we are interested in the problem of the causes of revolution. *First,* we take several case studies. Any of a number of historical descriptions might be selected. The objective is to obtain a variety of societies and timepoints so as to maximize the generality of the theoretical statement. We might follow Brinton's (1964) example and take the revolutions in Great Britain (1642), the United States (1776), France (1789), and Russia (1917). However, to make our task easier, we should also select time periods, perhaps arbitrarily, when revolutions have not occurred, preferably in the same societies: Britain in 1742, the United States in 1876, France in 1889, and Russia in 1817. This contrast makes the selection of causes (or consequences, depending upon our problem) much simpler to detect. *Second,* we read these studies as rapidly as possible, always checking the order of events. *Third,* we write down all the possible causative factors in each case study. *Fourth,* we eliminate all those that are not common, that is, we ask if the causes of the revolution—in terms of general variables—are the same in 1642, 1776, 1789, and 1917. *Fifth,* we check to see if the supposed causes of the revolution of 1642 are absent in 1742, repeating this check for each of our comparisons.

The reader might notice that what we have here is the approximation to an experimental design. Here, however, our analytical unit is a society, a most interesting kind of real-life laboratory in which to conduct an experiment. The important point is to have cases in which our phenomenon exists and cases in which it is absent. If we are looking at a general variable, then we select instances where the scores are high and instances where they are low or relatively so. The important point is the contrast. Our causes should be present when there are revolutions and absent when there are not (higher in degree and lower in degree). It is easy to see that when we search for consequences, exactly the same procedure is followed.

If we find no common cause, then we might divide the concept of revolution into various kinds, a line of departure that some have pursued. If we find that there does seem to be a common general variable or two, then these become the basis of our new theoretical statements. The author's reading of the case studies of revolutions, specifically the American and the Russian instances, suggests that when there is an increase in complexity without a decrease in centralization, this produces increases in the conflict rate, what we call revolution. The usual problem with this technique is not the lack of common causes or consequences but the discovery of more than we care to deal with. But then this may be an epistomological fact that we may have to live with—the complexity of social phenomenon.

One does not need case studies whether by historians, sociologists, economists, and other social scientists. Journalists are perceptive people as well; newspaper stories can be just as useful, if not more so. (See Glazer and Strauss, 1967, pp. 176–183, for a discussion of library materials, another source.) The main criteria of selection are that the reports be longitudinal so that time-ordering is observed and that there be several diverse examples. Then the search for common causes and/or consequences becomes a fruitful one.

The success of this technique also depends upon a specific focus. One cannot have a vague interest in some problem. One's interest should be specified in terms of a concrete general variable, or at least a range of one. Otherwise the complexities and details will overwhelm us.

Employing Basic Paths

Recently, the addition of path analysis to our empirical armamentarium has called attention to the fact that when we have several variables, we have a large number of possibilities as to how they can be combined. If we consider all the possible bivariate combinations with 15 variables, where order does not make a difference, there are 105 theoretical statements. If order does make a difference, then there are 210 possibilities. Obviously, they are not all equally probable. Quite the contrary. We would hope that there are only a relatively few empirical connections, for, perhaps, theory begins when we say some combinations do not occur.

One way of proceeding is to ask what the approximate time-ordering of the variables is. This may result in a relatively simple diagram or flow chart of theoretical statements. Here Blalock's (1969, p. 72) block discursive model is a most useful one. The time-ordering of variables involves the recognition that there are chains of causes and effects, with some subsets of variables forming bivariate blocks. This may seem to be an impossible task because there are so many possible feedbacks, one of the reasons why the technique of comparing diverse case studies is advisable.

To help organize the variables into some path or chain of theoretical statements, and especially where time-ordering may not be at all apparent, the following tactic might help. *First*, divide the variables into the following elements or classes of variables:

1. Variables outside the collective.
2. Variables that represent resources or inputs of the collective.
3. Variables that represent structures of the collective.
4. Variables that represent integration processes of the collective.
5. Variables that represent performances of the collective.
6. Variables that represent outputs of the collective.

Then assume that the time-ordering moves approximately from (1) through to (6). This may not solve all problems and is clearly designed for the case of social collectives, but it can be a helpful model, essentially a systems model of input, through-put, and output (see Fig. 2.3). This model is one that visualizes a production process with stages, represented by elements or classes of general variables. It is this kind of basic path or diagram that is so essential for determining the path of cause and consequence.

Once a unidirectional flow is achieved, then the *second* step is to add the feedback effects, the chains that move in the opposite direction. Here, variables within general classes may form a block of interrelated variables. One example of such a block is the conversion of Weber's rational-legal authority reported in Figure 2.2; most of the variables are structural, and they are perceived as interrelated, at least by Weber.

Third, besides searching for blocks, one needs to consider particular feedback effects. For example, the possibility of feedbacks from performance variables to structural variables is a defining characteristic of system analysis, an example of which is found in Table 2.3. Another kind of feedback is from output back to resource. There are probably others.

In other words, first one starts with a simple one-directional flow organized around the idea of some production process. Then one searches for blocks, usually within a particular step in the production process, and finally, one adds feedback effects. This may sound like an impossible task, but once variables are written down on a piece of paper or a blackboard,

STAGES OF THE PRODUCTION PROCESS

Examples

Input	Structure	Integration	Performance
Education	Complexity or specialization	Communication	Program change
	Centralization	Coercion	Growth
Size	Formalization		

Implied paths

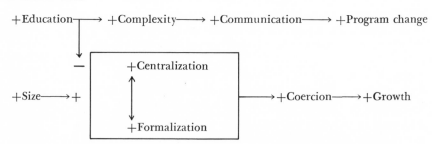

Figure 2.3   Using a Basic Path: The Case of the Production Cycle

theoretical statements connecting them should quickly come to mind. Finding the variables has always been the harder task. Here we are suggesting some guidelines for how one can establish a path diagram such as Blalock's block discursive design.

The suggested rules for social collectives will not work well for the microsociological level of analysis, that is, for concepts such as rank, position, role-relationship or role-set, and position performance. But for this problem we need some more general paths of flow models to guide us in our theory construction.

The reader might notice that rules for this technique are exactly opposite to those suggested for the technique of combining statements. There one assumes all variables are interrelated and perhaps eliminates only one or two of the double cause-and-effect connections. Here one assumes all variables fit into a single flow and adds as few feedbacks or double connections as possible. How can one reconcile these seemingly opposite approaches to theory construction? The answer is that the technique of combining statements is most appropriate when there are fewer than ten variables, most of which fit into one or two classes. For example, if all the variables are political or religious attitudes and behaviors, then that technique would seem to be the best way of proceeding. The intercorrelations are likely to be high, the time-ordering difficult to determine, and the delays in feedback of short duration. In contrast, when we have more than ten variables which cover three or more elements in some basic process, such as the production process, then the technique of path analysis is most advisable. The intercorrelations are more likely to be lower, at least between some variables, time-ordering is somewhat easier to determine, and delays in feedback are greater—important points to remember when constructing theoretical statements. The reader should consider these rules as rough and approximate at best. Path analysis is still a relatively new technique and we need more experience with it. Perhaps even more importantly we need other models or general paths besides the production process (Blalock, 1971).

As we have already noted, there are places for the logical statements of the kind "is" and "are" in a complete theory. Inclusion and exclusion reasoning is most appropriate when arranging definitions. Logical statements are also useful for what might be called the definitional premise. The idea is a simple one. Frequently, in a theory there is a place for a basic assumption about a need. Most functional theories rely on this assumption, either implicitly or explicitly. For examples:

(1) All societies need coordination (Durkheim, 1933).
(2) All organizations need achievement (Parsons, 1960, Ch. 1).

It is called a definitional premise because it asserts something about all members—whether individuals, organizations, or societies—of the analytical unit, and yet it is not part of the definition of the unit. An example from physics might make this point clearer. The first law of thermodynamics in its earlier formulation was the definitional premise that heat is work. Work does not define what is heat but by asserting some equivalence between these two concepts, some important implications follow. Likewise, coordination might *not* be a defining characteristic of society, but to assert that societies need or attempt to coordinate their parts allows us to make some interesting observations on how this might be done and how a method for achieving coordination might be selected. Definitional premises are a helpful first start in ordering our theoretical reasons into postulates as to the relationships between certain variables.

Similarly, just as there are qualitative differences with quantitative changes, there is a need for equations that stipulate threshold effects.

In verbal form, we might illustrate these ideas as follows: (1) Creativity is facilitated by conflict only in the range labeled competition. (2) Children will vote for the same party as their parents except when (a) they have reached the level of some college education, or (b) there is some deep societal crisis.

As can be seen in these examples, finding critical ranges is one way of formulating this kind of theoretical statement. There are other techniques as well which are discussed in other chapters of this book.

SUMMARY

Our task of finding theoretical statements is facilitated considerably if we recognize that concepts can be connected in an either-or way, such as with the verb to be and connected in a continuous way such as in the formulation, the greater the X, the greater the Y. For want of a better name we have called the former either-or statements and the latter continuous statements. The latter formulation allows us to be more subtle, complex, and informative in our analysis of sociological reality.

The ways of ferreting out continuous statements are easily grouped into three techniques. The first two help us to examine the existing literature for whatever statements may be buried in it. The conversion of constructs into continuous statements of a simple linear nature is quite straightforward once the general variables and their scores are identified. This can usually be done directly from the writing. In contrast, collapsing several statements into a more general one is a difficult technique because it requires changing levels of abstraction. The last two techniques are of much more general applicability. By reading carefully selected case studies, histories, and newspapers, we can isolate common causes and consequences. Again the focus of a particular general variable or even a range along it makes our work much simpler. If our cases are chosen so that we have cultural and temporal diversity and examples where our dependent variable scores both high and low, we are likely to discover some hypotheses. Similarly, by using general paths or models such as the one of the production cycle we can find a number of theoretical statements in some causal sequence, again assuming that we have some variables to work with. The last technique needs more development because as yet there are only a few general path diagrams.

Axiomatic reasoning, our third technique, has been much criticized. It can, however, be helpful under certain specified conditions. It is most useful when an area is new and relatively unknown. It is also most helpful when the number of variables is less than ten and when we have reason to believe that they are highly interrelated. This is most likely to be the case when the variables are from the same class of variables, what we have called an element.

The problem of searching for either-or statements we have deferred until later chapters. It is not nearly as important as finding continuous statements.

CHAPTER THREE

Specifying the Definitions

Concepts are the atoms of any theory, and the theoretical statements are the bonds between them. But a concept is not an irreducible minimum any more than an atom is. A concept, whether general variable or general nonvariable, dimension, or analytical unit, has several components or parts. These are the name, the theoretical definition, and the operational definition.

The most elegant operational definitions, and theoretical ones as well, are to be found in the work of Galtung (1966). Starting with a simple and nonexistent society of four people, he constructs precise definitions for the concepts of criss-cross, rank equivalence, and equality (see Table 3.1). The reason used and the discussion of the substantive significance of various scores such as 0 or −1 is insightful and very advanced. Although the measures and thus the operational definitions are for four-person societies, they teach us much about society in general. They also illustrate the advantages of having precise operational definitions, each definition referring to the same data. The relationships between these definitions can be stated in a straight-forward fashion as:

$$C = 1 - R^2$$
$$C = 1 - E^2$$
$$R = -E$$

None of these relationships is obvious. They come only from creating precise operational definitions.

Table 3.1   The Definitions of Theoretical Concepts: The Case of Galtung's Theory of Rank and Social Integration

Name of Variable	Theoretical Definition	Operational Definition
1. Degree of criss-cross	The degree to which there are individuals who can serve as bridges between completely disparate conflict groups	$C = \dfrac{4(a+d)\,(b+c)}{N^2}$
2. Degree of rank equivalence	The degree to which the individuals have statuses of equal rank in their status set	$R = 1 - \dfrac{2(b+c)}{N}$
3. Degree of equality	The degree to which the individuals are similar in terms of total rank	$E = \dfrac{(b+c)-(a+d)}{N}$

SOURCE: Galtung, 1966.

A less elegant illustration—but one that represents an attempt to define a concept which is critical in the contemporary literature—indicates the dialectic between theoretical and operational definitions, namely, the degree of stratification (see Fig. 3.1). Here, it is important to observe the fit between the name, the theoretical definition, and the operational indicators. There is no operational definition telling us how the indicators are to be combined. The degree of stratification is the concept. The distribution of rewards is the theoretical definition, or nominal definition, to use Hempel's (1952) term for it. The theoretical definition specifies the meaning of the theoretical concept, which delineates a meaning space that, in turn, is filled by the indicators. In this instance, we have suggested three indicators. These represent what is actually measured. What is important to observe about these indicators is that they do not measure all of the meaning implied by the theoretical definition. This is a typical problem. Usually, we mean more by a concept than we can measure. Also a typical problem is that the indicators overlap somewhat, that is, they cover some of the same space or meaning. Thus, we would not necessarily want to add them in our operational definition, but perhaps in some multiple correlational way, that is, add only the independent contribution of each indicator. (The intercorrelations between these indicators are not exactly equivalent in importance. It seems reasonable to say that the distribution of assets might be more important—it covers more of the meaning of the distribution of rewards than the distribution of income. But the precise weighting of these is difficult to determine and thus the lack of an operational definition.)

Name of Variable   Theoretical Definition
Degree of stratification df = the distribution of rewards in society

Operational Indicators
1. Distribution of income among social groups.
2. Distribution of assets among social groups.
3. Distribution of leisure time among social groups.

Meaning Space of Theoretical Definition

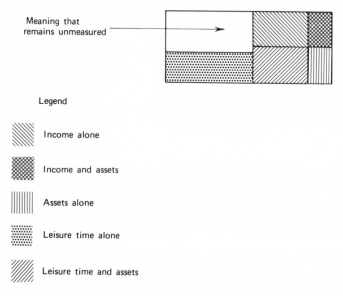

Meaning that
remains unmeasured

Legend

Income alone

Income and assets

Assets alone

Leisure time alone

Leisure time and assets

Figure 3.1   The Definitions of a Theoretical Concept: The Case of Stratification.

A particularly rich example of both theoretical and operation definitions is provided by Price's new book, *Organizational Measurement* (1972). The reader might study this book at some length, noting that Price carefully considers several alternatives, and then selects what he means for his theoretical definition. Usually, several operational definitions are given for each concept and discussed in some detail, indicating the exact questions or indicators, how they were combined into an index, etc. Since there are some twenty concepts, many of the important ones in the organization literature, one learns a great deal about the importance of theoretical and operational definitions by reading this work.

Also useful as an illustration of theoretical definitions is an early work by Price (1967). For example, he defines the division of labor as follows:

> Division of labor may be defined as the degree to which the tasks of a system are subdivided. A common measure of the division of labor is the number of different roles within a system. . . . "Role differentiation," "specialization," "fragmentation," "segmentation," and "fractionalization" are terms which mean approximately the same thing as division of labor. The term "complexity" is also used sometimes as a synonym for division of labor. . . .

Here, we are given not only a definition, which is clearly indicated in the text by a subsection heading, but we are told what other terms mean the same thing. We are also given at least one common measure for it.

Why do we want definitions for our theoretical concepts? The answer is relatively simple. Once we have developed some theoretical statements such as the greater the stratification in society, the greater the centralization, we need to know how to measure these variables and we need to know what is meant by the concepts of stratification and of centralization. This involves us in the task of specifying both a theoretical and an operational definition.

THEORETICAL AND OPERATIONAL DEFINITIONS

There are two strategies regarding the specification of definitions in sociological theory construction. The theorists have tended to emphasize the theoretical definition to the exclusion of the other. In contrast, researchers have been concerned primarily about indicators and indices or factors without any consideration of theoretical definitions. For example, Thompson (1967) in his work on organizations provides theoretical but not operational definitions. In contrast, Blau (1968) and Tannenbaum (1968) have been more concerned with the latter than the former. An exception is the work of Pugh et al. (1963 and 1968), where some attempt has been made to present both kinds of definitions. Most of the factor-analytic studies are indices without theoretical definitions (Sawyer, 1967; Seashore and Yuchtman, 1967; Empey and Lubeck, 1968), although, as always, there are exceptions (cf. Selvin and Hagstrom, 1965). An inspection of many of the recent journal articles makes clear that usually there are indicators, and sometimes theoretical definitions, but seldom both kinds. But the recent work of Price (1972) indicates how rapidly the field is changing.

Perhaps what is revealing is that most of the recent books on theory construction do not even consider this issue (Stinchcombe, 1968; Glaser and Strauss, 1967; Galtung, 1967; Zetterberg, 1963). The two that do, do so in an abstract way from the viewpoint of philosophy of science (Dubin, 1969; Willer, 1967).

The Advantages of Having Both Theoretical and Operational Definitions

There are good reasons why we want both. The two definitions are two different ways of comprehending our theoretical concept. Along with the name of the concept, they provide a triangulation in social space in much the same way that three astronomical fixes accurately determine one's physical location. In the world of sociology, where concepts are usually vague or trivial, this is not an inconsiderable advantage. We need the three elements of a concept, especially the two definitions, in order to make precise what is intended and aid in the search for the more profound.

Perhaps an extended illustration is necessary here. Suppose we take the rather difficult concept of centralization of society. One indicator that is frequently used is the frequency of turnover of parties in elections (Cutright, 1963; Lipset, 1961, Ch. 2). When we measure this indicator we see one thing and understand centralization in one way. Another indicator, suggested by Russett (1967), is the proportion of the total budget controlled by one government. With this indicator we perceive something else about centralization. Now suppose we say that we will define centralization of society *theoretically* as the distribution of power to make basic decisions about such things as the expenditure of national revenues, the appointment of key leaders, and the choice of national priorities. Notice how our theoretical definition again makes us perceive the variable centralization in a different way. It is not antagonistic to our two indicators and indeed each is a valid measure of what we mean by basic decisions, the former refers to the elections of the decision-makers and the latter to how much a kind of decision is in the hands of a single group; each is a qualification of the other. But the indicators and the theoretical definition exist at different levels of abstraction; they stimulate our thinking about the relationships between stratification and centralization in different ways.

The two definitions provide a critical and creative dialectic. Criticism is facilitated by the interaction between theoretical and empirical implications. It is much easier to decide if the indicators are valid with the presence of the theoretical definition, while indicators are a check on the utility of the definition. A concept can be measurable but not relevant because it bears little relationship to any other theoretical idea, as a number of factor-analytic studies have indicated. Similarly, a grand idea that is unmeasurable remains largely useless. Without a theoretical definition, the indicators can remain too specific. Without an operational definition, the meaning can remain too diffuse. We want to guard against the excesses of grand theory and empiricism, as noted by Mills (1959). This is best done by having two different kinds of definitions.

Perhaps the simplest illustration of the critical dialectic that can be created by having definitions both theoretical and operational is the example of stratification. Not everyone would agree with either definition suggested in Figure 3.1. Neo-Marxists (Kolko, 1963) might argue that perhaps we should define stratification as control over the distribution of rewards, really making it more akin to power. Some would prefer an even more general definition, namely control over resources, which lumps together in the same definition power, rewards, rights, and a number of other attributes. This would have the consequence of turning Marx's theoretical statement about stratification and centralization into a definition of stratification, a considerable alteration of his ideas. In the opposite direction, much empirical work has been done lately with the distribution of occupational prestige, and done on a different level of analysis, namely the positional level. We start the dialogue between these viewpoints by having both kinds of definitions, giving each a base from which to sally forth. Furthermore, the battle is considerably enhanced once we have stated the two definitions. This is the one reason why formalism in theory construction is an advantage. By having the format,

name, df = theoretical definition
          indicators

 no ambiguities about where each stands.
    ough there is not much evidence available, there does seem to be

another advantage in having two definitions for every concept. We actually make both these tasks simpler by having the two definitions. The presence of the theoretical definition helps us find empirical indicators and they in turn help us refine our definition.

Probably the greatest advantage of having two definitions is that the resulting clarity allows us to think more precisely and accurately about the concepts and their interconnections. The elimination of ambiguity facilitates the development of testable theories, speeding sociological solutions to mankind's problems. The extra effort of two definitions saves theory construction time in the long run because it can ease the discovery process of theoretical statements.

Specifying Theoretical and Operational Definitions

Our strategy here is to specify both the theoretical and the operational definitions, to have both meaning and measurement. Meaning by itself is not enough. Concepts must be measured as well. This entails an operational definition, a set of indicators with rules as to how they are to be combined into an index. By having both kinds of definitions, a theory can speak to both the humanists who are usually concerned about concepts losing their meaning in the hands of hard-hearted researchers and to the empiricists who usually have little patience for those who do not get on with the task of testing theories and accumulating knowledge. The theoretical definition allows us to maintain our purity while the operational definition, even if it is only one indicator, lets us be pragmatic. This is not a bad combination of virtues!

This is not to imply that all theoretical concepts must always have two definitions, one theoretical and the other empirical. In the beginning stages of development, theories might need a concept or two without an empirical referent. Sometimes it can be useful to have some fictions, ideas that are plausible but which, at a later stage, might prove false. It is difficult to provide examples in sociology because it would require guesses that some ideas current in the discipline might, at a later point, prove to be fictitious. But since this has occurred in other disciplines, it represents a possibility for our own. However, it is important to keep the number of fictions to a minimum. This is best done by striving to have two definitions for as many concepts as possible.

THEORETICAL AND OPERATIONAL DEFINITIONS OF GENERAL VARIABLES

Given that there are two definitions for each concept, the natural question is which should be constructed first? There is an element of taste in the answer. One might prefer starting with concrete indicators and then specifying the theoretical definition, or vice versa. The author has usually used the first approach, but the second might be faster and surer. The theoretical definition typically consists of a single word or phrase. We find it by selecting among several alternatives or possible meanings. The operational definition is more complicated; there is the problem of how to combine the indicators to say nothing about how to find more than one. The theoretical definition provides the basis for the search for indicators. It provides a focus, helping to solve that old methodological problem of choosing indicators. Although one can find theoretical definitions by using indicators, most people find it easier to move in the opposite direction. Each individual needs to experiment for himself to see which procedure works best for him.

We need techniques for both general variable concepts and general nonvariable concepts. In the following section are five techniques for specifying the definitions of general variables. The first two rely upon the literature; techniques for finding out what others have implied or employed in their work. The next two rely upon the existence of one of the definitions as the stimulus for the specification of the other. The last relies on the presence of more general definitions which can be employed to generate others. The problem of defining general nonvariable concepts is much more complex. As a consequence, no techniques are listed as such but several examples of the problems are given.

Searching for Theoretical Definitions

This first technique has considerable applicability. Implied definitions are buried in many sociological writings. The task is to find them, and then write them down, as Price has in his recent book (1972). Once committed to paper in the format,

name, df = theoretical definition,

we have a better grasp of what we mean by our concept. We will then discover that alternatives can come to mind.

One of the most brililant examples of the analysis of the theoretical definition of a concept, and the choice of one among several alternatives, is Merton's discussion of the word "function" (1957, Ch. 1). Merton studies several different possibilities indicating why he rejects each. He also examines several empirical studies, attempting to find the common theme implicit in this word. Finally, he comes to the conclusion that the essence are the words "objective consequences."

This is a surprisingly easy technique to employ. The essential task consists of skimming rapidly, searching for synonyms. They might be in the same sentence or they might be in different paragraphs. When we find a synonym, we have an implied definition. An example of this is from Parsons and Smesler's work, *Economy and Society* (1956, p. 20): "We wish to suggest that the two systems in question, the society and the economy, articulate in the following way; the economy is that sub-system of a society which is differentiated with primary reference to the adaptive function of the society as a whole." Thus we have—and this is an easy illustration— one definition of the economy:

economy, df = adaptive function of society.

On page 18 we are told that the adaptive function is defined as:

adaptive function, df = provision of facilities.

Therefore, we now can substitute and say:

economy, df = provision of facilities for the society.

The reader might work with the same book, specifying other definitions by reading rapidly and noting implied meanings in the sentences. Just searching for the definitions of each of the four major functional areas like the adaptive function can provide a number of insights into their book. As one does this, the logical structure of the book becomes more apparent and one can decide whether or not he accepts the basic set of concepts it offers.

We need not choose a single theoretical definition, as Merton did in his analysis of functionalism. It is entirely possible that several meanings are equally plausible; indeed, there may even be a conceptual argument about which is the better one. Under these circumstances, one takes both, constructing an operational definition for each of them.

An example of this is to be found in a recent article on centralization in organizations (Hage and Aiken, 1967b). Two theoretical definitions for the variable, degree of centralization in organizations, were considered. One was the participation in decision-making about basic organizational problems, the other was the relative autonomy over work decisions. Each of these denotations had a long history in the literature and, on *a priori* grounds, appeared to be an appropriate theoretical definition. Attached to each was a different set of indicators or index. This is an especially interesting example because the two indices also had high intercorrelations ($r = -.55$). However high this correlation, each index or set of indicators had different size zero-order correlations with a number of other structural variables. More importantly, when partial correlations were computed, holding constant all other variables, there were dramatic differences between the two theoretical definitions. One of them had consistently higher or stronger associations, as measured by the correlations between indicators, namely the participation in decision-making about basic organizational problems; but this was not known beforehand. In general, there is reason to believe that each theoretical definition is equally likely to be the "right one," and both can be employed in future research. Nothing is lost and much is gained.

As another illustration of the existence of multiple theoretical definitions for the same concept, we have the variable formalization. Some sociologists mean, how many rules have been written (e.g., Pugh et al., 1963). Others have suggested Weber's implied definition of codification, a not too dissimilar theme, but certainly a different meaning (e.g., Hage, 1965). Gouldner (1954) has stressed the importance of rules being actually enforced, still another theme. Hickson (1966) has offered the theoretical definition of specificity. Here we have a number of theoretical definitions, all referring to the same variable.

Clearly we could select the best or "true" definition on the basis of a pragmatic criteria, checking the size of partial correlations, as was done above with centralization. But the theorist can also weigh the theoretical consequences of different theoretical definitions. Here the mind considers how much conceptual mileage is possible with one or the other meaning. On theoretical grounds, one might argue that specificity is the best theoretical definition because the real import for an organization probably flows not from the presence or absence of a job description, or whether the jobs are codified or not, or written or unwritten, but how controlled a job occupant's behavior or job performance is. At least, this is suggested in Blauner's work (1964).

Searching for Operational Indices and Indicators

The literature is likely to have an abundance of indicators and few implied theoretical definitions. The technique of searching the literature for operational indicators is a relatively simple one which, again, requires rapid reading. By searching the indexes of books or the tables of journal articles we can quickly find a number of indicators (see Price, 1972). By listing all the indicators for the same concept, we begin to get some valuable insights.

Suppose the variable we are interested in is organization size, a common one in this literature. Various indicators that have been used are yearly operating expenses, number of books in the library, number of beds in the hospital, cubic feet of space, and number of participants (Barton, 1961). Each indicator suggests a different theoretical definition. The first is financial size, the next three are physical, and the last is demographic.

The reader might wonder what difference it makes if they are all intercorrelated? The answer is that even if they are, this does not mean that they will have the same theoretical and empirical causes and consequences, that is, the same correlations or partials with other variables. We have already given an illustration of this with the concept of centralization. More importantly, there may be good theoretical reasons for rejecting or accepting a particular theoretical definition. Population size might be most important for a theory of social structure à la Durkheim (1933), financial size might be more appropriate for an economic theory of competition.

The recent development of books listing scales, including instructions as to how the indicators should be combined into indices will help sociologists codify their operational indicators. This exactly parallels the development of psychology and its many large manuals on personality measures. As a consequence we need not worry about the problem of the literature search for indicators; many sociologists are working at this task.

Using Theoretical Definitions to Suggest Indicators

Once we have a theoretical definition, the technique of using it in specifying the indicators needed to measure the concept can be helpful. If one thinks about the definition suggested for the degree of stratification, namely, the distribution of rewards, indicators come quickly to mind. It doesn't take long to realize that income is one kind of reward, leisure time another, and so forth. The reason is that our search becomes focused once we are specific about what we mean. Only some indicators are valid—most are not.

The Case of Specifying the Indicators. If we select as the theoretical definition for deviance rate—a popular variable in sociology—the extent of rule violations per capita, then some indicators are valid and others are not. Crime rates and riots would be included, at least those that seem to involve some willful act to violate the law or custom of the society. But this meaning would clearly exclude such standard deviance indicators as mental illness rates because these are not rule violations in the normal sense of the words. Similarly, drunkenness, drug addiction, and gambling, topics found in the typical deviance courses, would not be included unless they specifically involved violations of the society's law or custom (Merton and Nisbet, 1966; Clinard, 1967). Suicide is more difficult to classify because it depends upon the particular society and its prevailing mores; egotistic suicide, for Durkheim (1951), is considered deviance, but not altruistic suicide. The theoretical definition clarifies a number of these issues, providing us with a standard by which judgments can be made. Students of deviance might not agree, but they can propose an alternative definition with arguments as to why it is to be preferred. In this instance, rule violations is the theme in Durkheim's famous *Rules of the Sociological Method* (1938), that is, deviance seen as a rupture of the collective conscience. Durkheim focuses on crime because of its significance for society. Thus, there is a theoretical reason for the selection of this particular meaning. Sociological consequences are most likely to accrue with this definition, that is, one that excludes all psychological problems, particularly those involving a lack of societal motive.

The procedures for thinking about our search for indicators are relatively simple once we have stated our theoretical definition. *First,* we list a number of examples, as was done above. In each instance we ask ourselves whether or not it belongs. *Second,* we ask how we can measure the content implied by the definition. This question is not always easy to answer but at least our definition starts us in a certain direction.

In the illustration of deviance, we might start with crime rates. But the problem is that different societies have different operational definitions. Some report crimes committed whereas some report crimes solved. Deviance experts have long noted the discrepancy between crimes committed as noted by the police and crimes committed. At best an imperfect indicator, crime rates must be adjusted in different ways in different societies. We have started to perfect our measurement but we cannot expect to complete this task even in one generation.

As another illustration of specifying indicators we might define conflict rate as the lack of control or disagreements about the structure of society (see Table 3.2). Conflict rate suggests a number of indicators such as strikes, demonstrations, and rebellions. Each of them can define a range, which itself can be refined by finding rates of participation (Tilly, 1969; Gurr, 1969). We would not include all internal wars (Ekstein,

Table 3.2   Specifying a Variable: The Case of Conflict Rate

Name of Variable	Theoretical Definition
Conflict rate, df =	Lack of control or disagreements about the social structure of society.

Operational Indicators

1. Absence of strikes, revolts, demonstrations, and groups plotting revolution.
2. Number of strikes per 100,000 working population.
3. Number of peaceful demonstrators against the government per 100,000 adult population.
4. Number of revolutionaries plotting overthrow of the government.
5. Number of days of armed conflict in revolution, revolt, rebellion, etc.

Index

Each indicator represents a threshold of conflict and is weighted accordingly.

1965) unless they involved some conflict over the distribution of rewards. Coups d'état and power struggles would also be excluded. Similarly, riots or crimes, when there is no inherent disagreement about the distribution of rewards, might be excluded. Admittedly, in practice, it might be difficult to draw distinctions between conflicts involving such disagreement and others. The important point is that the theoretical definition makes us aware of this boundary and the need to make a choice. We might not always make the right ones, but at least it does aid us in finding indicators, and thus, is a starting point in specifying our concept.

One popular concept in the literature is organization size. Here is one dimension that has a variety of meanings, and therefore, is an informative one to consider (Price, 1972). We might select as our theoretical definitions: all individuals who work to achieve the goals of the organization. This seems reasonable and what is usually implied. General indicators of this could be: (1) all full-time employees; (2) all part-time employees; (3) all volunteers; (4) all members of the various decision-making bodies, such as boards of directors, corporation officers, and liaison committees. The operational definition would include instructions that each part-time employee should be counted as equivalent to one-half of a full-time worker. The volunteers and the members of consulting bodies would be counted as equivalent to one-tenth. Or, the proportions might be determined on the basis of the average time each of these groups spent working to achieve the goals of the organization. As can be seen, our indicators can be quite general and still represent what is measured. This operational definition applies to all kinds of organizations in all kinds of societies.

The Case of Specifying an Index. Using theoretical definitions as a way of finding indicators is a relatively simple technique in comparison to the problem of constructing an index. What makes the latter difficult is that an index, that is, a complete operational definition containing rules about how the indicators are to be combined, involves a number of complicated issues. As soon as we have two indicators, the first operational problem is the relative importance of each of them. Should they receive equal weight? Should one be weighted twice as much as the other? Should they be scaled as in a Gutman scale?

Suppose we return to our illustration of deviance, a concept that has many measurement problems. We want to scale the indicators because different kinds of crimes involve different extents of deviance, that is, again that they have varying magnitudes. Some societal norms are more important than others and should be weighted accordingly. It would seem wiser to use the societal definition of what rules or norms are and not some "objective" judgment by the researcher sociologist. Certainly, murder is rated as a more serious crime than gambling in most societies, but not in all. In a particular society, what we might call murder might not be defined as such and therefore should not be counted. One simple operational solution is to rank the crimes in order of their maximum sentences. This would work at least in societies in which sentences are codified. One could use the behavioral modal sentence in those societies without a written procedure. Riots are obviously also deviance within the definition of a disruption, a violation of societal norms, although they are not normally included in deviance courses. They would seem to be more serious ruptures of the social fabric than crime, and therefore, should be weighted accordingly. This is an illustration of quantitative differences allowing us to make a qualitative distinction.

Note that our theoretical definition gives us a hint here as to how to combine the indicators. Since we have defined deviance as the extent of rule violations, we are given two different ideas of how to begin our task of constructing the index. One approach is to consider the number of people involved and weight the indicators according to this quantitative standard. The other approach is to consider the relative importance of the rule being violated. The former approach is an indicator of scope, and the latter is an indicator of intensity. As a measure of intensity we might decide to take the average length of sentences. If the average sentence for murder is five years and the average sentence for burglary is six months, we would then weight the murder rate as ten times as important. We can combine this approach with the first one by multiplying the number of murders per 100,000 population by ten and the number of burglaries per 100,000 population by one. Similarly, we could take each of the other major crimes, adding them to our index after multiplying by the ratio of their average sentence relative to burglaries.

The advantages of having a theoretical definition when constructing the index are even more apparent in the operationalization of the conflict rate. Here each indicator specifies a separate threshold or level of conflict (see Fig. 3.1). Note how easy it is to build in qualitative differences in our quantitative measurement when we make our index. We can be somewhat arbitrary about how to weight our indicators if there are good theoretical reasons to do so, the importance of the theoretical definition. In particular, we might reason that the difference between indicator two and indicator three in Table 3.2 is greater than the difference between 2 and 3. In this case we might want to create an artificial log scale by saying that indicator 2 gets a weight of 1, indicator 3 a weight of 10, indicator 4 a weight of 100, and indicator 5 a weight of 1,000. This is one way of operationalizing the old phrase that quantitative differences make big qualitative ones. Whether these ratios are correct could only be ascertained with research when we test theoretical statements using this index for the conflict rate. Here our main concern is to indicate a way in which one can think about the construction of the index and not necessarily to suggest that this is the correct operationalization for conflict rate. Indeed that is still an unsolved problem.

There are several additional guidelines that can be given for constructing an index. *In general, one wants to strive for as many points along the dimension as possible.* As has been suggested, the operational definition provides the cutting points, and wherever possible, we want to maximize them. Even though we might combine a number of qualities, such as different kinds of crimes and riots, we still want to measure each of these qualities in some quantitative way so that we have an interval or ratio scale. In general, one can use the qualities as one way of establishing the subscales or ranges in the dimension. Unfortunately, it may not always be obvious how to establish them.

As can be seen from the above, it is better to avoid indicators that are nominal categories or nonvariables. To add a number of nonvariable concepts together and call it a variable defeats most of the advantages that have been claimed for this kind of concept (see Pugh et al., 1968). It gives us the illusion of having a variable when, in fact, we do not have one. In measuring a variable like the degree of complexity, it is better to have one indicator, such as the number of occupational specialties, which can vary from zero to infinity, forming a nice ratio scale, than some twenty nonvariable items, such as presence or absence of a library, presence or absence of managers, or presence or absence of in-service training, even if they should happen to scale.

Using Indicators and Indices to Suggest Theoretical Definitions

This may be the harder technique to apply than the preceding one because we must move up in levels of abstraction. An illustration is provided by Selvin and Hagstrom (1965). After doing a factor analysis of a number of group properties, they decided that there were two implicit theoretical definitions, instrumental integration and expressive integration.

Since factor analysis has been less successful on so many occasions, it might be worthwhile to specify some guidelines for how to use it in searching for theoretical definitions. It would seem to be most helpful when the indicators have the following characteristics: (1) mutually exclusive; (2) mutually exhaustive; (3) the same level of abstraction; and (4) involve only one variable. The last characteristic is the most important. The general assumption of factor analysis is that things that do not correlate are not measuring the same thing. A variable such as conflict rate, described in Table 3.2, could never be constructed by factor analysis because the different thresholds are not intercorrelated; a society that has a revolution does not necessarily have peaceful strikes. Similarly, the correlations between indicators A_1 and B_1 can and may indeed be higher than between A_2 and A_1, or between B_1 and B_2, where A and B are different concepts. A perfect example of this problem is Sawyer's (1967) dimensions of society. Some of his power indicators are in his wealth dimension, and vice versa. Indeed, his article illustrates how the violation of the fourth guideline makes factor analysis a most useless approach for specifying either conceptual meaning or measurement. However, for one variable, factor analysis can indicate hidden subscales or indices.

In their research in organizations, Aiken and Hage (1966) factor-analyzed a hierarchy of authority scale and a rules scale developed by Hall (1963). What they found was a factor structure that suggested the following subdimensions of formalization (see Table 3.3): (1) rule observation, and (2) job codification. An analysis of their consequences for

Table 3.3 Using Indices to Find Theoretical Definitions: The Case of Formalization

Variable	Implied Definition	Indices
Job codification	Definition of the job	1. I feel that I am my own boss in most matters.
		2. A person can make his own decisions without checking with anybody else.
		3. How things are done here is left up to the person doing the work.
		4. People here are allowed to do almost as they please.
		5. Most people here make their own rules on the job.
Role observation	Enforcement of regulations	1. The employees are constantly being checked on for rule violations (reversed).
		2. People there feel as though they are constantly being watched to see that they obey all the rules (reversed).
Job specificity	Concreteness of definition of work	1. Whatever situation arises, we have procedures to follow in dealing with it (reversed).
		2. Everyone has a specific job to do (reversed).
		3. Going through the proper channels is constantly stressed (reversed).
		4. The organization keeps a written record of everyone's job performance (reversed).
		5. We are to follow strict operating procedures at all times (reversed).
		6. Whenever we have a problem, we are supposed to go to the same person for an answer (reversed).
Routine technology	Variety of work	1. People here do the same job in the same way every day (reversed).
		2. One thing people like around here is the variety of work.
		3. Most jobs have something new happening every day.
		4. There is something different to do every day.
		5. Would you describe your job as being highly routine, somewhat routine, somewhat nonroutine, or highly nonroutine?

NOTE: With the exception of No. 5 of Routine technology above, replies to these questions were scored from 1 (definitely true) to 4 (definitely false), and then each of the respondent's answers was averaged. Thus, for example, a high score on the first index means high job codification.

work alienation and expressive alienation indicated that they indeed did have different consequences. It is unlikely that the authors would have found these subscales without the help of a factor-analysis technique.

Factor analysis may also be helpful when two concepts, or at least their measures, appear to be so similar that one wonders if indeed their distinctions are not meaningless and sterile. Hage and Aiken (1969), in constructing a scale for routine technology, considered whether the items were different from the previous definitions of rule observation and job codification. This factor analysis—which included additional items and another scale developed by Hall (1963)—replicated the previous one and in addition provided two new factors called routine technology and job specificity. This lead to the recognition of these theoretical definitions: routineness of work means the variety of work; job codification measures how well-defined the job is; rule observation is, as its name suggests, enforcement of regulations; and job specificity is how concrete the job is.

The procedures are as follows. *First,* glance at the indicators to see if there is a common term. A good example of this is routine technology where the words different, variety, new, and nonroutine are clearly synonymous. In fact, this is very much like the technique of searching for the implied common definition (Ch. 1). *Second,* examine the indicators to see if they are on the same level of generality. This is a difficult judgment to make but one that is necessary if there are no instructions about the weight of particular indicators. In the example of Table 3.3, most of the indicators seem of approximately equal importance. References such as job, work, and technology—the indicators for routine technology—appear to be on the same level of abstraction.

There are several precautions that one must take in employing factor analysis to find theoretical definitions. For example, in the particular analysis set forth in Table 3.3, two indicators, a measure of rules manual and a measure of job descriptions, which had important theoretical meaning relevant to the concept, degree of formalization, were *not* combined in any of the factors. Thus, experience indicates that even with the above guidelines, one must exercise judgment and prudence. In particular, it seems advisable to see if there is a theoretical definition that makes sense and has meaning for each factor generated. One must also always check the unused indicators to see if there are more important ones not included. This check is both to see their theoretical relevance to some concept and their empirical pattern of association with the indicators of other concepts. If these precautions are taken, then factor analysis can be another useful tool in theory construction.

There are other methodological techniques for scaling indicators but each of them has approximately the same advantages and disadvantages as does factor analysis. Here we are concerned with using the constructed index or scale as a spur for specifying the theoretical definition. The necessary precautions that we have indicated for factor analysis apply to the other techniques as well.

Using General Definitions to Suggest Specific Ones

Just as we can use very general concepts to help us find more specific ones (see Ch. 1), we can use the same procedure as a way of generating definitions. This technique allows us to borrow both theoretical and operational definitions from other specializations within sociology, provided we recognize or know the general meaning and measures.

This is illustrated in Table 3.4 with the definition of social structure

Table 3.4   Using General Definitions to Suggest Specific Ones: The Case of Social Structure

General Element	General Definition	
Social Structure df = Distribution of some attribute among social positions or social categories		
Basic Dimension	Variable	Theoretical Definition
Knowledges	Complexity	Distribution of knowledges among social positions
Powers	Centralization	Distribution of powers among social positions
Rewards	Stratification	Distribution of rewards among social positions
Rights	Normative equality	Distribution of rights among social positions

as distribution. It is clear here that this means some variance measure, such as a standard deviation, or lorenz curve, or a proportion. Thus one can borrow the operationalization technique for measuring stratification in society, the distribution of income with a lorenz curve (Kutznets, 1963), and transfer this measure to the study of stratification in organizations. Once one recognizes that the general procedure is to compute a proportion or a lorenz curve along some attribute like income among a population, then any variable which is a structural variable should have this kind of operationalization.

Another illustration comes from a typology of role-relationships

(Hage and Marwell, 1968). If we define scope as the number or quantity, we can then cross-classify with each of our basic elements, generating the following theoretical definitions:

1. Number of partners, or degree of uniqueness.
2. Number of activities, or degree of specificity.
3. Number of locations, or degree of availability.
4. Number of times, or frequency of interactions.
5. Number of goals, or degree of purposefulness.

This example is an interesting one because most of the theoretical definitions were generated before the names of the variables since, in many instances, there was no name in the existing literature.

Similarly, one can use general indices and indicators, moving them to different theoretical contexts, as a way of generating new ideas. Cutright's (1963) index of national political development can be used to suggest indicators inside an organization, at least those that have elections, such as labor unions. Conversely, a participation in decision-making index (Hage and Aiken, 1967b), a measure of centralization, can be instructive when studying societies. Likewise, the work done in small groups can provide insights into other social collectives, and vice versa.

PROBLEMS IN DEFINING GENERAL NONVARIABLES

Although we want both an operational and a theoretical definition for our analytical units, major elements, and particular qualities—the three principal categories of general nonvariables—they are much, much harder to define and operationalize. Perhaps the best proof of this is to compare the large number of alternative measures for the distribution of power in organizations with the total absence of any measure for the existence of an organization itself. Or, consider the problem of defining charisma, revolution, or social structure. Each of these concepts is a popular one, and yet we have many more difficulties in agreeing upon meaning and measurement than we do with ideas like the degree of stratification, organizational size, or conflict rate, not that these are easy concepts to define by any means.

There are several reasons for this. General variables, even those like centralization, growth, and involvement, typically have only one relatively simple theoretical definition, even if they have several subscales. In contrast, general nonvariables, at least in sociology, require a long and complicated theoretical definition. It is necessary to specify all their properties.

To point to a group requires listing a number of defining characteristics: it is small, intimate, diffuse, etc. In this sense, sociology is no different from biology. It is much easier to define variables like body temperature than a nonvariable like man or bird—biological units of analysis.

The operationalization is also more difficult because the definition should specify the *exact* point at which the phenomenon crystallizes— when an aggregate becomes a group, for example, or an organization a society. The black-white demarcation is always harder to draw than the continuous gray. When is a man living or dead? Biologists have worked for a century on the problem, but there is still much imprecision in their operationalization, as the recent controversy over heart transplants makes apparent.

In view of this, the general procedures for specifying the definitions for nonvariables are almost the reverse of those for variables. In other words, (1) include a number of properties in the theoretical definition and do not be selective as to one key property, and (2) specify only one cutting point, which can be a small range of scores, for each indicator or for the index as a whole.

To illustrate this approach, let us consider the definition for social collective, a critical and fundamental concept. If one considers each of the major approaches to the study of social collectives as a starting point for discovering properties, we start with the following ideas: (1) certain inputs or resources (2) distributed among individuals (3) who perform different activities (4) which are integrated (5) and who share certain attitudes (6) that have performances and outcomes (7) that occur in certain places and at certain times. Possible empirical limits for each property are specified, first for a group, and then for an organization, in Table 3.5. The limits specified are intended only to illustrate how it might be done and to indicate the complexity of the problem of defining general nonvariables.

The suggested theoretical definition of a social collective has the advantage of including particular intellectual traditions. The first and third properties allude to the famous Hobbesian problem of order, while specifying the major ingredient in any social collective, namely, individuals. The second and third properties refer to the famous problem of coordination and control when there is a division of labor. The property of performances allows for functional analysis, while the property of location and time allows for ecological analysis. One usually wants to include the major intellectual traditions as implicit in the theoretical definition for an analytical unit; the more general the unit of analysis, the more this is true.

Table 3.5   Specifying Analytical Units: The Case of Organization and Group

Collective Property	Suggested Operationalizations Group	Organization
Number of individuals	3–20 typical	20–200,000 typical
Variety of acts and positions	Few acts and two positions such as leader and follower, that is, a simple division of labor	A great variety and a number of positions, that is, a complex division of labor[a]
Integration Mechanisms	Informal	Formal[b]
Performances and outputs	Expressive, that is, concern about social relationships	Instrumental, that is, concern about specific tasks to be accomplished[c]
Locations, times	Variable	Fixed, specified

[a] Etzioni, 1960 and 1961b.
[b] Blau and Scott, 1962, Chapter 1.
[c] Parsons, 1960; Hage and Aiken, 1970, Chapter 1.

One advantage of specifying the dividing line between a group and an aggregate of individuals, operationally speaking, as we have tried to do in Table 3.5, is that it makes us aware of the complexities of social phenomenon. Some sociologists would accept two interacting individuals as a group, others would prefer three or more. The example of the group also illustrates that our indicator may specify a range, say an upper limit on the number of individuals that a group can have before it becomes something else. Other combinations of ranges and limits can be used to define other kinds of social collectives. We have included the example of an organization, but one might want to add voluntary associations, programmatic organizations, neighborhoods, crowds, mobs, etc. Most of these could be generated by a manipulation of the word "certain" in terms of precise quantities. As we do, we begin to obtain a typology of analytical units.

As another illustration of how the definition of a general nonvariable involves a more complicated task, we may take the concepts of revolution and/or rebellion (Brinton, 1965; Ekstein, 1965; Moore, 1966; Tanter and Midlarsky, 1968; Davies, 1969), where the variety of interpretations is overwhelming. Some have suggested that we just forget the concept, and perhaps this is not a bad idea. But before we do, we can recognize the following. Revolution is a qualitative range along a quantitative dimension, namely, conflict rate. Like all collective events, it involves individuals, acts, places, and times, the essential coordinates of social action. These can be employed to suggest theoretical and operational definitions.

Revolution is defined as a sizable fraction of a society's population who are engaged in the violent overthrow of the existing government, which is not territorially based, and which does not cease for at least several months. Civil wars are territorially based. Rebellions can be and frequently are of much shorter duration than those events we typically call revolution, although there is a tendency to refer to civil strife, that is, unsuccessful revolutions as rebellion, while revolutions are seen as successful. Again our various properties cross-classified give us a typology of conflict.

Again, this will not satisfy everyone. The concept of change has been left out, and the idea of violence has been retained. Revolution has been used in both senses, as in the industrial revolution and the American revolution. But the attempt to specify a theoretical and operational definition makes clearer the areas of disagreement and difficulty, and this is all to the good.

SUMMARY

Instead of only one definition, it is better to have two for each concept. In this instance both a theoretical and an operational definition provides us with much more than twice one definition. The two kinds of definitions provide two ways of perceiving our concept. The theoretical definition gives us meaning and the operational definition measurement. A dialectic between meaning and measurement makes each definition easier to specify and produces a creative evolution towards better measures and sharper meanings. In turn, this facilitates the development of theories and especially theoretical statements.

Theoretical definitions can be generated in three basic ways: by searching the existing literature for implied meaning; by using indicators or indices to suggest a theoretical definition; and by employing more general theoretical definitions to derive less general ones. Likewise, the same three methods exist for generating indicators and indices: the existing empirical literature, the theoretical definition as an aid in searching for indicators, and more general operationalizations from which less general ones can be derived. Little attention is paid to the various scaling techniques because they are well described elsewhere. However, several rules are suggested for making factor analysis helpful in the construction of definitions.

CHAPTER FOUR

Specifying the Linkages

Concepts are not the only part of a theory that can be decomposed into parts. Theoretical statements are also more complex than our discussion in Chapter 2 suggested. Just as the concept is only a name until there are definitions added, theoretical statements are only verbal phrases until we add some content to them by specifying the rationale for the statement and the precise parameters connecting the concepts. There are two basic components: the theoretical linkage and the operational linkage. The word linkage is used to distinguish it from the idea of definition; as we have noted already, concepts are literally connected in theoretical statements. The linkages, in turn, specify how and why this connection is to be made. The operational linkage tells us how and the theoretical linkage why.

Zetterberg (1963) has called attention to the idea of linkages between what he calls the determinants and the results. Among other linkages, he has noted reversible and irreversible, deterministic and stochastic, sequential and coextensive, sufficient and contingent, and necessary and substitutable. These represent the ways in which X causes Y to occur in some theoretical statement but they are not the same as what is meant by a theoretical or even an operational linkage. The operational linkage specifies the *parameters* of the equation part of the theoretical statement including limits, coefficients, powers, etc. The theoretical linkage represents the *reasons* why the variables should be linked in some fashion; this provides the theoretical rationale part of the theoretical statement. Zetterberg's distinction can still be helpful for those concerned about connections; his term linkages is a good one and one that we shall employ.

The components of a theoretical statement or hypothesis are set forth in Table 4.1. The theoretical linkage is the rationale, the argument, or

Table 4.1   The Components of a Theoretical Statement

Verbal Statement	The higher the degree of complexity, the lower the degree of centralization.
	There is a limit to how much one can know.
	With specialization comes the need to consult the men who have the requisite knowledge.
The theoretical	Consultation with specialists increases their manipulating of information.
linkage or rationale	Increased specialization increases communication rates.
	As communication rates increase, power is dispersed.
	The greater the rank on education, the greater the desired rank on power.
The operational linkage or parameters	$+ \alpha$ complexity $= - \beta$ centralization

reasons why the variables make a viable statement. The reasons can be either more general premises or assumptions or some intervening variables.

In this instance, several premises, that is, more general theoretical statements, are involved. The limits of knowledge and the desire for rank consistency are highly abstract assumptions about men. In contrast, the concepts of consultations and communications are intervening variables. They are on approximately the same level of abstraction, and they occur in time between changes in complexity and changes in centralization.

An excellent illustration of intervening variables is to be found in Price (1967, p. 96). His hypothesis is as follows: "Organizations with a high degree of autonomy are more likely to have a high degree of effectiveness than organizations which have a low degree of autonomy." In explicating why the proposition is plausible, Price suggests, on the basis of several case studies, that a high degree of autonomy leads to greater adaptiveness to changes in the environment, which in turn influence effectiveness. He also speculates that low autonomy leads to low morale, which, in turn, reduces effectiveness.

Perhaps the best example of the use of very general assumptions, which are then applied in a variety of contexts, is Homans' *Elements of Social Behavior* (1961). Here, utilitarian theory—the desire to maximize profit—as well as several principles from reinforcement theory are employed to explain a wide range of human behavior. Regardless of whether one uses premises or intervening variables, the addition of a theoretical linkage provides a new dimension to a theoretical statement.

The operational linkage specifies the precise parameters of the equation: the form, whether curve or line, the coefficients, the direction, and the limits, etc. This is quite distinct from the theoretical linkage, just as the indicators of a concept, their scaling, and the rules for index construction are different from the theoretical definition.

Another illustration might make this point clearer. Suppose we take another theoretical statement:

$$(\alpha\ \text{Complexity} - (-\ \beta\ \text{Centralization}))^x = \gamma\ \text{Conflict Rate}$$

This is a more complex operational linkage because there are three variables instead of two, and we are using a power function, the x, instead of simple addition and subtraction. But there is no theoretical linkage provided. There is an absence of reasons specifying why these three concepts should be connected at all. This is the essential difference between a theoretical and an operational linkage.

In this instance, the theoretical linkage might be the premise that all men prefer consistency in ranks. Also implied is the premise that if men do not receive rank consistency, they will fight for relative rank equality. The addition of educated men, that is, new specialists, without corresponding changes in the power distribution creates conflict. Conversely, if men are given power without income, conflict will also occur. Naturally, all other variables are held constant—no increases in coercion or other mechanisms of social control, for example, or no migration of the dissatisfied.

In this instance, the operational linkage is far more complicated than the one in Table 4.1, even though the theoretical linkage is essentially the same as the previous one. There are three concepts connected by a power function for a discrepancy score. In other words, conflict grows at an accelerated rate as the discrepancy widens.

THEORETICAL AND OPERATIONAL LINKAGES

Recently, there has been some attention paid to the problem of specifying operational linkages. Blalock (1969 and 1971) devotes considerable attention to various ways in which variables can be connected, especially from the perspective of regression analysis. Stinchcombe (1968) suggests some typical kinds of formulations. However, to date, most of the emphasis has been placed on operational linkages and very little on theoretical ones. Blalock's perspective is that of the various problems associated with machine solutions, Stinchcombe's concern is the specification of particular theoretical orientations. The difficulty with machine solutions, especially current regression techniques is that we are likely to remain at the level of adding variables together instead of specifying nonlinear relationships such as curvilinear or power forms, more complicated linkages. And while the specification of particular theoretical formats is a helpful step, we want to move beyond this by developing techniques that apply in situations where the theoretical orientations are not appropriate.

The Advantages of Having Both

Perhaps the easiest linkage to justify is the operational one. Operational definitions make our theories measurable but not necessarily testable, appearances to the contrary. We can connect concepts operationally in a wide variety of ways. A simple illustration of this is in Figure 4.1, where three basic forms combining two concepts are diagrammed.

It is worth examining what each of these lines or curves states verbally. Furthermore, the reader should not be concerned by the word mathematics. I am not a mathematical sociologist, but instead interested in how mathematics can aid us in theory construction. In algebra and in calculus in particular are various ways of thinking about the linkages of concepts. It is this that we want to borrow; this does not require much knowledge outside of a few single diagrams such as in Figures 4.1 and 4.5 and the definitions at the beginning of the third section. It is the possibilities of *thinking* about linkages in different ways that is of more value and importance here.

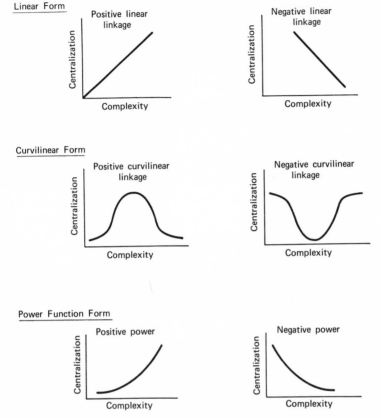

Figure 4.1   Forms of Operational Linkages for the Same Variables: The Case of Complexity and Centralization.

A linear linkage just means that as complexity increases so does centralization. The opposite, namely, as complexity increases, centralization decreases, is also a linear, or straight-line linkage. A curvilinear linkage means that as complexity increases, centralization increases to a certain point and then starts to decline. As a matter of fact, this very nicely describes the emergence of the nation-state, including the concentration of power in the king, and then the movement towards more democratic forms of government in at least the Western democracies during the past 500 years. In this case, it is a positive curvilinear relationship; we could make it negative by turning the peak upside down. Stated in words, as complexity increases, centralization decreases until a certain point and then starts to increase. A power function gives us change at an accelerated rate. Figure 4.1 shows both a positive and a negative power. The negative form is stated as this: as each increment of complexity is added, centralization decreases at an accelerated rate.

If we can see how different these three basic operational linkages are, then we appreciate the very critical difference between operational definitions and linkages. Measuring complexity and centralization does not tell us anything about whether the operational linkage is a linear one, a curve, or a power. Nor does it tell us where the peak is in the curve, the size of the power, or anything about the coefficients and limits. *Operational linkages provide us with testability.* They tell us how to use our computers effectively. If we can distinguish, for the computer, between linear, curvilinear, and power relationships, we have made great strides, and the rest of the problem of an operational linkage becomes simple since there are curve fitting programs. There are other forms of curves and lines than these, but many of them can be seen as combinations or variations of these three.

Why do we need a theoretical linkage? *The theoretical linkage tells us why two or more concepts are linked or connected in some theoretical statement. It gives us plausibility.* The first major advantage of having both an operational and a theoretical linkage is that they increase the probability of having a theoretical statement that will hold up upon research. One way of reducing the trial and error process in our search for a valid hypothesis is to search for as many theoretical reasons as possible for linking the concepts. The more reasons we have, the more difficult it is to be wrong on all counts. Correspondingly, the theoretical statement is less likely to be in error. Admittedly, in an age when an emphasis is placed on how much is published and not on how good it is, and when data articles are more likely to be accepted because they contain something tangible, the pressures are great to avoid this hard work. Finding a sound justification does take time. Perhaps if reviewers for the journals would start counting the number of reasons given for theoretical statements and demanding that hypotheses, whether post or predata analysis be included, the gap between theory and research would be closed fairly quickly. We need reasons why a correlation exists or should exist, and not just the correlations. This involves recognizing the importance of theoretical linkages.

Another advantage of having as many reasons as possible is that when we eventually integrate a set of theoretical statements into a theory, we are more likely to find some common themes or arguments. Indeed, the theoretical rationales became the basis for building what Willer (1967) calls the model of the theory, a set of basic premises that can be used to derive the specific reasons for the various operational linkages or equations.

These two linkages speak to different issues in science: *explanation and prediction*. The theoretical definition, to repeat, attempts to explain. When it involves an intervening variable, then there is some question whether or not there is real explanation (at least in the sense in which it is used by philosophers of science). Intervening variables, however, do point in the direction of explanation if they do not always reach this objective. The fact that the operational linkage predicts is easily seen from the previous examples. The various linkages in Figure 4.1 attempt to predict the degree of centralization by knowing the degree of complexity. It is clear how different our predictions become depending upon whether the relationship is positive or negative, linear or curvilinear, and depending on the nature of our coefficients and limits.

Similarly, as we have already suggested, if we know the basic form of the operational linkage—linear, curvilinear, or power—we greatly simplify our data-processing time. Even with high-speed computers we cannot search for all possible combinations, especially as the number of variables grows. In any case, it is more efficient to know, at least, where to begin our search, and this is what the three basic forms can tell us.

Many of the reasons given for the advantages of having both theoretical and operational definitions apply to linkages as well. The two linkages are two ways of comprehending our theoretical statement. This is quite apparent from Table 4.1. Similarly, although perhaps with less force, the two linkages provide a critical and creative dialectic. A curvilinear relationship as an operational definition might make us rethink some of our theoretical reasons as to why the variables are interrelated. Likewise, theoretical reasons sometimes suggest particular operational linkages, as we have seen in the example of Galtung's work. But the relationship between the two linkages is much more indirect than it is between the two definitions. Finally, the two linkages make us think more clearly about our concepts and their definitions, and vice versa.

Specifying Both Theoretical and Operational Linkages

Many of the recent propositional inventories do not contain any theoretical linkages, except perhaps as implicit in either the discussion or in the use of intervening variables. No one has suggested that this be done, perhaps because it was not recognized as a problem until recently. Willer (1967), for instance, has suggested that theories contain models, that is, extended rationales for the phenomenon involved. Others have focused on this problem in their own theory fragments (Homans, 1961; Hage, 1965), indicating an increasing recognition for the need for this part of a theory.

In contrast, as we have already noted, more work is being done on operational linkages. Although sociology has generally relied upon linear or straight-line operational linkages, slowly but surely an increasing sophistication and a movement towards more complicated linkages is developing. Atchley and McCabe (1968) provide in verbal form several ways of operationally linking variables on the subject of prisons. Pierce's article (1967), testing Durkheim's ideas on anomic suicide, should stand as a classic on the consequences of employing different kinds of curves when testing the same connection. MacRae (1969) and Kadane and Lewis (1969) also show what can be done with more complicated equations. A particularly brilliant example of how one kind of power curve, the Poisson distribution, can be used to investigate the efficacy of a number of theories is illustrated in a recent article by Spilerman (1970). He finds inadequate a number of traditional conceptions about the causes of riots in the light of the operational linkage that he uses to test them.

While sociology does not have a marginal-utility curve, it is clear that more and more sociologists are moving towards more complex operational linkages. This then is an argument for exploring nonlinear operational linkages. Insofar as more advanced disciplines such as economics have found their reality being analyzed with complex arrangements, then perhaps this says some things about the nature of social reality. Thus, our recommendation is to specify both theoretical and operational linkages. As we do so, we fill in the lacunae that presently exist in our theories and we move towards more complex conceptions of our social phenomenon.

SPECIFYING THEORETICAL LINKAGES

There are three important techniques for specifying theoretical linkages. The first is to specify the intervening variables. Frequently, these can be found by a rapid review of the literature. The second technique is to specify very general statements called premises or assumptions from which we derive the reasons for a particular lower-order statement, variously called theorem, corollary, or hypothesis. The third technique consists of thinking aloud, as it were, about why two or more variables might be interrelated.

Specifying Intervening Variables for the Theoretical Linkage

This is perhaps the simplest way of beginning when specifying a theoretical linkage. My own approach is to develop some theoretical statements and then do a rapid review of the literature, especially journal articles, reading and rereading. Invariably, I have found that things I previously ignored suddenly appear relevant. Isolated sentences in case studies or their conclusions can give hints or even reasons for the theoretical linkages. Certain facts in other contexts can lend some weak empirical support. The framing of the statement makes one sensitive to those aspects of our environment that are relevant. This is one of the major reasons why the mere writing of a theoretical statement is a step forward. Once stated, assuming we are looking for theoretical reasons, the theoretical linkage can accumulate if the statement is a worthwhile one to begin with.

For example, Weber (1947, p. 337) in his model of bureaucracy argues that the reasons it was likely to be more efficient were, "It is superior to any other form in precision, in stability, in the stringency of discipline, and in its reliability." Each of these reasons can be seen as an intervening variable. The idea of intervening variables has been discussed empirically by Lazarsfeld and Rosenberg, in *The Language of Social Research* (1955, pp. 115–125).

Similarly, one may find in other research studies the connection between A and B, or between B and C, when the theoretical statements connect A and C. Indeed, scanning tables is very helpful in finding intervening links which can be used to strengthen the plausibility of a theoretical statement. In this way, chains of reasoning are developed.

As an illustration, studies that point toward higher communication rates with specialists (Dalton, 1950; Landsberger, 1961) suggest the intervening variable between complexity and centralization, which is probably what Thompson (1961a, and 1961b) did when he first developed his insight.

The procedures are as follows. *First,* we start with a theoretical statement. *Second,* we do a rapid review of the literature, searching for variables that occur in time or causally between the two variables in our statement. This technique has the advantage of helping us to synthesize our own ideas with those of others.

In our search, two different situations, each of them interesting ones, can occur. One is that we might find some variable that seems to cause both the variables in our statement. For example, low income might cause both low education and low power. If our original statement was: the lower the education, the lower the power, we might want to recast it as: the lower the income, the lower the power. In this instance we would use education as the intervening variable or theoretical linkage.

Another possibility is that we might discover that the linkage between our two variables only occurs when another variable is present (or absent). To continue with the same example, suppose we believe after our review of the existing literature that the lower the education, the lower the power is true when there is also no income. Then we would reformulate our theoretical statement as follows: the lower the education, when there is little or no income, the lower the power. This is a more interesting statement because we have moved away from a simple two-variable hypothesis to one containing three theoretical concepts. In this instance, we would have to search for a new theoretical linkage. This process can reach a point of diminishing returns. As the variables become more and more concrete, the search for theoretical linkages will become more and more difficult.

With a few exceptions, the richest resources for intervening variables remain the classical theorists, such as Marx (1959), Weber (1947), Durkheim (1933, 1938, 1951), and Wolff's (1950) edition of Simmel and Simmel (1955). As they attempted to push their analyses further, they became involved in the problem of trying to find justifications for particular connections between variables. This is most apparent in the work of Marx (1959) and Durkheim (1951).

There are some other examples of how the search for theoretical linkages leads to an ever expanding set of concepts and statements. Perhaps the best illustration and one worth studying at length is March and Simon's *Organizations* (1957, Ch. 3, 4), in which there are many chains of propositions. One example is provided in Figure 4.2. Perceived prestige of the group is then seen as affected by a large number of variables. Many of the theoretical statements are put in both verbal and diagram form so that the reader has an opportunity to see as well as read about causal flows of ideas or chains of reasoning. In addition, for some of the very general models, operational linkages are suggested.

Using Premises to Generate Theoretical Linkages

Another possible source in the literature are articles dealing with premises. Gouldner's (1959) strain toward functional autonomy, Zetterberg's (1966) motivational assumption about rank, and some premises listed by Galtung (1966) are possibilities, as is the work of Homans (1961), Blau (1964), and Davis (1963). The contemporary literature tends to be a better

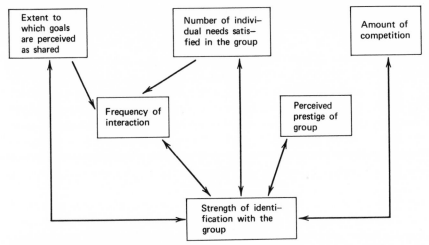

SOURCE: March and Simon, 1957, p. 66.

Figure 4.2 Specifying Theoretical Linkages by Searching for Intervening Variables: The Case of March and Simon's Factors That Affect Group Identification.

source for very general theoretical statements, the classical literature for intervening variables. Although, as always, there are exceptions.

As an example of how one can use general premises, we can turn to an article about interorganizational relationships (Aiken and Hage, 1968). In Table 4.2 are the very general theoretical statements that attempt

Table 4.2 Specifying Theoretical Linkages From More General Premises: The Case of Aiken and Hage's Assumptions About Organizational Interdependence

Premises

1. Internal organizational diversity stimulates organizational innovation.
2. Organizational innovation increases the need for resources.
3. As the need for resources intensifies, organizations are more likely to develop greater interdependencies, such as joint programs with other organizations.
4. Organizations attempt to maximize gains and minimize losses in attempting to obtain resources.
5. Heightened interdependence increases problems of internal control and coordination.
6. Heightened interdependence increases the internal diversity of the organization.

SOURCE: Aiken and Hage, 1968.

to explain how organizations become involved in interdependencies. The very general concept of diversity suggests a number of less general concepts including the degree of complexity, the degree of decentralization or the idea of a diverse number of power groups, and the degree of deformalization or the idea of a diverse variety of positions. Likewise, innovation suggests a number of less general concepts including new programs, new technologies, and new forms of organization arrangements. Thus, the first general theoretical statement or premise suggests some six less general ones. If the reader thinks of more concepts reflecting diversity and innovation, then he has generated additional theoretical statements. We can think of less general concepts for some of the other very general terms used in these premises, that is, the words of resources, interdependencies, and coordination. In the process, additional statements are generated.

Once we have these less general statements, we can begin to build a theoretical linkage. This might be thought as telling a story. This rationale or argument is necessary because our very general premises are a bare-bones form of explanation. Much of the flesh and blood is lost without the explication of all the implied details. Then too we find that communication with others becomes much easier when these theoretical linkages are made explicit. For example, behind or beneath the first premise of Table 4.2 is the following theoretical linkage:

> In several ways internal diversity creates a strain towards innovation and change. The conflict between different occupations and interest groups, or even different theoretical, philosophical, or other perspectives, results in new ways of looking at organizational problems. The likely result of this is a high rate of both proposals for program innovations as well as successful implementation of them (Hage & Aiken, 1967). But organizational diversity also implies a greater knowledge and awareness of the nature of and changes in the organizational environment, particularly when organizational diversity implies not only a spectrum of occupational roles in the organization, but also involvement in professional societies in the environment by the incumbents of those occupational roles, itself a type of organizational interdependency. Together the internal conflicts and awareness of the nature of the organization's environment create strains towards organizational change (Aiken and Hage, 1968, p. 915).

The authors do much of the same for each of the other premises. As can be seen, this theoretical linkage is not immediately obvious in the premise and yet it is suggested by it.

The procedures are as follows. *First,* one starts with some very general premises. These are obtained either by the second technique of Chapter

2 or the various techniques suggested in Chapter 6. This is, of course, the hardest part. And this is one reason why the contemporary literature contains the more general theoretical statements. It takes a great deal of time to move to higher levels of abstraction; we are slow to recognize the more general assumptions that underly our theoretical statements. *Second,* once one has the more general premises, then they can be used to generate less general ones by deducing all of the less abstract concepts that are implied as was done above. *Third,* these less abstract statements are then weaved together into a story, the set of theoretical rationales.

Another variation on this technique and perhaps a variation that is much simpler to employ is the borrowing of basic statements or premises from one area of analysis and transporting them by the expedient of dropping references to the particular kind of social collective. For example, in Table 4.2, we could substitute the word society for organizations or, even more general, the words social collective. However, the premises may not be true in the new contexts. One must always exercise caution. Do we think the same set of premises in Table 4.2 helps explain how societies become involved in interdependencies such as NATO, UNESCO, and other kinds of joint programs? I suspect that they do. If so, then the premises can be applied in the new situation. As we generalize, we proliferate more and more theoretical statements for each of the various kinds of social collectives.

Asking Why

Given the relative paucity of theoretical rationales in the literature, perhaps the best tactic for the reader is to focus on why the variables should be interrelated.

Why is population density related to the deviance rate? When we stop and think about this, a number of ideas come to mind. Under crowded conditions, individuals become more aggressive. With large numbers of people, it is difficult to provide adequate surveillance over their behavior. There are also more opportunities for deviant acts to occur when there are more people. This is the idea of some critical mass in physics or of demand in economics. It is exactly in the most populated areas where one might find bookies, prostitutes, and criminal gangs. Certainly, population density affects one's opportunities to learn deviance from criminals, as Sutherland has suggested. It also affects the likelihood of groups being formed, a factor that seems important in juvenile delinquency, an idea of Cohen (1955), and also of Cloward and Ohlin (1960).

When Durkheim (1951) attempted to understand why people's tendency to commit suicide increased as the day got longer, he implicitly suggested that interacting with strangers creates a stress or pressure. We might rephrase this to say that, as the population density increases, the ratio of interactions with strangers increases relative to known individuals, and therefore there is less integration and a greater propensity for deviance, as well as a greater stress.

We have provided a number of theoretical reasons that can explain why population density and deviance might be interrelated. They were developed by thinking about the two variables at hand and, admittedly, drawing upon previous literature (see Merton and Nisbet, 1966; Clinard, 1967). We are now organizing our thoughts relevant to these variables.

To take another example, suppose we hypothesize that increases in communication rates lead to decreases in deviance rates, all other things being equal. We might think as follows. As communication rates increase, more people are likely to be integrated in the society, that is, to have more role-relationships with greater frequency and duration of interaction (Durkheim, 1951). The role-relationships act as a conservative influence because of fear of social rejection or sanction. The constant exposure to communication results in better socialization to societal norms and values, creating a stronger commitment to them (Parsons, 1951), and this commitment, presumably, is reflected in conformity. Communication rates also affect knowledge about the relative efficacy of the police force and other deterrents, thus encouraging individuals to avoid at least those acts of deviance that carry good probabilities of severe sanction; certain kinds of communication, for example, pornography, violent movies, or mysteries, can provide an escape valve for some of the tensions that normally affect deviance rates—they are outlets for sexual and other kinds of frustration. (This argument in reverse has been used to suggest how communication can increase deviance.) Communication can provide information leading to the elimination of conditions causing deviance—in other words, the elite can find out what needs to be done if the communication is two-way (Kornhauser, 1959). The prospective deviant might find out about certain mechanisms of control and choose these himself, thereby depressing rates of deviance (what impact does knowledge of tranquilizers, for example, have on crime rates?). The communication can be entertainment and also a mechanism of social control itself—television appears to be used in this way with mental patients.

It goes without saying that perhaps not all these reasons are valid, nor is the theoretical statement necessarily tenable. But, as we find more and more plausible arguments for why two concepts are linked in a theoretical statement, the more likely some of them are to be verified in research.

The major stumbling block to the development of theoretical link-ages is inexperience with them. We are often so busy collecting data, we do not take time to think how the data should fit together (operational linkage) and why it should (theoretical linkage). The reader might try, as an experiment, thinking about why several variables are interrelated.

In thinking about the theoretical linkage, one place to begin is with the indicator or operational definition. Since the operationalization is more concrete, it can provide clues as to why two or three variables should be linked in some way. For example, if we measure formalization by the proportion of jobs that are codified and the range of variation allowed within jobs, and centralization by the proportion of jobs that include decision-making as well as the number of areas in which decisions are made, then these more empirical translations can provide clues. It be-comes easier to see that if there are jobs that are codified, there are fewer decisions to be made, and that these can be made by a smaller number of people. Similarly, when power resides in the hands of an elite, the pres-sure of decision-making will encourage specification of rules, or recorded, recurrent decisions. The development of codification allows an elite to control job performance more effectively and to do this in a larger number of areas.

While linking indicators can help individuals to think about the connection of variables, it is most important that each variable have a single definition. Perhaps the biggest barrier to thought is concepts that have multiple meanings. Associations become so complicated that a theo-retical linkage relating two concepts becomes almost impossible to find. It is important to narrow the scope of the concept by definitions, espe-cially if the concept is a very abstract one. It considerably simplifies our task of thinking.

It is not necessary to work with the indicators. The theorist can free-associate, keeping in the back of his mind the question why these concepts should be linked. But again, its success is dependent upon a clear concep-tion of the variables involved in the theoretical statement and an interest in the problem at hand. The reader should not conclude that the reasons always come rapidly. My own experience has been that some statements require years of working on an off-and-on basis. But once this process is started, it tends to continue.

SPECIFYING OPERATIONAL LINKAGES

The simplest way to approach the problem of operational linkages, and especially for those who have some fear of mathematics, is to recognize that there are only a few general possibilities. Indeed, most mathematical sociology can be seen as several typical equation models that are applied to a variety of situations. Similarly, economists have found many applications for the marginal utility curve. Engineers use the technique of families of curves, and, indeed, this represents one way of attacking the problem of how to specify an operational linkage.

Before we start explicating particular techniques for specifying operational linkages, we might begin by discussing the various parts of an operational linkage. For ease of discussion, we shall call the independent variable X and the dependent variable Y. The convention in drawing diagrams is to make the X axis horizontal and the Y axis vertical as in Figure 4.5. We have already suggested that for the purposes of theory construction, it is useful to think in terms of three basic forms or six if one wants to count negative and positive separately. In the technique of using trace lines, we shall broaden this conception to include some combinations. We shall also want several modifications of this basic form.

The first modification is the addition of coefficients. All these do is make a slight modification in the relationship between the two variables of X and Y, by saying a change in X produces more or less of a change in Y. A coefficient changes the relationship from 1 to 1 to some other ratio. For example, suppose X is investment and Y is economic growth. One-half $X = Y$ means one change in X, investment, produces one-half a change in Y, economic growth; $2X = Y$ means one change in investment produces two changes in economic growth. In the example $\frac{1}{2}X = Y$ we could say that it takes twice as much growth in investment to get the same percentage increase in economic growth (G.N.P.). In Figure 4.3, we have illustrated how coefficients can change the positive linear, curvilinear, and power forms. It might be noted that coefficients seem to be like powers but they are not. A power is a coefficient that keeps changing. This is a much more dynamic idea. One way of thinking about the difference is to remember Malthus' Law about arithmetic growth in food and geometric growth in population. The latter is an example of a power whereas the former can be expressed as a coefficient. The coefficient changes the slope of a straight-line making it more or less horizontal.

We could add the idea of constants as well, but since all they do is move our forms up and down relative to the X axis and sideways relative to the Y axis, they are not as important as the coefficient which does affect the slope of the line as opposed to where it is drawn.

The second modification of our basic form is the limit or the range. This states that the theoretical statement only holds within a certain range along our variables. We might argue as Walter Rostow does, to

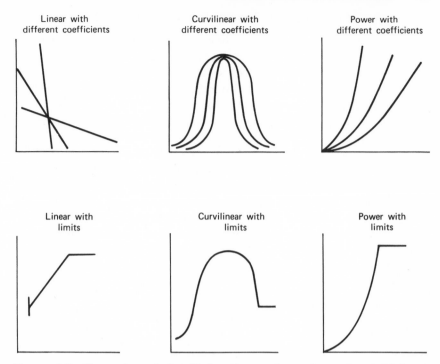

Figure 4.3   Examples of the Major Parts of an Operational Linkage:
Coefficients and Limits.

continue with our example of economic development, that investment is related to growth *only* after a certain level of development has been reached, what he has called the take-off point. This is another way of saying that the linkage operates above a certain threshold. Range is the total area, and it is defined by the upper and lower limits. Investment might affect growth only above the lower limit of $100 per capita level of development and not after the upper limit of $10,000 per capita level of development.

To recapitulate, we have broken our operational linkage into four basic parts. *First,* there is the form, and we have suggested as a start that there are three basic types. *Second,* there is the direction, and there are only two, positive and negative. *Third,* there are the coefficients, and *fourth,* the limits. If these ideas are understood and we have the picture in our mind as to how they affect our diagrams, then we can begin to think about operational linkages in a more precise way.

Using Trace Lines to Specify the Operational Linkage

This technique, like the first one in the previous section, depends upon the literature, in this instance, some reported data. We use a part of the data as a way of estimating the operational linkage. This estimate is then tested on other sections of the data. The data tested in this way may also be data we have collected ourselves.

Suppose we are developing operational linkages about the relationship between the proportion of time spent in research and the amount of research productivity (Andrews, 1964). We can take the trace line that exists, let us say for one subgroup, the Ph.D.'s and then use this as the basis for an estimate of the operational linkage (see Fig. 4.4). We make our estimates in four parts. In this instance, the form is a curvilinear one, positive, the coefficient of X has to be some fraction because big changes in the portion of time produce smaller changes in scientific contribution, and the limit would seem to fall between 40 and 100 percent time in research. This linkage can then be tested in each of the other subcategories or with other samples of Ph.D.'s.

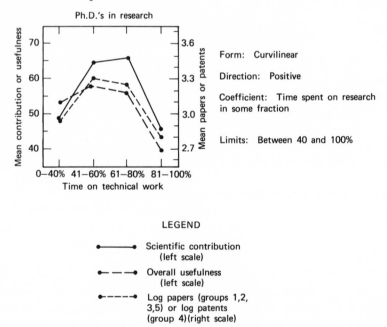

SOURCE: Andrews, 1964, p. 188.

Figure 4.4   Using Trace Lines as Estimates for Operational Linkages: Andrew's Productivity Study.

If this illustration is clear, then we can go on to observe that there is only a finite number of trace lines, as long as one puts an emphasis on general form. This is the idea of families of curves or lines and it is a very useful idea. If we can see that one section of data bearing on a particular hypothesis seems to fit one of these basic patterns or families, then the rest becomes much easier. Engineering has developed a large number of these, each with their own trace line. This is a stage that sociology has not reached. However, we can start thinking in terms of some of the more fundamental patterns, recognizing that, in most instances, they are variations on a line, curve, or a power, or some combination of them.

As a start, the six trace lines in Figure 4.5 should be helpful. These are suggested on the basis of their frequence of occurrence in the literature, at least as implied in the social change literature (Wilbert Moore, 1963).

The first variation on the theme of a linear relationship is what is called the step function. A more interesting case is one that applies to variables that increase a certain amount before they produce a change in another variable and then remain constant (see Fig. 4.3). An example might be the relationship between education and attitudes; the significant ranges or steps are from grammar school to junior high to senior high to college to graduate school. Or, the degree of stratification might be conceived as having significant ranges, which we can call middle class, working class, and upper class. Again, the point is that once a certain threshold is reached, there is a jump along some other dimension.

A very common trace line in the development literature is the power curve, or accelerating or exponential curve. Most inputs and outputs tend to fit this kind of trace line. In particular, the current measures of knowledge, technology, and energy consumption are best described by this curve form. A modification of the "ever upward and onward" equation is the problem of ups and downs as we march onward and upward, most typical of variables like investment and industrial production and gross national product. Note that we are adding curvilinear cycles to our basic power form. Whether one feels that one or the other is the most appropriate linkage depends upon the time span as well as the variables. The longer the time period, say 25 years and more, the more likely the power curve is a satisfactory approximation. When the period is 10 years or less, we become more and more aware of the episodic fluctuations, the booms and busts, the seasonal flows, etc., and this requires some curvilinear combinations.

A most interesting pattern is the curvilinear trace line. The marginal-utility curve is a variation on this theme, as are most cybernetic

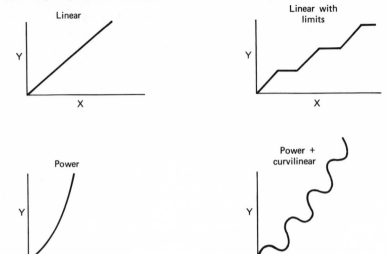

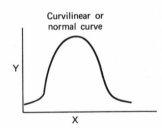

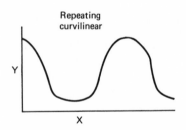

Note: Y can be any set of variables and X can be a time function as well as any other complex set of variables.

Figure 4.5   Specifying Operational Linkages: The Technique of Trace Lines.

control relationships (Ashby, 1956). Similarly, it applies to those situations where we have too much as well as too little of a good thing. A trace line that is similar is the repeating curvilinear relationship or sine curve; this is most appropriate where we keep repeating the ebb and flow, the good times and the bad. It applies to a large number of fashion situations —skirts go up and down throughout the century. It applies to the Pareto model of elites, lions replace foxes who are replaced by lions, etc. Perhaps the oscillation in methods of socialization in toilet training between permissiveness and authoritarianism (Miller and Swanson, 1958) fits this form of trace line as well.

There are, of course, many more forms than these, but these six cover a wide range of situations. As we have already noted, Moore (1963) suggests in his review of the literature on social change that these six forms plus two others cover all the major theories of social change. If so, and he appears to be correct, then we have indeed a good beginning; an intellectual arsenal with which to attack the problem of operational linkages.

The procedures for this technique are as follows. *First,* treat the trace line as the dependent variable—with this idea, the independent variable can be considered as some complex set of variables. *Second,* consider which of the six forms seems to best fit the case at hand. *Third,* adjust the general form by making it positive or negative, adding coefficients and limits.

It always seems advisable to start with the simplest and most general linkage possible. This is one reason why it is better *not* to use machine solutions at first; they tend to be too specific when one wants a linkage that will work in other social collectives and at other points in time.

The more difficult task is the other side of the equation, especially the multivariate case, that is, three or more variables. (This is an area where we need much more experience before we will be able to move to the kind of complicated sets of equations used in econometrics.) Throughout our discussion of the discovery of concepts and connections, we have considered several possibilities, but this is only a start on the problem.

The reader will note that we have not considered some of the other branches of mathematics, such as set theory, or some of the other kinds of models for analyzing data. They appear to be less applicable to the problem of operational linkages.

Regardless of the source, our idea is that there are several general models or forms. We should shop around, finding a likely fit for the theoretical statement at hand. Insofar as we can think of familiar illustrations, the more easily we can, in some substantive issue that concerns us, plot the trace line. We can say, Oh, this is like the marginal utility curve and a curvilinear form of trace line drops into place. The addition of coefficients and limits is then relatively easy. Then one can go to a mathematical expert for the finishing touches. For the more adventuresome, there are graphic solutions with machines. These can be most insightful because they concentrate our attention on the idea of families of trace lines or curves, which is the important first step in constructing an operational linkage.

Using Tables to Specify the Operational Linkage

Another example of how one can think about operational linkages comes from an article that is probably seldom read, and yet contains many, many rich ideas. Barton and Anderson (1969) worked with a case study, specified the implicit concepts, their interconnections, and finally *hypothetically* explored several different operational linkages. They are listed in Table 4.3. The substitution of different numbers allows us to try different kinds of linkages. Here they have experimented with different coefficents. They did not have any data whatsoever. The conclusion is that we can try these different possibilities on our own to see intuitively if one makes more sense.

It is worth commenting about the didactic possibilities of their work for understanding mathematical concepts. For most of us who have not received much training in mathematics, a concrete example such as this is the best way of thinking about the significance of a coefficient or a power or some other mathematical concept. For the sociologist, this is the main issue and not the study of mathematics per se.

Only simple equations have been included in Table 4.3. Barton and Anderson (1969) also suggest a dynamic model with the following equations:

$$H_t = WA_t + xH_t - 1$$
$$P_t = 2A_t$$
$$D_t = H_t - P_t$$
$$R_t = W - H_t$$

With these, they substitute numbers and observe that, while in the short run, the rate of prison disorder (D) increases faster than the rehabilitation rate (R), a new equilibrium point is reached with the disorder returning to the previous level, and the rehabilitation rate being much higher. This corresponds closely to what actually did happen as reported in McCleery's case study (1957).

Table 4.3 illustrates how experimentation with numbers leads to reasonable estimates of operational linkages, in the first instance, a coefficient, and in the second, an additional variable, hostility (H). We could also experiment with other forms of equations, substituting numbers to see if they empirically made sense to us.

Asking How

Another way of specifying operational linkages is to recognize that there are several finite questions that can be explored. The four basic

Table 4.3 Tables of Numbers and Operational Linkages: The Case of Barton and Anderson's Analysis of Prison Disorder

If $H = A + F$, $P = A$, $D = H$, $R = W - H$.

Administration Arbitrariness (A)	Prison Frustration (F)	Activities Attraction (W)	Prisoner Hostility (H)	Inmates Elite Power (P)	Prison Disorder (D)	Rehabilitation Activity (R)
20	20	40	40	20	20	0
10	20	40	30	10	20	10
0	20	40	20	0	20	20

But if $H = A + F$, $P = 2A$, $D = H - P$, $R = W - H$.

20	20	40	40	40	0	0
10	20	40	30	20	10	10
0	20	40	20	0	20	20

SOURCE: Barton and Anderson, 1969, pp. 540–557.

questions have already been outlined in the introduction to this section. What basic form is the linkage—linear, curvilinear, or power or some combination of them? Is the direction positive or negative? As for the coefficients in the independent variable X, are they fractions, close to a ratio of 1, or some larger number? Are there limits, whether upper or lower or both?

Of these questions the easiest to answer is usually the second because this one is typically contained in the theoretical statement. The greater the degree of stratification, the greater the rate of conflict is a positive relationship, whereas the greater the centralization, the less the integration is a negative one.

The hardest part is to select the basic form. Here, thinking in terms of families and the examples of the technique of using trace lines, might help. My own approach is to start with the linear form and at least consider the possibility of curvilinearity or power forms. One starts with a linear approach because so many of our machine programs are written for it and so much of our thinking is dominated by it. But one distrusts the linear form just because there are so many small correlations. My hunch—and it is only a hunch, since this is another relatively unexplored area *in sociology*—is that the following classes of variables might, more often than not, fit into one of the three forms noted in the beginning of the chapter.

When the variables appear to be highly interrelated, that is, when a change in one would appear to produce quickly a change in another, linear solutions seem the best. This is most likely to occur when the variables fall with the same class or element. In Chapter 5, we have suggested a number of classes: resources, structures, integration processes, performance, and outputs on the collective level; individuals, activities, place, times, and goals on the microsociological level. There are others. The same situations that seem appropriate for axiomatic reasoning are those where linear forms are recommended.

As soon as we move to the complexities of some system or across these very general elements or classes of variables, then we probably need more complex operational linkages. Again, certain classes of variables seem most appropriate for curvilinear relationships and others for power relationships. Any variable such as an input or output probably requires some power linkage. The rest are probably more likely to be curvilinear in form. In other words, the most ubiquitous linkage may be variations on the curvilinear relationship. The normal curve has done as much for abnormal psychology as the utility curve has for supply and demand in economics. The normal curve and the utility curve are two kinds of curvilinear relationships. Sociology might give it a try.

Admittedly, these questions do not always produce answers, but they do provide guidelines for our thought processes. We are here attempting to indicate some useful beginning steps in our struggle to specify operational linkages.

In thinking about coefficients, for example, we are asking how much change in X is going to produce how much change in Y. How much does per-capita wealth have to increase before there is a slight change in the distribution of wealth (Kuznets, 1963)? How much does the frequency of interaction have to increase before there is a change in the degree of sentiment (Homans, 1950)?

Is the relationship good only on a particular level or threshold or within a particular range or set of limits? Perhaps the idea about increasing specialization leading to greater decentralization is only true for professional specialties that require more than four years of college education. This is the idea of a threshold. Marx and Engels (1959) expressed a similar idea when they expressed doubts about the lumpen proletariate ever revolting. Similarly, perhaps Weber's (1947, p. 330) idea that centralization and formalization gives us more efficiency is only true for a range of these two variables. Beyond a high degree of formalization lies the inefficiency of red tape, as we know from watching postal slowdown strikes where postal clerks enforce all the rules and an exceptionally high degree of centralization can produce a paralysis of indecision, as did Hitler's tactical control over tanks in the latter stages of the Second World War. Thus, it is always worth asking what is the threshold, and what is the range, in which these variables articulate.

Through our discussion, we have been concentrating on the problem of interrelating just two variables. In practice, we can and do expect our operational linkages to be more complex than this. The diagrams and forms refer to the effect of X on some Y where X can be a combination of variables. For example, X might be the level of government spending and some Z the level of consumer saving. If our hypothesis is that $X + Z = Y$, we still have a linear relationship and we can draw it but, in this instance, the X axis represents the sum of variables X and Z, that is, government spending and consumer saving. Similarly, we can do the same for the other two curves. Except in the latter two cases, things become more complicated. Powers are more likely to be the products of two or more variables. And curves can be formulated in a large variety of ways.

For the present, the problems of time go beyond the limits of our current development. However, some are beginning to work on them (Blalock, 1969, 1971; Coleman, 1965).

SUMMARY

If our theoretical statements are to be put on a sound intellectual basis, they must have two linkages, one theoretical and the other operational. The former helps us explain social phenomena and gives our statements some theoretical plausibility. The latter helps us predict social phenomena and gives our statements some testability. Together they can be a winning combination because if we have seriously taken our time to specify both linkages, we increase the probability of making our research more productive.

There are three techniques for specifying theoretical linkages and three for operational ones. The simplest technique for the former is to do a rapid review of the relevant literature looking for intervening variables. More difficult is the technique of employing general premises to generate the theoretical linkages. The technique with the broadest application and yet not necessarily the most difficult is to ask why the two variables should be connected in some statement; in this way, one finds both intervening variables and premises.

The three techniques for specifying operational linkages are somewhat different. The first technique for specifying operational linkages is the diagnosis of which family of curves applies. Beyond the three basic forms, another three were suggested. Many more could be added but the six families cover a wide variety of cases. The second technique is to substitute numbers into various formulations until we obtain a result for the dependent variable that seems reasonable. This is also helpful for understanding better what impact coefficients, powers, etc., have on our dependent variable. Finally, we can think about the likely nature of our linkage by breaking our problem into four separate tasks: the search for the form, the search for the direction, the search for the coefficients, and the search for the limits. Of these, the first is perhaps the hardest, but with practice one becomes accustomed to thinking in terms of families of curves and drawing analogies. This is the art of asking how two or more variables are linked. Again, these techniques are most effective when used in conjunction with each other.

CHAPTER FIVE

Ordering Concepts
and Definitions

As we add more and more variables, we gradually come to realize the need for conceptual order. Sometimes even a single concept such as role makes us aware of the need for some conceptual arrangement. Sometimes, and more probably, our recognition of the need for a more formal scheme of concepts occurs after a period of rapid development, when a number of facts and ideas have accumulated in a particular area of the discipline. The present attempts at theory construction in several areas are reflections of this stage. Irrespective of what prompts the attempt to order concepts and definitions, it is another important task in constructing theories.

Any discussion of conceptual ordering is aided by the basic distinction between primitive and derived terms, as suggested by philosophers of science (e.g., Bunge, 1967). Their definition is simple. Technically, primitive terms do not have definitions. They are instead explained by illustration, as in geometry, or they are intuitively obvious to us on the basis of experience. Once understood, primitive terms are used to provide the definitions for the derived concepts. If one were to construct a dictionary in a language which no one knew, it would be necessary to start with a few words that could be understood either by illustration or intuitively. In this sense, all words have definitions. The critical point is whether the definition lies inside or outside the theory. All the remaining terms are then defined with the primitive terms or with combinations of them and other terms already defined; thus, the definitions of the derived terms are within the theory and the definitions of the primitive terms are outside the theory.

We have already seen some illustrations of this. In Chapter 1, where we discussed the use of basic elements to create new variables, we used primitive terms to generate new variables. We did the same thing in Chapter 3 when we discussed the technique for specifying definitions. Any ordering of concepts by levels of abstraction requires recognition that some terms are more primitive than others. In the existing literature, the best example is probably that by Davis (1963).

Table 5.1 shows the primitive and derived terms that form the heart of Davis' formalization of several existing literatures. The first eight terms are in one sense only formal, specifying the terms used in a balance graph. What is more critical are the specification of Person, Other, X (some social object), liking, unit formation, and similarity. Once these are understood —Davis uses other terms to explain them—they can be employed to generate the concepts of peers, friends, clique, group unity, etc. His work is well worth extended study for understanding something about the ordering of concepts into very general and less general ideas.

Another illustration of primitive and derived terms is given in Table 5.2. This is a typology of general variables, created by the cross-classification of the primitive terms of occupants, activities, locations, occurrences, goals, scope, intensity, integration, independence, and value. For example, the cross-classification of the row integration with the column locations suggests the general variable of the communality of locations. Social places differ in the number of role relationships that typically interact in the same location. The intersection of the row independence and the column activity is the variable formalization, which is defined as the choice of activities; this might be thought of as the idea of ritualization in relationships, a concept quite important in Goffman's work (1961). The critical point is that role relationships vary considerably in the amount of ritual that occurs, the king-servant relationships at one end of the continuum, and the servant-servant relationships at the other end. By stipulating a definition of each of the primitive terms as well, one can also generate the definitions for each of the derived variables. In turn,

Table 5.1 Primitive and Derived Terms: The Case of Davis' Structural Balance

Primitive Definitions

1. A linear graph, or briefly, a *graph*, consists of a finite collection of *points*, A, B, C, . . . , together with all unordered pairs of distinct points. Each of these pairs (e.g., AB) is called a *line*.
2. Lines may vary in *type* (or "kind" of relationship) and *sign* (plus or minus) or *numerical value*.
3. The *net value* of a line of two or more types is the sum of the values for each type.
4. A *path* is a collection of lines of the form AB, BC, . . . , DE, where the points A, B, C, D, and E are distinct.
5. A *cycle* consists of the above path together with the line EA.
6. The *value* of a *cycle* is the product of the net values of its lines.
7. A cycle with a positive value is *balanced*, a cycle with a negative value is *unbalanced*.
8. The *net value* of a *graph* at point P is the sum of the values of the cycles in which P is a point.
9. *Person (P)* is the individual whose behavior is predicted by the theory, the point whose net value is being considered.
10. *Other (O)* is some additional individual.
11. *X* is some value or social object, sometimes a third individual.
12. *Liking* refers to a person's evaluation of something, as when *Person* likes or admires, approves, rejects, or condemns.
13. *Unit Formation:* "In addition, there is a unit relation . . . the parts of such units are perceived as belonging together in a specially close way. But also two (or more) separate entities can form a unit. The two entities may be related through similarity, causality, ownership, or other unit-forming characteristics."
14. Considering *P* and one or more *O*s, and a set of social attributes including *X*, the *similarity* between *P* and *O* (symbolized by r_{PO}) is the correlation between *P* and *O* over all the attributes other than *X*.

Derived Definitions

15. *P* and *O* are peers if r_{PO} is positive.
16. If *P* likes *O* and *O* likes *P*, *P* and *O* are friends.
17. A subset of group members whose average liking for each other is greater than their average liking for the other members is a *clique*.
18. The *unity* of a group is the reciprocal of the variation (variance, standard deviation, etc.) in value of the member-member likings. The opposite of unity will be called *fragmentation*.
19. *Innovation* is a situation where initially the members either do not possess or have no degree of liking for a given *X*, and an attempt is made to introduce *X* into a group.
20. *Attitude change* is a situation where initially most or all of the members possess *X* or hold a given attitude and an attempt is made to reverse the situation.
21. *Conflict* is a situation where initially the members differ in their liking of *X*, some liking it, some disliking it.
22. *X* is a value if everyone in the group likes *X* or if everyone dislikes *X*.

Table 5.2   The General Variables of Role Relationships

BASIC DIMENSIONS	BASIC ELEMENTS				
	Occupants	Activities	Locations	Occurrences	Goals
Scope of the relationship	Average number of occupants (uniqueness)	Average number of activities (specificity)	Average number of locations (availability)	Average number of occurrences (frequency)	Average number of goals (purposiveness)
Intensity of the relationship	Average distance between occupants (compartmentalization)	Average act effort	Average location compactness	Average duration of occurrences	Average goal drive
Integration of the relationship	Average occupant overlap (common role-sets)	Average act dovetailing (articulation)	Average communality of locations	Average simultaneity of occurrences	Average goal compatibility (legitimacy)
Independence of the relationship	Average degree of occupant choice (replaceability)	Average degree of activity choice (formalization)	Average degree of location choice (movability)	Average degree of occurrence choice	Average degree of goal choice (freedom)
Value of the relationship	Average value of partners (sentiment)	Average value of activities (pleasure)	Average value of locations	Average value of occurrences	Average value of goals (importance)
	(who-whom)	(what)	(where)	(when)	(why)

SOURCE: Hage and Marwell, 1968.

the scope of occupants becomes the number of occupants; the scope of activities, the number of activities; the scope of locations, the number of locations; etc. Table 5.2 contains the definitions in the scope and independence rows. Where a cognate term exists, which can be seen as a synonym for the name of the variable, then it is placed in parentheses. Thus, the variable, scope of occupants, is defined as the average number of occupants or role partners in role relationships. A cognate term in the literature might be the uniqueness of the role partner. The same procedure was not used with the other three rows but it could be. Once we have a definition for intensity, then it becomes the definition or a part of it in every cell of the intensity row. The same procedure can be employed for each of the elements, which are easier to define.

One might wonder why so much ordering of concepts? Might we not be losing our meaning as we attempt to arrange our concepts into some scheme? What advantages, if any, are there to this procedure?

AD HOC AND ORDERED CONCEPTUAL SCHEMES

There is a danger in ordering concepts. To arrange and systematize concepts and definitions too quickly in a field or discipline can create conceptual sterility, imposing blinders and barriers. Not all the generated variables discovered for role-relationships are included in Table 5.2. Of course, additional dimensions, along with appropriate primitive terms could be added. But this does not say anything about the stray concept that does not fit neatly into the basic framework. *Typological arrangements tend to exclude in the process of being exhaustive.* Where is the variable of visibility, one that at least Merton (1957, Ch. 9) would argue is basic? In this instance, it can be derived by combining several of the variables in the typology, namely the variables of integration of places and integration of times; this is the meaning of visibility. But we are not always so lucky. Key concepts can be excluded in the process of generating a typology and indeed must be if they are on a different level of abstraction.

The Advantages of Ordering Concepts and Definitions

Despite some of the dangers noted above, there are distinct advantages to having a conceptual scheme in a theory. The first major advantage is the *elimination of tautology*. Tautology exists when two or more operational indicators and/or theoretical definitions overlap. A few minutes reflection makes apparent why this is a problem. Suppose we have a theoretical statement to the effect that all proletarian workers in capitalist countries are alienated. Leaving aside for the moment that we have an either-or statement, let us also suppose we measure presence of capitalistic countries by whether or not there is private ownership. Likewise, we measure alienation by seeing if the workers own the means of production; if they do not, we then score them as alienated. This is tautology. In general, the simplest way of determining whether there is an overlap in concepts is to see if the indicators of two concepts are the same or cognate ideas; if so, then there is conceptual tautology. Our correlations are higher but we do not have much of a theoretical statement, which is the connection between two or more concepts. If two concepts are defined by the same indicator or index, then we do not have two different concepts nor, therefore, a statement.

As we order our concepts into primitive and derived terms, we reduce the danger of tautology. It becomes easier to detect overlapping definitions and the distinctiveness of each theoretical concept when we juxtapose them.

When we order our concepts and definitions, there is also the crucial advantage of locating *new definitions for familiar ideas.* A case in point is the example of defining social structure as the distribution of some attribute (see Table 3.4). This leads to the insight that stratification and centralization are distributions and thus could only have certain indicators. Since the theoretical definitions are systematically derived when concepts are ordered, there is always the possibility of locating new meanings. The exercise of arranging ideas into some system will force us to think about our theoretical concepts in new ways. In some arrangements, we will find ourselves dissatisfied because the real meaning is lost in the attempt at logical rigor. But in other cases, we may discover that the force of logic has led us to a truer meaning, or at least a better definition than the ones current in the field.

Another advantage of systematizing and structuring our concepts and definitions is that *the primitive terms are exposed to view.* We are led to analyze our primitive terms more carefully. Perhaps precisely because they do not have definitions, at least within the theoretical scheme, we wonder more about their meaning. The contrast between them and the derived concepts becomes apparent. In particular, we are forced to question whether there are more basic concepts or ideas. What is the definition of activity, location, or time, to take some illustrations from the typology of role-relationships? Can we find terms more primitive than these? As we think about this, we are grappling with basic intellectual problems with far-reaching consequences. Indeed this is one way that the real revolutions in a discipline or a specialty occur. When we add a primitive term or take one away, we alter our entire system of thought. Consider the suggested definition for a social collective (see Ch. 3). The subtraction of the primitive term attitudes eliminates value analysis, the concept of norm and the problem of consensus—ideas that many in the discipline would consider basic. Similarly, the addition of a primitive to a definition as basic as that for social collective brings in a whole new approach or specialty.

The Strategy of Ordering Concepts

All things considered, there is more to be gained than lost by the ordering of concepts, but only when the theory involves more than ten variables. Certainly, physics profited a great deal by Newton's attempt to logically arrange concepts, an insight he obtained from studying Euclid's geometry. Indeed, probably more is to be achieved by the earlier attempts at ordering than the later ones. Conceptual schemes are usually constructed when the theory is fairly well established, after most of the concepts have been discovered. Individuals look upon the new arrangements as being somewhat sterile, a reshuffling of ideas, and nothing more. This criticism is avoided when the scheme produces new ideas or indicates some errors in thought, as occurred with the periodic table in chemistry. For the main purpose of systematizing ideas is to discover new ones, as well as to understand better their conceptual interrelationships. The role-relationship typology of variables is a case in point. The discovery of new ideas is more likely to occur when concepts are ordered relatively early in the development of a particular subject matter.

This strategy is not always appropriate. As we have noted, it becomes more desirable as the number of general variables increases beyond ten. It is then that we are most likely to have some overlapping definitions. As the number of concepts increases, it becomes more and more difficult to make this judgment without a tight logical scheme. Furthermore, we always want to use the strategy of ordering concepts with caution, checking the scheme against the existing set of concepts in the literature. If too many are left out, we would do best to stick with the *ad hoc* arrangement.

ORDERING CONCEPTS AND DEFINITIONS

We have discussed techniques for ordering concepts and their definitions in Chapters 1 and 3. It is essential to recognize that they represent different levels of abstraction (Blalock, 1969; Dubin, 1969; Galtung, 1967). We might imagine this process as going up and down an intellectual ladder, as we move from more basic to less basic and from primitive to derived. As has been suggested several times, this process is a difficult one for most people. And this may be the reason why typologies of general variables are so rare. For this reason, some additional discussion is included about levels of abstraction below as one of the basic techniques. Another technique is the cross-classification of primitive terms to create either typologies of variables or typologies of nonvariables or both. This technique requires the recognition of four basic kinds of primitive terms, three of which we have encountered in previous chapters, although not defined: elements, dimensions, modes, and operatives.

Logic may be suspect in constructing hypotheses, but it is most desirable in constructing a conceptual scheme. Each of the techniques below is built upon logical manipulations of one kind or another. The attempt to arrange terms into primitive and derived concepts and definitions is nothing more than the basic inclusive and exclusive reasoning that Aristotle made so famous. If we see the order in matter, living matter, animal, and man, we are ready to order sociological concepts into primitive and derived terms.

Arranging Theoretical Concepts Into Levels of Abstraction

One way of practicing and developing a skill for perceiving different levels of abstraction is to practice with a dictionary. As we read down a column of words we keep asking whether one word is more or less general than the ones before. Part of the argument over the meaning of stratification is an argument about the level at which the theory should be tested. Resources is a more general word than instrumentalities because there are resources that are not instrumentalities. Likewise the latter is more general than resources, which in turn is more general than the concepts of money and prestige. Practicing the ordering of words like this serves one to develop a feeling for levels of abstraction.

There are a few illustrations of this in the literature. One scheme of levels has been proposed by Parsons and his colleagues (Parsons, 1960; Parsons and Smelser, 1956; Smelser, 1959) etc. This might prove insightful to some readers because of the variety of ways in which it has been employed. Indeed one of the best tests of a conceptual scheme is to see if it has wide applicability.

Another and much older illustration is to be found in the Parsons and Henderson translation of Weber (1947). Starting with the four social types of action (see Ch. 1), Weber proceeds to bring in several other basic primitive terms and then defines a number of types by cross-classification. Indeed almost the entire book can be arranged into several typologies, all stemming from the first initial concept of the four types of social action. It is regrettable that Weber died before this work was finished because he might have had a chance to fill in the various lacunae that exist in it. If the reader systematically works through all the derivations he will discover a number of missing categories, which are suggestive.

The difficulty with both of these illustrations is that we have them after the hard work has been completed. We do not see how one moves from the most general to the less general, nor are we told how the most general ideas were obtained in the first place. In practice, one suspects that most people start with the concrete and then move up in levels of abstraction and then down again, constantly reworking their set of concepts and definitions.

If the variables have definitions, then the set of procedures becomes much easier. As we have already suggested in the use of other techniques, we *first* start searching for the most general term in the definition. Once we discover it, we ask ourselves *second* if it can be applied to other concepts and their definitions. *Third,* we search the names of our concepts to see if some include or subsumed others. *Fourth,* we work backwards seeing if combinations of particular terms produce the desired result, our derived concepts. For example, does the cross-classification of scope and integration really produce the communality of locations. *Fifth,* we repeat and repeat this process until we have as few primitives as possible and as many derived terms as possible, or at least until we have more derived concepts than primitive ones.

One way of developing levels of abstraction in sociology is to explore the indexes of textbooks for the most common themes. The themes can be detected—assuming there is some order in the book—by the number of cross-references reported. It quickly becomes apparent, when one studies the index of a book, whether there is any system of thought and what elements and dimensions are most important in it. This is particularly easy to see when the indexes of several books on the same subject are compared. Most of the basic texts have tried to impose some conceptual scheme. They are interesting because they suggest some of our primitive concepts. Wilson (1966) uses the ideas of rules, roles, and relationships as a way of organizing his approach to the field. Broom and Selznik (1963) systematically use a more complicated list of basic ideas. Johnson (1960) attempts to combine Merton's and Parsons' more fundamental concepts.

Cross-Classifying Primitive Terms

If we are lucky enough to have a set of primitive terms, then we can employ them to generate other ideas. In choosing primitive terms, we should keep in mind that there are four kinds. Each is needed if we are to avoid the common problem of a barren conceptual scheme.

Elements define inherent branches or classes which must always be present in any concrete situation. *Dimensions* define quantities, which again must always be present but, unlike the elements, are capable of variation. *Modes* are qualities which, unlike the elements, are not always present. Finally, *operatives* are words that complete the definition, for example, prepositions such as in or between, and words like same or different. These four kinds of primitive terms allow us to specify more easily the techniques for manipulating the terms to create other concepts, especially the technique of creating a typology of general variables.

Examples of elements exist in the typology of role-relationship variables—individuals, activities, location, and occurrences, the journalist's famous who, what, when, and where; they are potential candidates for primitives at this stage of development in many different kinds of conceptual schemes. The primitive why, or goal, has been left out, but it can be added, especially if the researcher is interested in the purposes of social action.

For those interested in the analysis of social collectives, the elements of social resources, social structures, integration processes, social performances, and social outputs might be a useful start. They appear to be quite general and cover some of the major problems that interest sociologists.

Elements which represent the basic components that must always be present in any concrete situation will always be few in number. For basic dimensions, again, there are several different sets that one might consider. The discussion of role-relationships supplies us with the primitives of scope, intensity, integration, and independence. Another set that will probably prove useful in sociology is knowledges, powers, rewards, and rights. In selecting dimensions, one searches for continua that have the same generality and do not overlap. These characteristics are essential if tautology is to be avoided.

The Case of Deriving a Typology of General Variables. Once we have sets of both elements and dimensions, then the task of deriving a typology becomes easier. *The major procedure consists of cross-classifying elements with dimensions.* This creates a typology of variables. Table 5.2 provides one illustration. Another is given in the extended example in the next section, where a typology of collective variables is derived.

As we develop our typology, we keep checking it against the existing literature to be sure that major concepts are not being excluded. This prevents us from going too far afield. Insofar as we are able to order most if not all of the major variables, then we have some assurance that we are on the right track. We should note cognates or synonyms to aid us in appreciating the connection between the primitives and the derived concepts. This is particularly important because the derived definitions often have a quite abstract quality that makes comprehension difficult. To put it another way, if people carry in their heads *ad hoc* sets of concepts, which is what all of us do, then some ordered scheme becomes very difficult to understand until we have lived with it for some time. My own experience and that of students has been that it is most difficult to keep the variables within the typology on exactly the same level of generality or abstraction. This requires constant reworking.

Definitions are easily added in the typology by defining the primitives. As we have noted, primitive terms technically have no definition, but synonyms can be added as a way of making the scheme richer. This point becomes much clearer in a large conceptual scheme such as the one in the next section. But in a typology this is not necessary.

We can increase the number of our variables by adding modes. In particular, they allow for the consideration of dimensions and variables that might otherwise not be included. Even though there are probably dimensions underlying these modes or qualities, they may be difficult to express at a particular stage of theory development. This third kind of primitive allows for some relaxation of the typological arrangement and the consideration of other kinds of ideas. But its only advantage is the broadening of the scheme.

For example, we might cross-classify instrumental and expressive with scope, intensity, integration, and independence. The idea of instrumental and expressive integration is an old one (Selvin and Hagstrom, 1965), but the other combinations appear to be new ideas. They would have to have their own definitions—both theoretical and operational—thus establishing that they are indeed distinctive.

As another illustration, we might cross-classify the mode of formal versus informal with the dimensions of knowledges, powers, rewards, and regulations, creating the following ideas (Hage and Aiken, 1970):

	Mode	
Dimension	Formal	Informal
Knowledges	Education	Apprenticeship
Powers	Authority	Influence
Rewards	Income	Status
Regulations	Rules	Customs

Formal knowledge implies the idea of education, while informal knowledge implies the idea of apprenticeship. It might also suggest the concept of experience, since this is another way in which knowledge is informally acquired. In other words, the combinations of words might lead to more than one label because most terms in the language, even sociological language with all of its attention to jargon, have more than one denotation or meaning. Which one is best is a question of the fit between the product of the two primitives and the label—a question of judgment, admittedly.

The Case of Deriving a Typology of General Nonvariables. This is the instance most readers are familiar with. Usually, it is nonvariables that are being ordered into types and our analytical units that are being derived.

The procedures for this are much easier. One cross-classifies elements by elements, a technique already discussed, or elements with modes. Modes are well known in sociology. We have, for example, instrumental versus expressive (Parsons, 1951), or urban versus rural (Redfield, 1941). Each of these dichotomies can be expressed as opposing ends of a continuum, and yet their nature is different from that of a dimension. They are an either-or classification, that is, nonvariables. Zetterberg's terms (1962), the modes of executive and emotive, another way of saying instrumental and expressive, illustrate this point nicely. Science and art are not really ends of a continuum, but instead opposite ways, hence the word modes, of doing the same thing. Modes, at least a few of them, always appear to be necessary in the development of a classification scheme. Chemists have found the distinction between organic and inorganic to be empirically essential. At some later time, these modes might be replaced by one or more dimensions, but at this stage, they seem necessary.

As an example, we might cross-classify instrument and expressive, two modes, with occupants, activities, locations, and times, to continue with our same illustration. This would give us eight types. Some of these are more interesting than others. Instrumental activities might be construed as work whereas expressive activities might be leisure. An elaborate procedure to produce a banal idea! Yet, if the procedure did not have old ideas as well as new, bright ideas and banal ones, it would be suspect. The objective of a conceptual scheme is to organize insights and this always means uninteresting ideas as well as insights. For example, instrumental occupants and expressive occupants is a more intriguing idea and one involved in the research of Bales (Parsons, Bales, and Shiles, 1953, Ch. 4).

Conceptual schemes and perhaps especially typologies of nonvariable concepts require constant checking against the developments of the field. This is so because they are so easy to generate and yet the question remains whether the product is worthwhile.

The Case of the Complete Conceptual Scheme. We can combine the two procedures above and elaborate an entire conceptual scheme. The four kinds of primitive terms allow us to indicate clearly how the technique of derivation works. *First,* cross-classify the elements to create a number of nonvariable concepts. *Second,* add some equivalences for the elements, allowing for the systematic derivation of the theoretical definitions as well. This also allows for a richer exposition. *Third,* cross-classify the elements and the dimensions to create variable concepts. The theoretical definitions will be specified at the same time. *Fourth,* work from the most general to the least general in deriving both variable and nonvariable concepts, especially the latter, and then work back again. *Fifth,* use modes to broaden the system of classificatory concepts. It also expands the number of variables. *Sixth,* use the fourth kind of primitive to add what operative words are needed in the theoretical definitions.

The fourth kind of primitive term is one that indicates the kinds of operations that are possible in the system. Students of formal logic usually worry about this the most and yet it is probably the least important. Sociologists need to think carefully about the other three kinds of primitives but can safely assume they can select the operations that they need. (After all, there is not much choice in logic!) Perhaps this is so precisely because logicians have worked on this problem. The reason why the operatives are not that important is because, in the final analysis, how the derived terms were created, whether by cross-classification or some other logical operation, is not important.

In the final analysis, the choice of primitives on *a priori* grounds, that is, without inducing them from derived ones or from reality, depends upon the nature of the problem. We have indicated some sets of primitives that are designed to handle general issues in sociology. But the reader might prefer to systematize the concepts involved in the sociology of the economy. Under these circumstances, primitives like money or market or machine might become important. The subject matter of the theory will determine the choice of primitives. But again, the hope is that by making the distinction between primitive and derived concepts and definitions, the reader will attempt to organize his concepts into some coherent scheme. This is the important thing.

AN EXTENDED EXAMPLE IN SOCIOLOGY

The purpose of this extended illustration is to indicate some of the advantages and disadvantages of imposing some conceptual order on the discipline. Its primary focus is on the analysis of societies although a number of microsociological concepts are included as well for didactic purposes. This particular scheme was developed over a period of several years in response to the problem of building some system for attacking the analysis of social change. Thus much of its focus is pointed towards the issue of how to describe and analyze the biographies of societies without becoming an historian.

While each reader will find things wrong with this particular exegesis, hopefully each reader will also find his imagination stimulated by some of the juxtapositions and derivations. For, in the final analysis, this extended example should be more than just an illustration but a serious attempt to bring some order into the conceptual chaos that presently exists. But, in the final judgment, it is not whether there is more order but more progress that is important with a scheme such as this one.

Choice of Primitives

One wants to have as few primitive terms as possible, and at the same time, be able to derive as many concepts and definitions as possible. Thus, the task is to know where one wants to end before one begins. This is one reason why searching for primitives or higher-order concepts is so important. If we can move up in levels of abstraction, then we can isolate the primitives we want.

In this illustration, although the focus is mainly on societal change, some microsociological primitives are included to indicate how one can move between these basic levels in sociology. We shall use two sets of *elements*: for macrosociology, the primitives of input, distribution, integration, performance, and output, that is, the major parts of the social system, and for microsociology, the primitives of individuals, acts, attitudes, locations, and times.

Only one set of *basic dimensions* will be used at this time, namely, knowledges, powers, rewards, and rights. This is a set that is helpful for both levels, although it is primarily designed for the analysis of social systems or collectives. One could also add scope, intensity, integration, and independence, but this would make the example too complicated.

For *modal primitives,* the terms instrumental and expressive are flexible ones. There are other ideas that one could use as well: Zetterberg's (1962) executive and emotive, for example, Toennies' (1955) gesellschaft and gemeinschaft, or Redfield's (1941) folk and urban—but they place the accent on other ideas rather than on the relative emphasis on getting a task accomplished and paying attention to the feeling of social relationships, the interpretation given here.

There appears to be no need for selective operational primitives, our fourth kind of primitive, such as number or the logical concepts of inclusion or exclusion. It does not seem necessary here because our main concern is with the sociological content of our definitions and not their logical manipulations.

The Derivation of the Properties of a Social Collective

We have already defined a social collective, and we will repeat the definition here. This is the major starting point because our strategy will be to differentiate kinds of social collectives primarily in terms of their outputs. Furthermore, we are interested in specifying some of the major macro and micro components of social systems.

Definition 1.0: A social collective exists when
    (1) there are inputs
    (2) distributed among individuals
    (3) who do different acts
    (4) which are integrated
    (5) and who share certain attitudes
    (6) and the result are certain performances and/or outputs
    (7) that occur in certain places and at certain times.

This is a complicated unit of analysis since there are seven defining properties. But as we have already observed, it is necessary if we are to include the major branches of analytical interest.

A few moments of reflection about this particular definition indicates that we have included some major branches within sociology. The inclusion of attitudes—property (5)—allows us to do value analysis. Structural analysis is brought in by property (2). Ecological analysis is possible with property (7).

The Definition of Microproperties. What defines our many social collectives is, of course, how the word "certain" becomes quantified. We have suggested some definitions for groups and organizations. Here we are concerned with societies. But before we suggest some measures, we need other definitions of microproperties.

Definition 1.1: Members, df = individuals in the same collective, e.g., employee, citizen.

Definition 1.2: Rank of member, df = the input of knowledges, powers, rewards, and/or rights of a member.

Definition 1.3: Elite, df = members with high rank.

Definition 1.4: Lower participants, df = members with low rank.

Definition 1.5: Social position, df = similar acts that are repeated in time by some members of the collective, e.g., leader and follower, worker and foreman.

Definition 1.6: Position rank or status, df = input of knowledges, rewards, powers, and rights for a social position.

In general, positions are named and therefore easily detected (Nadel, 1957). We sometimes use the word "location" as a consequence (Bredemeier and Stephenson, 1962). However, despite the imagery of this meaning, it is important to recognize that there are common acts performed by different individuals. Thus, all teachers lecture, grade papers, answer questions, etc. The style with which these are done—whether a teacher speaks slowly or rapidly, whether he avoids questions or welcomes them— are reflections of personality.

Definition 1.7: Occupants df = members of a position.

Definition 1.8: Interaction df = shared acts between any two occupants.

We frequently lose sight of the fact that not all acts for the achievement of collective objectives are done together. Managers do much paper work at their desks, while students probably spend more time reading than listening to lectures, and perhaps wisely so. Indeed, positions vary considerably in the amount of time spent in interaction, as do occupants within them.

Definition 1.9: Role, df = similar acts of the occupants of one position in an interaction, e.g., the role of foreman when interacting with a worker.

Definition 1.10: Role-relationship, df = the interaction between two or more roles, e.g., student-teacher, prostitute-customer.

Definition 1.11: Role-set, df = all roles attached to the same position.

We have already cross-classified scope, intensity, integration, and independence with the major elements of role-relationships. The reader might observe that the same basic elements and dimensions could be employed to generate a typology of variables for social positions. The cross-classification of activities and scope gives us job complexity, a key idea in the writings of Victor Thompson (1961a, 1961b) and implicit in Andrews (1964). Similarly and more simply, one could use these basic dimensions to generate some useful properties of rank—rank scope, rank intensity, rank integration, and rank independence.

The Definition of Macroproperties. We could define a number of other microproperties, but we have already obtained the more common ones in the literature, especially those found in elementary textbooks. What we need now are some of the more essential macrocomponents.

Definition 2.1: Social structure, df = distribution of knowledges, powers, rewards, and rights among social positions in the same collective.

This is the major concept that unites micro- and macrosociology. Structure is more than the distribution of some social resource among individuals, it is distribution among social positions that is important, and which goes to the heart of a number of major assumptions in sociology, and more particularly, in the premises suggested in the next chapter. However, this is not the only major organizational concept.

Definition 2.2: Social network, df = integration of role-relationships in the same collective.

Definition 2.3: Social organization, df = social structure and social network.

The last unites two major traditions and, indeed, two ways of conceiving of social structure. The definition 2.1 is the German tradition, especially that of Marx and Weber, while 2.2 is French, more specifically Durkheim, although Simmel, a German, also belongs here. Anthropologists have suggested that social organization is really the two combined, and this seems like a sensible suggestion.

Still another major tradition in macroanalysis is the problem of concensus. There are a number of schools that focus on particular kinds of collective attitudes as a way of understanding and predicting collective behavior. The more important are:

Definition 2.4: Social beliefs, df = shared knowledge attitudes.
Definition 2.5: Social norms, df = shared attitudes about the acts of occupants.
Definition 2.6: Social expectations, df = shared attitudes about the interactions of role occupants.
Definition 2.7: Social values, df = shared attitudes about the desired outcomes and performances.
Definition 2.8: Ideology, df = shared attitudes about the distribution of knowledges, powers, rewards, and rights.

Frequently, norms and expectations are used interchangeably. The purpose of the above is to make each a separate unit of analysis. Similarly, sometimes values and ideology are seen as synonymous. But in splitting apart what is frequently lumped together, we begin to understand more profoundly what is involved. This is not to say the definitions are correct, but only to say we are now forced to think about them.

These are not the only approaches to the study of macrosociology, however. In addition, we need to add the following concepts:

Definition 2.9:   Social function, df = performance or output.
Definition 2.9.1: Functional, df = an increase in a performance or output.
Definition 2.9.2: Dysfunctional, df = a decrease in a performance or output.
Definition 2.10: Territory, df = location of the collective.

With these macrodefinitions, we now have some of the major theoretical traditions. Structural-functionalism relates social structural and sometimes social organizational variables with functional variables. Ecological analysis looks at the territory and, to a lesser extent, the temporal continua of a collective. System analysis might be seen best as the combination of these various traditions, although other concepts, like feedback, are involved (see Ch. 8). In addition, there are particular kinds of variables within particular elements of variables that define schools of thought, such as size, technology, conflict, but these are derived below. Again, there are a number of other concepts that could be derived, but for now we need concentrate on only illustrating some of the more important ones.

The Derivation of Kinds of Social Collectives

The simplest way to distinguish social collectives is in terms of their outputs. Here, and implied in the primitives, is the idea that *every* collective produces something, even if it is just the pleasant glow of companionship. Then the next issue becomes, what are the most important kinds of outputs, and which kinds of collectives produce them?

Definition 3.1: Information, df = an instrumental knowledge output.
Definition 3.2: Artistic creation, df = an expressive knowledge output.
Definition 3.3: Sovereignty or independence, df = an instrumental power output.
Definition 3.4: Population, df = an expressive power output.
Definition 3.5: Industrial production, df = an instrumental reward output.
Definition 3.6: Relaxation, df = an expressive reward output.
Definition 3.7: Rehabilitation, df = an instrumental right output.
Definition 3.8: Charitable production, df = an expressive right output.

Here is an excellent illustration of how the procedure of combining modes and either dimensions or elements can result in some seemingly strange ideas. One way of understanding the concepts is to go back to the original conception of the primitives. We suggested instrumental meant getting a job done whereas expressive meant being concerned with the feelings of the relationship. This would seem to be a fundamental distinction, albeit each of these are probably variables and all social situations have various degrees of each. It makes some sense to say that knowledge concerned with getting a job done is information, or a concern with facts. Its counterpart, knowledge about the feelings, or concern with what is evolved, would seem to be artistic creation. Both are descriptions and analyses, but their objectives, in terms of the modality of instrumental and expressive, is different. This same parallel is continued with the basic dimension of power (see Table 5.3). Instrumental power suggests the idea of independence or sovereignty; the power to get a job done. Power relative to feelings is what is implied by the process of socialization, the production of adults capable of feeling. There is no term quite adequate except perhaps population, but the idea is more than just the demographic problem of births and deaths; the output of societies is socialized adults, something different and something quite sociological.

Definitions 3.5 and 3.6 might be seen as another way of saying work and play. Rehabilitation and charitable production require more explanation. Here our concern is with those collectives that denote time or

Table 5.3   The Definitions of Institutional Outputs

Outputs	Theoretical Definition	Specific Indicators for Society
Information	Instrumental knowledge	Amount of discoveries or ideas produced, such as number of journal articles, research reports, number of college graduates
Artistic creation	Expressive knowledge	Amount of art objects produced, such as number of novels, sculptures, paintings, etc., executed, number of artistic performances
Sovereignty and independence	Instrumental power	Size of territory; ratio of foreign troops to native troops
Socialization	Expressive power	Functioning adults
Production	Instrumental rewards	Index of agricultural production; index of industrial production
Relaxation	Expressive rewards	Average vacation, average weekly time off
Rehabilitation	Instrumental rights	Number of health and welfare recipients, average amount of payment, average longevity
Charitable production	Expressive rights	Number of people helped by charity; church attendance

NOTE: Many of these ideas are suggested by Zetterberg, 1962.

money for various worthy causes, that is, philanthropy. It is defined as an expressive right and an obligation because our charity represents our feelings and social concern about others in some group or society. Rehabilitation is easier to understand. Again, individuals do define as a right the repairing of certain wrongs in society. In fact, this is how charitable production and rehabilitation are akin—a repairing process.

How do these ideas compare with other schemes concerned with the same problem? Although these matters are always subject to interpretation, there is some correspondence between these major outputs and the Parsons-Bales scheme of functional alternatives, except that there are four pairs rather than just A., G., I., and L. (Parsons, Bales, and Shills, 1953). A comparison perhaps makes the above ideas clearer. Adaptiveness is similar to information and artistic creation; goal achievement to sovereignty and socialization; integration to production and relaxation; and finally, rehabilitation and charitable production are similar to pattern maintenance, that is, they involve a form of preserving present capabilities and potentialities.

With these kinds of outputs, we can now define kinds of collectives in institutional and societal analysis.

Definition 3.9:   Institutional realm, df = all collectives concerned with the production of the same output.

Definition 3.9.1: Scientific realm, df = all collectives concerned with the production of information.

Definition 3.9.2: Artistic realm, df = all collectives concerned with the production of artistic creation.

Definition 3.9.3: Political realm, df = all collectives concerned with the production of sovereignty.

Definition 3.9.4: Familial realm, df = all collectives concerned with the production of people or socialization.

Definition 3.9.5: Economic realm, df = all collectives concerned with the production of industrial and agricultural products.

Definition 3.9.6: Leisure realm, df = all collectives concerned with the production of relaxation.

Definition 3.9.7: Welfare realm, df = all collectives concerned with the production of rehabilitation.

Definition 3.9.8: Religious realm, df = all collectives concerned with the production of charity.

This raises the issue of how one would operationalize this, and therefore, the societal and institutional indicators are included in Table 5.3. Not all of the meaning is measured, but enough is included so that the concepts are concretized. More elaborate indicators are given below.

Naturally, societies differ on the other six properties of collectives as well. They have all eight inputs, which are defined below. They tend to be very large in size and also have a wide variety of activities, that is, a complex division of labor. There are less complex collectives. Finally, with the exception of nomadic societies, they have fixed territories and tend to endure for very long periods of time. Perhaps the most important difference is that they produce all eight outputs, and thus are largely self-sufficient, that is, relatively less dependent upon the environment than other kinds of collectives.

Definition 3.10: Society, df = a social collective with all eight outputs.

A comparison of this definition with the existing ones indicates that most of the traditional ideas are included. New ones have been added, making the definition a much more complex description of a society. But perhaps this is all to the good. Here the accent is placed on society as producing eight essential outputs, making them relatively self-sufficient. The definition does not exclude the concept of exchanges because there is no assumption that the society produces everything within each output that it needs. To argue that society requires the production of goods, the variable, industrial production (which is intended to include agricultural production) is not to say that all the wheat or chickens or carbon or steel that it consumes are produced internally. Thus, this definition is not inconsistent with a conception of societies as relatively open social systems. Another advantage of this particular definition is that it combines the old conception of institutional analysis with the new model of system analysis where the accent is placed on through-put, or some idea of production.

The Derivation of Variables for Describing Social Collectives

There are a number of behavioral variables as well as the eight outputs we have defined. To help distinguish each of these elements or classes of variables, the word level will be used for inputs, degree for distributions, rate for integration variables, and amount for performances and outputs.

Definition 4.1.1: Level of education/technology, df = the input of instrumental knowledge.

Definition 4.1.2: Level of taste, df = the input of expressive knowledge.

Definition 4.1.3: Level of autonomy, df = the input of instrumental power.

Definition 4.1.4: Level of familial investment, df = the input of expressive power.

Definition 4.1.5: Level of investment, df = the input of instrumental reward.

Definition 4.1.6: Level of leisure, df = the input of expressive reward.

Definition 4.1.7: Level of welfare, df = the input of instrumental right.

Definition 4.1.8: Level of charitable investment, df = the input of expressive right.

The simplest way of thinking about inputs or social resources is in terms of expenditures, that is, how much does a society invest. The word is clear in the economic institutional realm. However, we seem to lose sight of the fact that technology is an investment as is population and autonomy.

In Table 5.4 we see the essential technique of cross-classifying an element with a dimension. Social resources, the idea of an input, is cross-classified with the eight kinds of outputs, to generate eight inputs. Instrumental knowledges, as inputs, suggests the critical concepts of education or technology. Education in turn, can be measured by looking at the expenditures on education and how many people work as teachers or scientists. (Table 5.5 shows the suggested indicators.) Likewise, leisure is seen as involving expenditures, whether public or private for activities, such as sports, nightclubs, television, resorts, and amusement parks. This is a whole industry, which is quite different from industrial production.

One can make a distinction between short-term and long-term expenditures, such as salaries or buildings in each of these institutional sectors, but that is a refinement that is unnecessary. It should be understood that investment or expenditures is intended to cover both of these kinds. More importantly, this distinction, which is common in economics, is applicable in each of the institutional sectors. Thus, we build schools and pay teacher salaries, we build aircraft carriers and pay naval salaries, we build resorts and pay for entertainers.

Many of the measurement problems of both inputs and outputs, including those for areas that are usually ignored, are to be found in Sheldon and Moore *Indicators of Social Change* (1968). They note many problems which cannot be considered here.

The next 12 variables are in sets of four instead of eight. We could continue the basic dichotomy between instrumental and expressive, but there does not seem to be any advantage to this as long as our indicators cover both instrumental and expressive institutional sectors. Indeed, for structural variables, integration processes, and social performances we want to describe what is happening in all eight sectors and their interrelationships. It is precisely this that changes the meaning of a variable like centralization from being a political science concept. Similarly, complexity refers to the distribution of managers and professions in each of the eight sectors.

Definition 4.2.1: **Degree of complexity, df = distribution of knowledges.**

Definition 4.2.2: **Degree of centralization, df = distribution of powers.**

Table 5.4 A Typology of 28 Social Indicators for the Analysis of Societies

Basic Dimensions (Quantity)	Social Resources (Level of expenditure)	Social Structure (Degree of distribution)	Integration Processes (Rate of control)	Social Performances (Amount of effectiveness)	Social Outputs (Resource production)
Knowledges	R_1 Level of education R_2 Level of taste	S_K Degree of complexity	C_K Rate of communication	P_K Amount of institutional change	O_1 Amount of information O_2 Amount of artistic creation
Powers	R_3 Level of autonomy R_4 Level of familial investment	S_P Degree of centralization	C_P Rate of coercion	P_P Amount of growth	O_3 Amount of sovereignty O_4 Amount of socialization population
Rewards	R_5 Level of investment R_6 Level of leisure	S_R Degree of stratification	C_R Rate of consensus/conflict	P_R Amount of efficiency	O_5 Amount of production O_6 Amount of relaxation
Rights	R_7 Level of welfare R_8 Level of charitable investment	S_N Degree of normative equality	C_N Rate of conformity/deviance	P_N Amount of membership participation	O_7 Amount of rehabilitation O_8 Amount of charity
	Inputs	Arrangements	Articulations	Adequacies	Accumulations

Definition 4.2.3: Degree of stratification, df = distribution of rewards.
Definition 4.2.4: Degree of normative equality, df = distribution of rights.
Definition 4.3.1: Rate of communication, df = integration by knowledges.
Definition 4.3.2: Rate of coercion, df = interaction by powers.
Definition 4.3.3: Rate of consensus/conflict, df = integration by rewards.
Definition 4.3.4: Rate of conformity/deviance, df = integration by rights.
Definition 4.4.1: Amount of institutional change, df = adequacy of the distribution and integration of knowledges.
Definition 4.4.2: Amount of growth, df = adequacy of the distribution and integration of powers.
Definition 4.4.3: Amount of efficiency, df = adequacy of the distribution and integration of rewards.
Definition 4.4.4: Amount of membership participation, df = adequacy of the distribution and integration of rights.

Again, the essential technique is to combine an element, such as social structure, with a dimension, such as knowledges, to generate a variable, what in the literature is called "social indicators," a term quite different from the way in which it is employed in this book. When we combine power and structure, we obtain the familiar centralization. The basic concept of stratification is generated by combining structure and rewards. We have already noted how the new concept of normative equality was obtained with this procedure.

Likewise, familiar concepts like communication, conflict, and deviance have their place in the typology of variables for societies. The four performance variables are less familiar but tap what appear to be essential ideas for societal analysis. One might think of growth as akin to the economists' gross national product, albeit it is measured in a very different way. Membership participation represents the conservation of human resources, efficiency represents the conservation of economic resources. Finally, institutional growth refers to the development of new disciplines, welfare programs, industries, art forms, etc. In each of these, as noted above, we are averaging across all eight institutional sectors.

If we were concerned with the analysis of a particular institutional sector, such as science and education, we could apply the same set of variables, but their indicators would be different. For example, we would look at the complexity, centralization, and stratification of this realm. It would have its own four integration variables, performances, and so forth.

The theoretical definitions have been created simply by cross-classifying the definitions for each of the five elements of variables—social resources, social structure, integration processes, social performances, and social outputs—with the four basic dimensions (see Table 5.4).

The operational indicators, along with some examples from the literature, are provided in Table 5.5. The specific indicators, when compared with this definition, make clear how little of the meaning is being measured, but they do represent a start, and perhaps that is all that we can ask for at this moment. Again, this helps concretize the discussion and indicates that our very abstract and general primitive terms have arrived at some quite useful ideas. Several comments about the indicators are in order. First, these indicators are only appropriate for societies. One would need different but very similar ones for organizations or groups or institutional realms. This is one advantage of general variables with general theoretical definitions. They allow us to have different indicators for different kinds of collectives, a considerable gain in flexibility. It also allows us to see more clearly parallels among the analyses of social collectives, thus aiding us in finding theoretical and operational definitions.

A second observation to make is that these indicators represent one being employed in an on-going research project involving historical documents. Thus, they are designed to be practical in the sense they make use of what is relatively available for the past several hundred years, in industrialized societies at least. The indicators could be made more general but at the risk of their losing the appearance of being concrete. Finally, a third observation is that a variety of indicators have been suggested for each concept so that the interplay between theoretical definitions and operational indicators can be appreciated. In addition, one can explore the relative strength of alternative indices, a most important consideration when doing research. And, the fact that we have not only one index but several for the various collective variables gives us some confidence that our formal scheme of primitive and derived terms is not divorced from social reality. A quick check of a number of measures currently being employed in sociology, economics, and political science indicates that indeed this is the case.

Another test of the typology of collective variables, one might argue the heart of this conceptual scheme, is how many of the key concepts in the literature, or at least the literature on social change in societies, have been captured. Naturally, not all the critical concepts are included. But a number of them have been—complexity or structural differentiation, education, stratification, growth, conflict, and deviance are included, and are important concepts in their own right. This is perhaps the most im-

Table 5.5   Societal Indicators for the Social Collective Variables

Social resource variables (expenditures)

R_1 Level of education and technology (expenditure of instrumental knowledges)
  1. Expenditure for education
  2. Expenditure for science
  3. Number of teachers in education
  4. Number of scientists in research institutes, industry, etc.

R_2 Level of taste (expenditure of expressive knowledge)
  1. Expenditures for art
  2. Number of artists

R_3 Level of autonomy (expenditure of instrumental powers)
  1. Expenditure for the military
  2. Expenditure for government, excluding health, education, and welfare
  3. Number of personnel in the military
  4. Number of civil servants, excluding health, education, and welfare

R_4 Level of population size
  1. Family income
  2. Number of families
  3. Expenditures for para-familial activities (day care centers)
  4. Number of para-familial workers

R_5 Level of investment (expenditure of instrumental rewards)
  1. Capital investment in industry
  2. Capital investment in agriculture
  3. Managers and industrial workers
  4. Farm owners and workers

R_6 Level of leisure
  1. Expenditure for leisure time activities (sports, entertainment, vacations)
  2. Number of people in leisure time industry

R_7 Level of welfare (expenditure of instrumental rights)
  1. Expenditure for health
  2. Expenditure for welfare
  3. Number of medical personnel
  4. Number of welfare personnel

R_8 Level of charitable investment
  1. Expenditure for religious activities
  2. Number of religious personnel
  3. Expenditures for charitable activities other than religious
  4. Number of personnel other than religious

Table 5.5 *(Continued)*

Social structure (distributions)

S_K Complexity (distribution of knowledge)

Percent of population in managerial and professional occupations
Percent nonagricultural (of working population)
Percent in labor unions (of working population)
Percent in agricultural associations (syndicate)
Percent in professional associations
Percent in cities of 10,000 or more
Percent in cities of 100,000 or more

S_P Centralization (distribution of power or decision-making)

Proportion of total national income spent by central government
Proportion of instrumental sectors controlled by national government (budget)
Proportion of instrumental sectors controlled by national government (appointments)
Proportion of population eligible to vote
Proportion of representatives in national government from working class
Number of changes in political party in government in ten year period

S_R Stratification (distribution of rewards)

Lorenz curve on land among social groups
Lorenz curve on income among social groups
Lorenz curve on assets among social groups
Lorenz curve on vacation time among social groups

S_N Normative equality (distribution of rights)

Similarity of educational opportunities among social groups
Similarity of legal rights and political privileges among social groups
Similarity of life expectancy among social groups
Similarity of unemployment rates among social groups

Integration processes (control)

C_K Communication (integration by knowledge)

Number of messages sent per capita per annum (mail, telephone, telegraph)
Number of hours spent consuming media per capita per annum (radio, newspapers, television, etc.)
Number of miles traveled per capita per annum (car, bus, plane, and train)

C_P Coercion (integration by power)

Number of police per 10,000 population
Number of penal days per 1,000 population
Number of executions per 1,000,000 population
Number of preventive arrests per 1,000,000 population

Table 5.5 *(Continued)*

Number of political prisoners per 10,000 population
Number of applications of martial law per annum

C_R Consensus/conflict (control of rewards)

Percent of labor force involved in strikes
Number of political crimes per 1,000,000 population
Number of violent disturbances (see Tilly, 1969)
Number of attempted or actual political assassinations
Number of mass strikes or demonstrations
Attempts at violent overthrow of government

C_N Conformity/deviance (control of rights)

Total lesser crimes per 100,000 population
Total major crimes per 100,000 population
Total number of riots per 100,000 population

Social performance variables (adequacy)

P_K Institutional Change
Number of new disciplines created in one year
Number of new governmental responsibilities created in one year
Number of new industries created in one year
Number of new welfare fields created in one year

P_P Growth

Average percent growth in output across all eight outputs

P_R Efficiency

Average percent growth divided by percent investment

P_N Membership Participation

Emigration per 100,000 population
Desertion rate

Social output variables (resource production)[a]

O_1 Education and Science Output
Number of university degrees granted annually
Percent literate
Percent population ages 17–21 in universities
Percent of children ages 5–17 who are in school
Number of scientific journals and publications

O_3 Sovereignty output

Gains or losses in territory

---

[a] Not all of the indicators for the outputs have been specified, only the more important ones, the instrumental outputs. But the logic would be the same for the expressive outputs.

Table 5.5 *(Continued)*

Gains or losses in the ratio of foreign to native troops
Gains or losses in the proportion of military equipment from foreign sources
Gains or losses in the size of the army

O_5 Industrial output

Industrial production
Agricultural production

O_7 Welfare output

Infant mortality ratio
Life expectancy of population

---

portant check on our formal procedure of arranging primitive and derived concepts.

It is for the reader to judge whether the conceptual scheme and especially the typology of collective variables and their indicators has added any additional comprehension without losing the essential meanings.

Thus, starting with ten elements, four dimensions, and two modes as primitive terms, we have generated many of the ideas that people consider essential to an analysis of societies. This is perhaps the best test of our attempt to bring conceptual order to a specialty that does not have much of it.

The techniques employed have been those discussed at various places in the previous chapters. What one sees here is a logical arrangement after the fact. The *only* critical procedural point is that one cannot use a concept that has not yet been defined, unless it is a primitive. The ordering emerges at the same time that one is searching for the most primitive terms. In addition, there are some other guidelines that one can follow. The two most critical tasks are the definition of the properties of the unit of analysis and the definition of the variables for describing the unit. These ideas can then be employed to derive other properties and variables, as was done here. When defining the unit of analysis, one attempts to combine analytical traditions. Similarly, some of the derived variables should have representation in the literature. If these rules are followed, then a conceptual scheme can be creative and critical and not just a formal exercise in logic.

SUMMARY

As the number of concepts proliferates, we find it necessary to arrange our concepts and their definitions into some conceptual scheme. Although there are some risks in doing this, the gains in rigor and, more importantly, the opportunities of seeing new concepts and definitions would seem to outweigh the possible disadvantages. Paradoxically, although conceptual ordering tends to be a sign of a mature discipline that has developed some knowledge, it might speed the growth of sociology, if more attention were paid to the arrangement of concepts.

The techniques, all two of them, rest on the basis of logical reasoning. We are attempting essentially to combine primitive terms to create derived ones as well as to surmise primitive ones from less general concepts. The first technique is the arrangement of concepts by levels of abstraction, working from the least general to the most and vice versa. The second technique is the manipulation of various kinds of primitive terms to derive particular kinds of schemes. The cross-classification of elements and dimensions generates a typology of general variables, the most important part of any conceptual order. The cross-classification of elements with elements or with modes generates a typology of general non-variables. Combining these procedures creates a complete conceptual scheme.

Since there are relatively few examples of conceptual schemes in the literature, an extended illustration is offered. Although primarily designed to handle the problem of societal change, a number of the basic concepts in both macro- and microsociology are defined. Both theoretical definitions and empirical indicators are derived for a basic typology of 28 variables, a set of continua for describing societies and other social collectives. With these a number of fundamental concepts in institutional analysis and societal change can be derived. This example makes apparent the advantages and disadvantages of a conceptual order.

At best, arranging concepts by level of abstraction is a difficult procedure. The more elaborate the scheme, the more variables it contains, the more difficult it is. Our tendency to think always at one level of abstraction is a major stumbling block. In addition, it takes a long time for most of us to fully comprehend the concepts and their definitions. As we start to arrange them in some scheme, the definitions, and even some of the concepts, are being altered. New ones are added, others are borrowed, and some are dropped. We need then to rethink our position on these matters and this requires time, much time. But this time is worth the investment because the added benefit is an increased comprehension of a number of ideas and an extension of our thought in many directions. Our entire scheme becomes more profound, and as a consequence so does our understanding.

CHAPTER SIX

Ordering Statements and Linkages

If the proliferation of theoretical concepts forces us towards some conceptual scheme, an abundance of theoretical statements has the same result. As our theoretical statements multiply, we need to organize them in some way so that we can understand better the causal argument or flow of events and avoid the danger of inconsistent reasoning. If we don't, we might find ourselves using opposing statements in the same theory. The ordering of theoretical statements requires the recognition of two levels of abstraction: premises and equations. Premises are very general assumptions, sometimes called axioms or postulates, that explain why. Equations are less general formulae, sometimes called corollaries or derived hypotheses that predict how. The premises might be thought of as the organizaton on a higher level of the theoretical linkages whereas the equations represent the ordering of the operational linkages.

We have already seen several examples of premises. Another illustration, from Davis (1963), is shown in Table 6.1. Here, one can observe that three relatively abstraction assumptions provide the reasoning for a wide number of derived statements. Only 13 statements are included here, but Davis derives some 56 statements from his basic three postulates or premises, and with the aid of the definitions of Table 5.1. The derived statements do not contain operational linkages and therefore are not equations, but operational linkages can easily be added.

Table 6.1 Ordering Statements: Davis' Structural Balance

Premises
- A. People prefer positive net values.
- B. Liking has a positive value.
- C. Unit formation has a positive value.

Derived Statements
1. The more similar Person is to Other, the more Person will like Other.
2. Friends tend to become similar in activities.
3. Friends tend to become similar in attitudes.
4. If Person and Other are friends, but differ in their degree of liking, the one with the greater degree of liking will imitate the one with the lesser, rather than vice versa.
5. If the relationships between Person and Other and between Other and X (where X is a third individual), are both marked by dislike, the relationship between Person and X may be friendly.
6. If Person likes Other and Other dislikes X, Person will tend to dislike X.
7. If Person likes Other and Other likes X, Person will tend to like X.
8. If Person dislikes Other and Other likes X, Person will tend to dislike X.
9. To the extent that Person has equal positive ties to two Others who have equal and opposite degrees of liking for X, the net value of any attitude toward X approaches zero for Person.
10. The more equal the opposite values, the weaker Person's liking toward X.
11. If Person does adopt a positive or negative attitude toward X, it will be the attitude of the Other with the strongest degree of liking or disliking toward X, provided that Person's bonds to the two groups are equal.
12. If Person does adopt a positive or negative attitude toward X, it will be the attitude of the Other to whom he has the stronger positive tie (liking or similarity), providing that the strengths of the Other's attitude toward X are equal.
13. If Person does adopt an attitude toward X, he will tend to lower his liking for the Other with whom he is now in imbalance and increase his liking of the Other with whom he is now in balance.

SOURCE: Davis, 1963.

The best examples of the ordering of premises and equations exist in the physical sciences, especially in physics. There are general premises, such as the laws of thermodynamics or the laws of motion, and a large number of equations that can be derived from them. These are perhaps the clearest illustration of a tightly-knit arrangement of linkages.

Sometimes these higher-order assumptions or premises are called axioms (Galtung, 1967; Blalock, 1969), but this is a confusing name because it evokes the idea of axiomatic reasoning. All of the examples of the latter (Zetterberg, 1963; Hopkins, 1964; Hage, 1965) in the literature have theoretical statements that are on the same level of abstraction. Like geometry, one can start almost anywhere and construct the same set of theorems and corollaries. Here, premise is understood to mean higher-order theoretical statements from which a variety of theorems and corollaries can be deduced, the meaning used by Galtung (1966). It is therefore important to recognize that there is a considerable difference between axiomatic reasoning as practiced and the ordering of statements into premises and equations. And, as we have suggested in Chapter 2, axiomatic reasoning is best seen as an *interim* technique for developing statements—when there are a small number of variables. In contrast, the ordering of theoretical statements into a system of premises and equations is most appropriate as the number of statements becomes large and thus cumbersome to handle.

AD HOC AND ORDERED STATEMENTS AND LINKAGES

The ordering of statements and linkages into premises and equations is not very common in sociology. Perhaps the best-known example of premises to date in sociology is the work of Homans (1961) on exchange behavior. The premises are psychological in nature but the entire effort indicates how our need to organize our thoughts requires that we develop some higher-order premises. Indeed Homans' discussion of this need in his introduction is an apt description of the intellectual biography of many of us. In the past decade a number of isolated premises have appeared.

Another symptom of the changing emphasis in sociology is Willer's book (1967), which discusses the three types of what he calls theoretical models, one of which corresponds to the idea of premises. This work is well worth reading since it too suggests the movement towards premises as the discipline accumulates more facts and strives towards more rigorous explanation.

The Advantages of Ordering
Statements and Linkages

Some sociologists, such as Glaser and Strauss (1967) have been critical of what they called logical, deductive theory. Yet, most of their criticism does not apply to the ordering of theoretical statements as defined here. As a matter of fact, logical, deductive theory has received a suspect reputation because of several conceptual schemes that do not have operational definitions. This is not what is meant by the ordering of statements. There is little point to developing an ordered set of theoretical statements and linkages without having indicators and parameters, problems that we have already discussed.

There are several other misconceptions about an ordered set of premises and equations, perhaps again because of the unfortunate terms "logical, deductive" and their various connotations. The most difficult problem is the confusion between syllogistic reasoning and the relationship between the premises and the equations. The equations are not logically derived as much as they are implied in the premises. This should become apparent from the example in Table 6.1. Twelve different equations are implied, each with different coefficients and different powers. We could have also added limits. The relationship between the two levels of statements lies in the connection between the concepts more than in the concepts, although it is true that the variables must be deducible from the terms in the basic premise. Since the point of any statement is its connection between several concepts, such as in the greater the X, the greater the Y, what is derived are various ways in which the connection can be formulated. But these are only implied and not clearly so. Thus our key point remains that the arrangement in Table 6.1 is not quite the popular conception of logical, deductive theory.

A number of advantages flows from the ordering of statements and linkages. With two levels of statements—premises and equations—we have the advantage of more flexibility. We can make the operational linkage fit the empirical world without being forced to explain why a particular parameter is necessary. For example, statements 7 and 8 in Table 6.1, although in verbal form very much alike, may have quite different coefficients or limits and other parameters. Person's liking Other may affect his regard for X much more than his disliking Other.

At the same time, the most general statements, the premises, can suggest other equations besides those that are part of the original theory. In the illustration given above, we could find other variables to describe the distribution of other kinds of basic dimensions. These could then represent still more equations with different coefficients, powers, and limits. Or we might move from macrosociology to microlevel, taking variables describing the nature of social positions and role-relationships, but using the same premise. This creates the potential for future growth; this is most important since we are dealing with the complex reality of a sociological world which we only partly understand.

The two levels simplify our tasks in theory construction by allowing us to move simultaneously towards greater precision and greater generality. The goals of generality and precision flow from the objectives of science: explanation and prediction. The premises summarize the story or set of theoretical linkages as succinctly as possible. The fewer we have, the better. By making the premises very general and by not having to make them precise (which does not mean that they tell us nothing, for they still must connect two variables or nonvariables), we are able to simplify our problem of explaining. And, we are always interested in obtaining the most general assumptions as possible and thus the most general explanation as possible. In contrast, when we attempt to predict, we want as much precision as possible. This forces us towards less generality. We make our task of having both generality of explanation and precision of prediction much easier to accomplish, by being on one level, as general as possible almost to the point of being vague, and on another level, as specific as possible almost to the point of being pedantic.

The major advantage of ordering statements is that it facilitates criticism and creativity. We can check premises against equations and vice versa. This becomes particularly important when several premises are combined into a single testable conclusion. Again, the paucity of examples makes it difficult to prove this assertion, but it would seem to flow from the nature of the arrangement into two levels. Certainly, the construction of Euclidian geometry seems to have aided many people in organizing their thinking. Newton relied upon it heavily, with good results. While there are certainly differences between mathematics per se and science, two levels help facilitate the process of critical thought. Do the premises make sense? Are the equations appropriate implications of them? Is there a flaw in the reasoning? These and other checks are more readily made when all the premises and equations are listed on the same page, for all to praise or condemn.

Since the ordering of premises and equations facilitates critical thought, it is also a spur toward creativity, and thus, the development of knowledge. We constantly grapple with the imperfections as they become more obvious.

Indeed, the major reason why relatively tight arrangements of concepts, definitions, statements, and linkages work is that when all the ideas are condensed into a few pages we can more easily comprehend these ideas and alter them accordingly. One suspects that this is the major reason why mathematics has developed. Symbols are succinct. And, in succinctness lies the opportunity to understand what is happening. Furthermore, what is being advocated here is not symbolization for the sake of symbolization, but some succinct ordering so that the theory can be quickly grasped.

The Strategy of Ordering Statements and Linkages Into Premises and Equations

For all of the above reasons, it is worth our effort to order our theoretical statements and their linkages into some hierarchy of premises and equations. But again, just as with the ordering of concepts and definitions, one must take certain precautions. The advantages of ordering statements and linkages do not really become apparent until we have more than 10 of them. The problem of inconsistent reasoning is most likely to appear only as we get a complex theory. Furthermore, with fewer than 10 statements and sets of linkages, we do not gain much in comprehension and in critical thought because we will end up with almost as many statements as we had before. We would be better off in these circumstances with our *ad hoc* arrangement.

ORDERING THEORETICAL STATEMENTS AND LINKAGES

Surprisingly, there are more techniques for the ordering of statements and linkages than appear to be available for the ordering of concepts and definitions. Part of the reason is that the ordering of statements and linkages is less dependent on syllogistic reasoning. Another part of the reason is that I believe that this is a much more important task in theory construction, and therefore have searched for more techniques.

Here, we might note that the relationship between primitive and derived terms is much tighter than the one between premises and equations. The word derived quite literally describes the relation between primitive and derived terms, but equations are implied in the premises rather than derived from them. With concepts, we are ordering them into classes; lower abstract terms are included in higher-order ones. In contrast, with theoretical statements, the ordering is in terms of the connections. Usually, the higher-order premise is a statement, such as the greater the X, the greater the Y. Any number of different parameters are implied and can coexist at the same time. Thus, the word derived is less appropriate when ordering statements. It is true, however, that the concepts of the equations are included within the concepts of the premises. But this does not mean the connection between them is derivation as such, except to say that the premise allows for a vast array of parameters.

There would seem to be five major techniques for the ordering of statements and linkages: synthesizing several theories or parts of theories, generalizing lower-level statements into higher-order ones, ordering statements and linkages by levels of abstraction, extending incomplete sets of premises (and equations), and finally, what might be called the suppose-if technique. These techniques should by now be familiar to the reader because they are nothing but variations on ideas discussed in Chapters 2 and 5. Some important differences still exist. The first technique below seems very much like the technique based on axiomatic reasoning (Ch. 2), yet it is different because we can borrow premises from one theory and equations from another (see Willer, 1967). The second technique is like the technique of reducing several statements to a general one (Ch. 2), the third is similar to the technique of arranging theoretical concepts into levels of abstraction (Ch. 5). In both cases we are relying upon a capacity to move up and down levels of abstraction. The fourth technique has much broader applicability in that it is less dependent upon the literature and is somewhat akin to the technique of cross-classifying primitive terms (Ch. 5). It is based on the definition of four kinds of premises and the recognition that it is the action premise that is frequently missing from a theory. It is perhaps the most interesting technique because it goes to the heart of the matter of what might be a satisfactory set of premises for explanation. Finally, the last technique has the widest applicability, allowing our imagination free reign.

Synthesizing Several Theories

When we are working in an area that has been well developed, we have the opportunity of effecting our order somewhat easily by borrowing the equations from one theorist and the premises from another—sometimes with interesting results for the ideas of both. A simple illustration of this is stratification theory. The "Communist Manifesto" by Marx and Engels (1959) contains a number of verbal operational linkages as well as some theoretical ones on how increasing stratification can lead to increasing conflict and eventually a revolution of the proletariat. In

Capital, Marx argued that conflict represents an ever-increasing power with curvilinear episodes within this, thus like one of our six families in Figure 4.5. But nowhere is there a set of basic premises. We are left wondering why the capitalists will want to increase their share of the wealth and why the proletariat will revolt. There are intervening variables but much of his argument remains on the same level of abstraction as his statements. In shopping around for a premise, we can borrow, as did Davis from Heider's work. For example, Galtung (1966) and Zetterberg (1966) suggest that social groups strive for consistency in rank. However, although this premise and Marx's hypotheses are talking about the same phenomenon, they are not in complete accord. Marx and Engels' reasoning—once we juxtapose the premise, and begin to appreciate their thinking more easily—is that differences in rank, and more particularly rank in wealth, would cause conflict between social groups. Other premises explain why this wealth might vary from time to time; this is the familiar argument about the internal contradictions of the capitalistic system.

How do we reconcile the discrepancy? The answer is, of course, we alter the linkages or the premises according to which ones we think are the most accurate. We might call this the process of reconciling them. The power of this procedure should not be underestimated. Instead of saying one side is right or wrong, we begin to ask ourselves in what way might they be right and in what way they might be wrong. As we do, we are synthesizing theories. This is probably the major way in which theories alter across time, the recognition that several seemingly opposing ideas can be merged into the same intellectual framework.

This technique of synthesizing has several steps. *First,* we put down the linkages as suggested by one author. *Second,* we write the premises as suggested by another. *Third,* we reconcile the two according to our own understanding.

Naturally, there are many variations. One variation is to borrow different sets of equations from authors and reconcile them. This is more akin to axiomatic reasoning. Likewise, one can synthesize premises of different authors.

The reader might, on his own, experiment with some of the following combinations: synthesizing Durkheim's *Suicide* (1951) with Simmel's *Web of Group Affiliations* (1955) and his "Mental Health in the Life of the Metropolis" (Wolff, 1950); synthesizing the "Communist Manifesto" with much of Weber's work, which can be interpreted as a "yes, but," or combining Simmel's *Conflict and Web of Group Affiliations* (1955) with Marx's theory of stratification as has been done by Galtung (1966). At the end of this chapter, there is an extended illustration of an attempt to synthesize Durkheim's *Division of Labor in Society* and Marx and Engel's "Communist Manifesto."

Generalizing Statements and Linkages

If the reader checks the various reasons used in the theoretical linkage of Table 4.1, he will note that some are more general than others. The more general ones can then be used as premises.

There are several simple steps to follow. *First,* list all the reasons in a set of theoretical linkages. *Second,* pick out all reasons involving intervening variables, particularly if they are on the same level of abstraction, and convert them into additional equations in the theory. To return to our example of Table 4.1, communication rates is not used because this variable is on approximately the same level of generality as complexity, centralization, etc. *Third,* apply each reason in each theoretical linkage to all the statements to which it appears appropriate. When one reason makes sense, that is, theoretical sense, as an argument for more than one statement, we have some justification for assuming that it is more general. This procedure not only codifies the many theoretical linkages into a few coherent and consistent premises, but creates a parsimonious set as well.

In some instances, the theorist will discover that he has two or more antagonistic reasons. Indeed, one of the objectives of arranging hypotheses is to find contradictory statements. The problem is to determine which is correct. Again, the best criterion is scope: the premise that can be a reason in the greatest number of theoretical statements is more likely to be accurate. However, as always, we must make our judgments about this. It is not an automatic procedure.

We can generalize whole theories, premises, and equations as well. This is best done by determining what social collective or, more broadly, what social unit the theory applies to and then attempting to fit the same set of ideas to other social collectives or units. Do propositions about the family, for example, apply to other kinds of social relationships? Do small group experiments have something to say about the articulations of communities? We have seen this at work many times in social psychology, perhaps even more than in sociology. Ideas about conflict between individuals have been applied to conflict between nations, for example. Similarly, as was suggested, a theory about interorganizational interdependencies might be an adequate theory of intercollective interdependencies.

Ordering Statements and Linkages by
Levels of Abstraction

If the reader has developed a feeling for the different levels of abstraction involved in concepts, then he will find that this technique has some utility. The procedures are straightforward.

First, we arrange the theoretical linkages by level of generality. This is much akin to what was just discussed. *Second,* we arrange the operational linkages by temporal flow, putting first the variables that we think occur first, those that occur second, we put second, etc. This is very much like technique of creating a path diagram of operational linkages (Ch. 2). *Third,* wherever possible we subsume the less general theoretical linkages and operational linkages under the more general ones. *Fourth,* we check to be sure that there is a premise or set of premises for every equation in our path and vice versa, adding when necessary. *Fifth,* we order our premises to correspond to the ordering of the equations. *Sixth,* we check for additional implications of our premises and of our equations. This is illustrated in the third section of this chapter.

Perhaps the best illustration of the sorting out of very general premises and the arrangement of operational linkages into temporal flows, although not complete and now nearly 15 years old, is March and Simon's *Organizations* (1958). Chapters 3 and 4 are well worth the time to read and reread because there is a fine feeling for the problem of different levels of abstraction. Their diagrams illustrate how one can grasp complicated ideas quickly when everything is put on the same page.

Although Davis (1963) probably deduced his premises from many studies, their arrangement in the form of three postulates and 56 inferences indicates how far a few general assumptions can carry one (see Table 6.1). His work is so far one of the best examples there is in sociology. This is another illustration well worth extended study. Although we have the arrangement after the fact, one suspects that Davis used procedures somewhat akin to those outlined above. It can also be studied as an illustration of the technique of synthesizing theories. Consistency premises are borrowed from Heider and juxtaposed in a number of seemingly disparate areas. But, as we have already noted, there are certain overlaps in these techniques and in practice we employ them in combinations.

Extending Incomplete Sets of Premises and Equations

A very typical situation that confronts sociology today is that a theorist has a number of very general theoretical statements but not a complete set. To understand what is meant by a complete set, we must define four basic kinds of premises. Just as there are four kinds of primitive terms, we can make similar distinctions among basic assumptions needed for a theory. Although Willer's effort (1967) is quite suggestive, it does not make clear what might be a satisfactory set of premises. To define the kinds of premises, we must recognize that it is the action premise that is most critical.

Table 6.2   The Four Kinds of Premises: Societal Model of Integration

Definitional Premise	All social collectives need integration.
Mechanism Premise	Integration can be maintained by interaction and by punishment or force.
Action Premise	As collectives become more differentiated, integration is maintained more and more by interaction.
Operational Premise	The rapidity of change affects the ability to maintain integration in social collectives.

Examples of each kind of premise are provided in Table 6.2. Each deals with part of a model or set of premises concerning integration. As can be seen, these four basic premises are rather free interpretations of Durkheim (1933). Durkheim might not have agreed with the wording, but he would certainly have agreed with their spirit. Regardless, the differences between the four kinds of premises are easy to see. The definitional premise stipulates a property. Functional assumptions are frequently of this kind. The word need is not necessary but is useful for calling attention to a particular analytical orientation in sociology. The mechanism premise states the alternatives, or if there are more than two, the choices for fulfilling a particular need. This might be thought of as the specification of all roads to Rome. Similarly, in most social theories there is a variety of ways in which some need can be met, the channels or choices available to the social system. Merton's word mechanism is an apt name for it. The action premise involves some assumption about the direction of movement. In this particular case, we might have stated that as collective control becomes more concentrated, more and more integration will be maintained by force or punishment. Finally, the operational premise makes some assumption that implies the need for powers or constants, etc. Of the four kinds, it is the least important. The first three provide a complete set of premises in our sense of the term.

If this is so, then when we select premises, we may find it useful to select at least one of each kind so that the theoretical model will allow for a much more interesting story. In one sense, *the definitional premise tells us what must be done, the mechanism premise tells us how it can be done, and the action premise how it will be done.* Of these, the last, as Bergmann (1957) argues, is the most important. It makes the theory dynamic and allows us to formulate much more interesting kinds of explanations.

If we return to Davis' theory, we see that it is the action premise that is lacking. We need to be told what the alternatives are, given a negative net value (although they are clearly implied, change of friends or change of attitudes), and under which conditions one alternative is selected and, of course, which one. So, there are really two choices, given a negative net value. Here is an excellent case where we can add an action premise and gain a great deal. We might speculate that extroverts prefer to maximize liking and introverts prefer to maximize unit formation. The search is then for different kinds of people who want to maximize one option in preference to the other. Or, one might specify different conditions when one or the other choice is likely.

An examination of Homans' exchange theory makes clear that it loses in explanatory power because we are not told the definitional premise, namely what are the various kinds of rewards and costs. It could well be that particular kinds of personalities have different rewards and costs, and if so, the explanatory and predictive power of exchange theory would be considerably extended. As it is now, each time we observe some behavior we can say that such and such a course of action is chosen because there are greater rewards and less costs. But this does not really let us know if individual A will take course X—the heart of prediction and explanation.

As an additional guideline in constructing complete sets of premises, it is useful to build in some dialectic or internal strain in the theory. We have already discussed this at the equation level with several aspects of Weber's model of bureaucracy. In constructing the premises, we should allow the set of equations to have more than one independent variable and allow these variables to work in opposite directions. In Blalock's (1969) terms, this would be more than one exogenous variable. To continue with the Davis illustration, cross-pressures on Person can be created by stipulating that, as his ego becomes stronger, he is more apt to keep his friends, despite different attitudes. But, we can also say that under the condition of few friends, he is more likely to change his attitudes. The system is open to forces that push in opposite directions, probably allowing for much better prediction and explanation.

The procedures for this technique can be seen as a supplement to those of the previous one. Our concern is to *first* check for the presence of the definitional premise, mechanistic premise, and an action premise. *Second,* we can make the theory more interesting and perhaps closer to social reality by stipulating several premises of action that work in opposite directions.

Suppose-If

One of the great advantages of labeling the very general level in theories with a tag such as premises or assumptions about the nature of the human condition is the increased awareness with which we can speculate about particular premises and see, at least in our mind's eye, where they lead us. Although this book has begun with the working assumption that it is better to begin with variables and then work up to premises, the construction of theories can begin with an assumption, tracing out all of its consequences. This might be called the suppose-if technique. It has certain advantages because it allows us to imagine many more possibilities than might empirically occur.

The four kinds of premises help us understand how the suppose-if technique can be extended to provide a more complete explanation. We can start with any one of the three kinds and then add the other two. Of course, the easiest place to begin is with the action premise, some general assumption very much like any theoretical statement discussed in Chapter 2, except on a more abstract level. If this point is clear, then this technique is more assessable.

Suppose we imagine that all social collectives attempt to be effective. Then, we might ask ourselves what are various ways of being effective, which kinds of social collectives adopt a particular approach. Another example is the assumption that all social relationships are controlled in some way. Then, we might ask ourselves who does the controlling, internally or externally? Which mechanisms are used internally and which externally? (See Table 6.3.) An action premise would tell which kind of mechanism of control internally is used by what kind of person or in what kind of relationship and similarly, which kind of mechanism is used externally in what kind of relationship and in which kind of social collective.

Table 6.3   Suppose-If Premises: The Case of the Problem of Social Bonds

Definitional premise
   A. All role-relationships are controlled either internally by the occupants in the relationship or externally by the society via mediating groups.

Mechanistic premises
   B. If role-relationships are controlled externally by society, the mechanisms of control are regulation with sanctions and/or visibility with socialization.
   C. If role-relationships are controlled internally by the occupants, the mechanisms are feelings and/or reciprocity of exchange.

Action Premises
   D. The more durable the role-relationships, the more likely that either visibility with socialization or feelings are the mechanisms of control.
   E. The more unpredictable the encounters of the role-relationships are, the more likely either regulation with sanctions or exchange are mechanisms of control.

An interesting illustration of some attempts to develop very broad premises is the book, *Social Theory and Social Practice* by Hans Zetterberg (1962). If one were to combine some of these ideas with, say, various personality theories, some interesting insights might be obtained. In any case, any one of these general assumptions is a good starting place for a suppose-if meditation. In particular, as other kinds of premises are added, the explanatory power increases enormously.

AN EXTENDED EXAMPLE IN SOCIOLOGY

An extended illustration can indicate how the various techniques for ordering statements and linkages can be combined. Here, our concern is to formulate a relatively general theory of social collectives, although the focus and all the examples refer to societies. The two concrete substantive problems are what causes development and what causes revolution. As is well known, there seems to be some relationship between the process of industrialization and the phenomenon of revolution, yet not all industrializing societies have a period of instability such as revolution. The problem becomes finding out what the causes are. What tips a society in one direction or another?

The substantive problems also articulate with a number of basic theoretical problems. How resources are allocated among social positions

—the causes of social structure; what structures appear to be acceptable, and which ones are not acceptable—the problem of social integration or consensus; the problem of effectiveness, and finally, the problem of survival.

In searching for answers to the second substantive problem, many insights can be obtained by synthesizing Marx and Durkheim. Marx offered a number of ideas about the causes of conflict, Durkheim developed a theory of integration, one that we have already seen in Table 6.2. Together they make for a much richer exposition of how societies might alternate between evolution and revolution or perhaps more correctly, how some go through an evolution and others a revolution.

The search for answers to the first substantive problem, the problem of development, comes from a synthesis of Weber (1947) and Toynbee (1946). Although they were concerned with different kinds of social collectives, Weber being interested in patterns of organizational authority and Toynbee civilization, if one ignores the unit of analysis and asks if the ideas can be transplanted, then some insights about societal development are obtainable. In terms of the theoretical problems listed above, we might say that Weber provides some assumptions about effectiveness and Toynbee some more about survival. It is Toynbee, however, who recognized that short-term effectiveness may mean long-term ineffectiveness and thus lack of survival. He has a more dynamic or process-oriented conception of the effectiveness problem. Again, the combination of the two provides a more complete theory of societies.

Since the substantive problems are highly interrelated—effectiveness affects revolution just as revolution affects survival—it is more appropriate to organize the premises into four sets, each of which relates to one of the four problems listed above. Fortunately, this just happens to fit a temporal order for the equations.

Resource Allocation

Table 6.4 shows the basic premises and equations they suggest for how resources become allocated among social positions, and thus how social structure is generated. The essential insight is from Marx. He felt that as the economy expanded, it produced not only material goods but that this production cycled backward in the form of investment which in turn generated the stratification system of society, the distribution of rewards among the haves and the have-nots. The distribution was unequal and thus a problem emerged. Premise 3 is akin to Marx's ideas, but we have broadened it to include the distribution of power and rights, and like him, assumed that as societies become more powerful, there will tend to be a movement towards greater inequality and not equality. The elites will gain and not the lower participants, to use again the very general concepts from the previous chapter.

Table 6.4 Ordering Statements Into Premises and Equations: The Problem of Resource Allocation

Premises about the Problem of Resource Allocation
  A. As inputs of knowledge increase, structural differentiation occurs, that is, there are more social positions.
  B. As inputs of powers, rewards, and rights increase, these tend to be concentrated among only a few positions, that is, an elite.
  C. However, occupants of social positions will attempt to maintain the same rank on knowledge, powers, rewards, and rights, that is, rank consistency.
  D. In achieving rank consistency, occupants of social positions will attempt to prevent a loss in rank.

Equations Regarding the Allocation of Resources Among Social Positions
  1. R_1 (education) $= S_K$ (complexity)
  2. R_2 (taste) $= S_K$ (complexity)
  3. R_3 (autonomy) $+ R_5$ (investment) $+ R_7$ (welfare) $= S_P$ centralization) $+ S_R$ (stratification) $- S_N$ (normative equality)
  4. R_4 (familial investment) $+ R_6$ (leisure) $+ R_8$ (charitable investment)$=$ S_P (centralization) $+ S_R$ (stratification) $- S_N$ (normative equality)
  5. $S_K = - S_P - S_R + S_N$
  6. $\triangle S_K^{1/t} = [S_K - (- S_P - S_R + S_N)]$
  7. $[+ S_K - (- S_P - S_R + S_N)]^x = - C_R$ (consensus) $- C_N$ (conformity)

But, as we all know, these are not the only forces for change in society, and here, we have the contribution of Durkheim. Writing 50 years after Marx, he saw the steady proliferation of occupations, what today we would call professional ones. While we do not agree that the cause is the increasing population, and increasing social and moral density, to use Durkheim's terms, it is true that by definition the creation of new social positions alters the nature of the social structure. The cause of increasing structural differentiation would seem to lie in the expansion of knowledge. The new positions are usually at the professional and managerial levels; it is here that specialization is proceeding. These occupants have high rank on knowledge—both formal education and informal experience—and they demand a similar rank in terms of powers, rewards, and rights. Furthermore, they usually get it. This results in an alternation of the social structure.

This gives us the basic dialectic that is important in theory construction, yet the source of the dialectic is not so much the antagonism of social classes, the Marxian model, but the creation of new professions and specializations, a key concept in Durkheim's first work. Because these social positions—usually occupational, but they could be political, religious, etc.—have high rank in terms of knowledge, they fight for a share of the other societal resources.

These four premises unite Durkheim and Marx with much of the recent work that has been done in stratification theory by Lenski (1966 and 1967), Zetterberg (1966), Galtung (1966), and others. However, note that for Marx the problem was the concentration of rewards, for Michel it was the concentration of power. More recently the problem of rights has come into focus. It might also be observed that consistency theory has been integrated into the theory, albeit in an unusual way.

The equations for instrumental resources and expressive resources are written separately, in part to demonstrate that the concepts in the premises are more general, and in part to suggest that the coefficients in the equations are probably different. These have not been specified because at this stage I am unsure of what they might be. Education is presumably a more powerful factor in affecting the division of labor than taste. Similarly, although it is not indicated, the concentration of powers —that is, either the variable of autonomy or the variable of population— is more likely to lead to the development of centralization, stratification, etc., than the growth of investment and/or welfare. These avenues are not ruled out, but what evidence there is does suggest differential size coefficients. Although there has been some discussion in the literature, at least organizational literature, about the relationship between growth in size and centralization—Michel's iron law of oligarchy—there has not been much about autonomy. This remains an unexplored area.

The first two equations in Table 6.4 are derivations from the connection of premise A. These variables and their indicators are for society (see Tables 5.4 and 5.5). We might have different forms for other kinds of social collectives. Certainly the coefficients might vary. Likewise equations 3 and 4 are derivable from premise B.

Equation 5 sets up the inherent strain when several of the resources are growing at the same rate and suggests how distributions of power and rewards are altered in society. In contrast, equation 6 indicates that the speed with which structural differentiation occurs affects the size of the discrepancy between the degree of complexity and the degree of decentralization. The symbol, delta (Δ), indicates the magnitude of change, while the power $1/t$ specifies the speed with which it occurs. In turn, as the discrepancy grows, it affects the rate of consensus and conformity negatively, that is, it decreases. In other words, if various groups in society, whether occupational, political, economic, or religious, do not have the same ranks on education, wealth, power, and privilege, then there is discontent, which manifests itself in increasing conflict and deviance, all other things being equal.

Coordination and Control

Other things, however, are never equal. This leads to the problem of coordination and control. Here, there are several points worth making. The variety of social positions, the different organizations, the eight institutional realms have to be coordinated in some way. Because the positions are occupied by individuals—and the same is true for organizations and institutional realms—these individuals have to be controlled. Thus, coordination and control are two sides of the same coin. The twin labels are used to emphasize this fact (see Table 6.5).

Table 6.5 Ordering Statements Into Premises and Equations: The Problem of Coordination and Control

Premises about Coordination of Positions and Control of Occupants:

E. All elites attempt to maintain coordination and control.

F. Coordination and control can be maintained by sanctioning and interaction.

G. As structural differentiation increases, interaction increases as a mechanism of coordination and control.

H. When powers, rewards, and rights are concentrated in a few positions, sanctioning increases as a mechanism of coordination and control.

Equations Regarding the Problem of Coordination and Control:

8. C_K (communication) $+ C_P$ (coercion) $=$
$$C_R \text{ (consensus)} + C_N \text{ (conformity)}$$

9. S_K (complexity) $= C_K$ (communication)

10. S_P (centralization) $+ S_R$ (stratification) $-$
$$S_N \text{ (normative equality)} = C_P \text{ (coercion)}$$

Since $S_K = -S_P - S_R + S_N$, equation 5
and $S_K = C_K$, equation 9

11. $\therefore -S_P - S_R + S_N = C_K$

Since $S_P + S_R - S_N = C_P$, equation 10
$\therefore -S_P - S_R + S_N = -C_P$, the negative of equation 10

12. $\therefore C_K = -C_P$

If Marx had a good insight about what made people discontented, Durkheim's work contains some more complex ideas about how coordination occurs and control is maintained. It is not only the heavy hand of repression, but also the more subtle method of socialization. Furthermore, different mechanisms are more or less used in different societies.

Again, we have built into our set of four premises, two action premises that can be moving in opposite directions. This means that in some situations one could expect both mechanisms of control to be present. In general, we would expect as noted in the equations that the emphasis on one implies a decreasing emphasis on the other. The exception is when there is increasing conflict, which, in turn, leads to high control being exerted.

Our equations indicate that usually consensus and conformity are maintained in society. This is one reason why revolution is a relatively rare phenomenon. Revolutions *cannot* occur if the government has the power to exert enough coercion, that is, plenty of police and paramilitary forces armed with weapons. But they do occur and therefore we need an additional set of premises to explain under what conditions the normal mechanisms of control and coordination might break down. These are suggested in the next two sets of basic assumptions.

Equations 11 and 12 illustrate how implications can be derived by the simple method of substitution, reasoning with algebra. One way of interpreting these equations is to say that in the long-term trend societies, as they become more complex move towards ever more reliance on communication as the primary mechanism of control and decrease their reliance on coercion of various kinds such as mass arrests, censorship, political executions, and so forth. This has manifested itself concretely in the declining use of capital punishment in most industrialized societies as well as the changing laws regarding police tactics.

Effectiveness

Weber's concern with the question of which organizational form would survive was answered by noting what factors seemed to lead to greater efficiency, his interpretation of the concept of effectiveness. Like Weber, we believe that everyone wants more effectiveness, but unlike Weber, we don't believe that efficiency or growth is the only way of demonstrating effectiveness; there are other performances as well. This raises the question of which kind of society opts for what kind of effectiveness.

Even in the most autocratic societies, it is necessary to indicate to the population that something is being done about various problems in the society. If this is not done, then gradually the members of the society become disaffected. In general, however, members of the society seem to be willing to accept sacrifices as long as at least some outputs are being emphasized.

This means that there is more than one road to success, a point frequently overlooked in the East-West debate, since there are at least four basic performances and eight outputs. The inspiration for premises I and J, in Table 6.6, is Bales' work (1950) on the internal dilemma between

---

Table 6.6 Ordering Statements Into Premises and Equations: The Problem of Effectiveness

Premises about the effectiveness of the collective

I. Elites must demonstrate effectiveness to the members of the society in order to maintain their participation.

J. Effectiveness is demonstrated by either an emphasis on rapid development with the production of powers, rewards, and rights outputs, or by an emphasis on innovation with the production of knowledge outputs.

K. As powers, rewards, and rights become more concentrated, there is a greater and greater tendency to emphasize rapid development and the production of powers, rewards, and rights as opposed to innovation and the production of knowledge outputs.

L. Each input expenditure affects the amount of each output produced.

Equations regarding the problem of effectiveness

13. $- P_K$ (institutional change) $- P_P$ (growth) $- P_R$ (efficiency) $=$
$$- P_N \text{ (membership participation)}$$

14. $- O_1 - O_2 - O_3 - O_4 - O_5 - O_6 - O_7 - O_8 = - P_N$

15. $S_P + S_R - S_N = P_P + P_R + O_3 + O_4 + O_5 + O_6$

16. $R_1 + R_2 + R_3 + R_4 + R_5 + R_6 + R_7 + R_8 =$
$$O_1 + O_2 + O_3 + O_4 + O_5 + O_6 + O_7 + O_8$$

Since $S_K = - S_P - S_R + S_N$

17. $\therefore S_K = + P_K + O_1 + O_2$

---

adaptiveness and integration. Here it is seen as the problem of choosing between a relative emphasis on innovation or development. Premise K is an important action premise indicating under what circumstances which option is selected; elites, particularly when they are small, are more likely to opt for a maximization of particular outputs, and especially rapid growth of the society.

The last premise seems a simple idea, but it is worth very careful consideration before one accepts it. It lies at the heart of all interinstitutional analysis and yet, it remains the one problem most difficult to analyze. Premise L goes considerably beyond the normal considerations of economists, concerning the relation between technology, investment, and even welfare to economic growth in suggesting that every output is dependent upon every input. Again, this is picking up on an essentially Weberian notion as best exemplified in his *Protestant Ethic and the Spirit of Capitalism* and extending it to the logical extreme. Simple as this premise may appear, it has broad implications for the survival of society because it suggests that regardless of the option selected to indicate effectiveness, there are going to be some long-term difficulties.

Equations 13 and 14 are derived from premise I and suggest that negative performances and declining outputs affects the willingness of the members of society to participate in society. This is how governments and other kinds of elites can lose their popularity. It might be observed that there is a certain parallel with the rising-expectations thesis of Davies (1969) except that it has been broadened to cover all outputs, and the emphasis is on a decline in the actual production of outputs as opposed to a decline in the expansion rate.

Equation 15 tells us that centralized societies prefer to maximize the outputs of sovereignty and production, in particular. We could split equation 15 into two separate ones, an equation for the instrumental outputs and another for the expressive ones, as we did with equations 1 and 2. But here our emphasis is on seeing that society is producing simultaneously a number of outputs. Equation 16, which is an extremely important one, is a very weak statement because we do not know the relative importance of particular resources for the production of particular outputs. We can easily imagine eight separate equations, each with different coefficients, one for each output. In other words, the costs in terms of these outputs for producing information (O_1) are quite different from, say sovereignty (O_3). Also, in the absence of any reason, we are postulating the simplest relationships, namely linear, without any interactions, which seems unlikely. One can easily imagine multiple effects here. But note that as we learn more from our research, we can make these alterations in the equations without disturbing our basic assumptions. Equation 17 is clearly implied in the set of premises as well.

Although the parameters in the equations are not well specified and although much of this is speculative, it does seem that these equations are at least pointing to some of the tensions inherent in modern societies. They cannot easily produce everything, while maintaining the same social structure. There are clear negative feedbacks implied: less emphasis on certain outputs begins to affect the production of other outputs (the importance of equation 16), and in turn, this decreases membership participation even more. The ruling elite begins to lose authority under these circumstances. This then brings us to the problem of survival.

Survival

The last four premises in Table 6.7 are much more speculative. Yet they are not totally without foundation in the literature. They are an attempt to codify a number of Toynbee's essential insights into more rigorous theoretical statements. The essential idea is that while rapid development is good in the short run, it is produced by an elite who tends to be nonadaptive and nonadjusting to changing environmental conditions. Gradually, this affects the success of the society, and then its

Table 6.7 Ordering Statements Into Premises and Equations: The Problem of Survival

Premises about the problem of survival

M. All societies must respond to internal and external changes in order to remain effective.

N. As power, rewards, and rights are more and more concentrated in a few social positions, there is less and less adjustment and adaptiveness.

O. As societies become more and more ineffective, it becomes more and more difficult to maintain coordination and control.

P. As coordination and control decline, it becomes more and more difficult to respond to internal and external changes.

Equations regarding the problem of survival

18. $S_P + S_R - S_N = -\Delta\alpha_{t_1-t_2}$

19. $S_P + S_R - S_N = -\Delta\beta_{t_1-t_2}$

20. $-\Delta\alpha_{t_1-t_2} = -P_K$
and $-P_K = -P_N$
$\therefore -\Delta\alpha = -C_R - C_N$

21. $-\Delta\beta_{t_1-t_2} = -O_1 - O_2$
since $O_1 = R_1$ and $O_2 = R_2$
$\therefore -R_1 - R_2 + R_3 + R_4 + R_5 + R_6 + R_7 + R_8 =$
$\qquad -O_1 - O_2 - O_3 - O_4 - O_5 - O_6 - O_7 - O_8$
$\qquad\qquad = -P_N$
$\qquad\qquad = -C_R - C_N$

22. $-C_R - C_N = -\Delta\alpha_{t_1-t_2} - \Delta\beta_{t_1-t_2}$

control mechanisms begin to break down. This in turn further increases the likelihood of nonadaptiveness and nonadjustment, and thus the eventual collapse of the society. Thus the start of the vicious cycle.

The reader might wonder what the definition of survival is. This goes back to the definition of what a society is. The suggested definition in the last section of Chapter 5 is that there is a production of eight outputs, one of which is sovereignty. As there is a decline in one or more of these outputs, the existence of the society becomes more and more in doubt. One contemporary example is the collapse of Poland at the end of the eighteenth century. The occupation of many countries during the Second World War, while of short duration, illustrates the point also. Although they lost much of their sovereignty, they continued to survive, in one case, for two centuries, until they finally regained some sovereignty as well.

Although it is not at all obvious from these abstract premises, they are suggesting that revolution, a possible outcome, can be adaptive for the society if the new ruling elite produces some structural change and an alteration in the priorities attached to particular performances and specific outputs.

We might consider the role of revolution in the process of survival. The answer is that it is frequently a heroic effort on the part of societal members. Russia and China, in this century, have both illustrated this process. After the revolution, Russia became more centralized and more coercive, which in turn meant greater development that resulted in a greater participation of the members in the society. However, the long-term consequences of this adaptive response have been less adaptiveness and adjustment to internal and external changes. The long-term consequences—as predicted by the premises—are increasing disaffection upon the part of the people.

The equations expressing some of the implications are more complicated than the ones we have seen so far. This is, in part, because they represent events occurring over relatively long time spans. It would be nice to be able to write then in terms of time, but this I cannot do at present. Equations 18 and 19 (Table 6.7) are derived from the combination of premises M and N. However, we need to define two special variables, alpha (α) and beta (β), which represent the distribution of priorities among particular performances and outputs respectively. The meaning of $t_1 - t_2$ is just the period of time in which these distributions remain relatively constant. Thus, equation 18 can be interpreted to say that centralized societies do not change their priorities among performances very much within some given time period, say a period of ten years. Although we have not discussed the problem of time in constructing theories and especially in connection with operational linkages, here is an example where the variable itself is taken across a particular time period. Both adjustment and adaptiveness are system feedback processes, regulative in the same sense in which control is but quite different from the latter processes (see Ch. 8 for a discussion of system analysis).

By combining equations 18 and 19 with the previous ones, we can, of course, derive a number of other implications. This is left for the reader. Suffice it to say that they would indicate that coercion reduces the magnitude of both α and β, that is, the magnitude of change in the priorities of performances and outputs, whereas both complexity and communication are associated with it. Perhaps this is a complicated way of saying that complex societies are more adaptive, one of the essential insights of Durkheim. However, the fact that these derivations do have some correspondence with the literature is a check that our ideas are not straying too far afield.

Since equations 20 and 21 are somewhat complicated, their derivations have been included. The ideas are simple, however. Not changing priorities means a decrease in the amount of innovation, which eventually (again the problem of time) has a deleterious effect on membership participation. In turn, this affects conflict and deviance. Likewise, a lack of change in priorities regarding the outputs has the same consequence. Although here, the negative feedbacks on the production of desired outputs hastens the end. One weakness of these equations is that the amount of time needed for these effects is not specified, so their predictive power is considerably reduced. Yet, hopefully, they indicate a way of thinking about societies that helps organize the many disparate facts.

Finally, equation 22 marks the beginning of the end. Given a large number of internal problems, the society loses what little ability to adapt and adjust it had, making it even more vulnerable. This corresponds to the two basic ways in which Toynbee saw civilizations collapsing, either because of internal difficulties or external ones. At some point, the society loses enough of its outputs, and that is its demise.

If we put these equations together, they can give us a continuous-process story about how societies either evolve or else move into some form of instability. If investment and autonomy expenditures grow faster than the level of educational expenditures, strong pressures exist for the society to become more centralized and stratified. In contrast, if there is a balance in these inputs, then the society will very slowly evolve towards more decentralization and greater equality of wealth. If the educational expenditures are considerably greater than investment, then there will be strong pressures for a rapid change in the social structure towards more equality. One implication of this thesis is that as some societies become more industrialized, they can also become much more autocratic than they were before, a process we have observed during this century (Flanigan and Fogelman, 1968).

Once there is a considerable degree of centralization in the society, then it is likely to become maladaptive and nonadjustive. The elites are myopic and remain unaware of problems in the production of outputs, even when there are danger signals. Furthermore, they respond to discontent of the population by exerting steadily increasing coercion. At some point, this control process can break down, especially if there is a declining production of outputs, just because there are less resources to go around as well as more discontent in the population.

As centralization increases, by definition, the basic decisions about society are made by a smaller and smaller elite. This elite is likely to maximize certain outputs to the exclusion of others, creating even more imbalances in the production of inputs and affecting the distribution of the social structure.

If we could make our operational linkages more precise, specifying the coefficients and limits to, say, nothing, about adding precise temporal estimates, we could answer interesting questions about societal biographies. For example, it may well be that there is a certain degree of centralization beyond which a society cannot evolve without a serious loss of flexibility, or ability to change. Likewise, the combinations of proportions of particular resources needed to produce particular outputs is an issue that needs much more thought and study and yet, it would seem to represent a critical way of extending Toynbee's interesting observations into a more econometric form of analysis.

One might wonder, if we cannot be more exact in our equations than we have been, then why bother? The answer is that in our research we need to be guided if we are not to waste our time. We cannot study everything, so we pick and choose among variables. Likewise, we cannot study every possible combination of these variables, so we pick and choose linkages between them on the basis of various techniques. This, then, informs our analysis. By at least specifying the forms of the equations and placing them in a temporal order, we have considerably lessened the task of analysis.

SUMMARY

Theoretical order is more than just arranging our concepts into primitive and derived terms. We must also order our theoretical statements into premises and equations. We feel this need for very general assumptions and very precise derived hypotheses as the number of statements in our theory multiply. After we order them into some hierarchy, we discover new benefits other than just a formal beauty. We avoid inconsistent reasoning, and we gain flexibility, simplicity, and creativity in theory construction. These advantages are unlikely to accrue, however, unless we already have at least ten theoretical statements.

There appear to be at least five techniques for ordering our statements and linkages. We can either synthesize existing theories or else extend them by adding a complete set of premises. All theories would seem to require a definitional premise, a mechanistic premise, and an action premise. The action premise is most important. We can also generalize our existing statements, or order them by levels of abstraction. Finally, even if we have no statements whatsoever, either our own or someone elses, we can suppose various premises and then see where they lead us. But again this makes more sense if we cast our imagination into one of the three molds: a definitional premise, a mechanistic premise, or an action premise.

PART TWO

Problems of Metatheory

CHAPTER SEVEN

Theory and Knowledge

There are three closely intertwined metatheoretical problems that can be conveniently handled in a single chapter. The first is the problem of what a theory should be. There are as many definitions of a theory as there are theorists, and each definition has implications for the process of theory construction. The metatheoretical problem of what is the *best* definition is not an easy one, but it should at least be considered as a fundamental issue in any book on theory construction. Its consideration makes clear our hidden values or desires of what we would like to see in a theory.

The second problem is what is a good theory. Again, there are many opinions about this and the opinion one selects has an effect on the kind of theory construction one will do. Here the intent is not to argue that every theory must conform to an ideal, but merely to raise these issues, to make more apparent how our present theories or theory fragments can be improved.

Finally, the relationship between theory and knowledge should be mentioned if not resolved. Implicit in this book is the conception of how theory relates to the development of scientific knowledge. This conception should be made explicit so that hidden assumptions will be more easily viewed and revised.

THE DEFINITION OF A SOCIOLOGICAL THEORY

There is general agreement that a theory is a set of propositions or theoretical statements (Zetterberg, 1963; Galtung, 1967; Reynolds, 1971, Ch. 5). It may be a path diagram, an axiomatic theory, or even a single hypothesis. Most theorists would argue that it has to be more than just a concept or even a set of concepts. The concepts have to be connected. There has been little additional discussion of what might be included in the definition. The elements of a theory that we discussed in the latter chapters of Part One are not usually included in a formal definition of sociological theory.

What is suggested here is that a theory should contain not only concepts and statements but definitions—both theoretical and operational—and linkages, again both theoretical and operational. The concepts and definitions should be ordered into primitive and derived terms and the statements and linkages should be ordered into premises and equations. What is crucial is why one would want to add more parts to a theory. It is not my preference. Quite the contrary! I would prefer the more simple notion of a set of interrelated concepts. What forces this definition upon us is the fact that each part makes a unique contribution to our understanding of social phenomena around us. This is probably why each component exists in the work of at least some people interested in constructing theories. Perhaps this is the most compelling argument as to why one needs each of these six components.

The Contribution of Each Theory Element

Each of the six components or parts of a theory makes a unique contribution to the whole theory (see Table 7.1). With theoretical concepts we see new sights. They are the descriptive lens of our theory, calling attention to otherwise neglected aspects of the social world. An excellent example of this is Merton's famous article on the role set (1957), an article that opened a whole new way of thinking about roles. An earlier example is Simmel's discussion of the stranger (Wolff, 1950), a social type with whom we are all familiar but who escapes our attention until we attach a label.

Table 7.1 The Contribution of Each Element of a Theory

Theory Part	Contribution
1. Concept names	Description and classification
2. Verbal statements	Analysis
3. Theoretical definitions	Meaning
Operational definitions	Measurement
4. Theoretical linkages	Plausibility
Operational linkages	Testability
5. Ordering into primitive and derived terms	Elimination of tautology
6. Ordering into premises and equations	Elimination of inconsistency

The development of some theoretical statements means that we have moved from description to analysis. As soon as two concepts are connected in some way, we can begin to make predictions and explanations, even though they may be of a very low level. Perhaps part of the power of Marx's writings is due to the many, many hypotheses buried in just a few pages of, for example, the "Communist Manifesto." When these are compared with almost any work in sociology, we begin to appreciate the great differences in analytical acuity. Indeed, it is a useful exercise to read theoretical works and count the number of theoretical statements in them. There are many that contain none.

Definitions add to our description of social phenomenon by providing meaning and measurement. As we have already noted, a definition may be implicit in the name of the concept, but the additional work to make it explicit is perhaps the most worthwhile work. It produces the best proof that something new is being added. Similarly, it may not seem like much to shuffle our concepts around until they are arranged into some order, but, as is clear to those who have tried, it is not easy. When we do order our concepts, we achieve still another objective, namely the elimination of tautology.

Linkages add to our analysis of social phenomenon by providing plausibility and testability. Again, adding this part is not easy but the gains are well worth the effort. Finally, ordering the statements and linkages into premises and equations helps us to discover whether we have been inconsistent in our reasoning.

Practically, a theory can be considered as fairly complete if it contains concepts, definitions, statements, and linkages. The ordering of these parts into some inductive-deductive arrangement is an elegance only slowly achieved in the sciences. It should represent a long-term objective rather than an immediate goal. Furthermore, as we have already noted several times, it is only when the number of concepts and statements proliferates that the advantages of ordering concepts and statements, and definitions and linkages accrue. Merton's (1968) advice about middle-range theory remains good advice, provided it is understood that a theory of this kind contains definitions and linkages as well as statements.

Some sociologists may want less in their theories and that is their choice. But, if our reasoning is correct, then they eliminate the particular contribution made by that part as well. We can avoid having theoretical statements, but can we afford being without analysis? Likewise, one can combine concepts and statements, the typical definition of a theory in sociology, thereby avoiding the specification of definitions and linkages. But in the process, one is losing meaning and plausibility as well as measurement and testability. Most sociologists would not argue against their inclusion and therefore definitions and linkages at least must be part of the definition of a theory.

This separation of what has been called the theoretical and the operational level in a theory has perhaps been the most unfortunate aspect of previous definitions of theories. Some would argue that theory, good theory, is only one or the other. Choosing one level and eliminating the other results in a one-sided approach. A concentration on operational definitions and linkages is characteristic of the school of thought which is called operationalism (Adler, 1947; Bridgeman, 1936; Dodd, 1943). The danger of this concentration is present in the proponents of path analysis. Whole path diagrams give us measurement and testability; they do not provide meaning and plausibility. Likewise, theories that cannot be measured and tested are not very desirable.

The Advantages of the Six Parts in Constructing a Theory

The arguments for including each of the six parts of a theory have already been made both in example and in exegesis. They need not be repeated here. But there is another reason why it is important to have all six parts of a theory included in the definition; a dialetic in the construction of a theory is created as each part is added. There is an interaction between the parts of a theory that results in the transformation of each.

The interrelationships between the six components are diagrammed in Figure 7.1. As can be readily seen, if we consider only bivariate relationships, there are 15 of these with six parts. Each arrow represents a creative interaction.

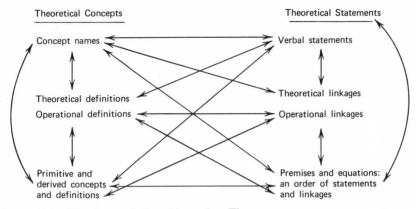

Figure 7.1   The Interrelationships of a Theory.

The interaction between theoretical concepts and statements requires little discussion beyond what was said in Chapters 1 and 2. As we discover some statement, we delineate our theoretical concepts in various ways, and vice versa. We find the idea of integration changing when combined with a statement about societal conflict as opposed to one regarding role conflict.

Once we add definitions, the number of interactions increases. We sometimes find it necessary to change both theoretical concepts and statements when we have operationalized one of the concepts. Indeed, one is continually struck by articles in the journals that appear to be testing hypotheses very different from those they say they are testing because their definitions are so different. Lazarsfeld (1959) has discussed a similar problem under the idea of expressive and predictive indicators. If one reads the indicators employed in journal articles this becomes clear. Hence, our point is that the addition of a theoretical and operational definition changes and sets limits on our concepts, which is obvious, and on our statements, which is less obvious. Here we may fall into the practice of seeing our theoretical statement as a connection between operational indicators, but it is more than that; it is a hypothesis relating two theoretical definitions as well. The inclusion of meanings influences our thinking about our statements in many ways.

The addition of linkages means three more interactions and thus three more checks on our reasoning. Both theoretical and operational linkages can and do alter considerably the content of our theoretical statement. We begin to appreciate that we may really want to talk about something other than what we were talking about. This becomes even clearer as linkages somewhat alter our concepts and their definitions. A discussion of the reasons why two concepts are interrelated reveals the necessity of using other concepts with different definitions. For example, if one discovers that the reason why an increase in the number of occupational specialties leads to a change in the distribution of power is because of horizontal communication channels undercutting the existing hierarchy of power, then one might change one's theoretical statement to an increasing emphasis on horizontal communications leads to a decrease in centralization. Naturally, one changes definitions accordingly. Or the use of different operational indicators for the degree of stratification creates very different operational linkages in almost any theoretical statement one might choose to use. Prestige rankings suggests one linkage, the percentage of income earned by the top 20 percent another, and the percentage of the bottom 20 still a third linkage. Also implied in these indicators, as we have already noted, are different theoretical definitions and thus, sets of reasons.

When we order our concepts into primitive and derived terms, we discover that there are again considerable limits placed on what can constitute the definition. We have already noted in the extended example in Chapter 5 how the primitives are anticipated in the particular derived terms that we desire to work with. Naturally, a conceptual scheme alters the reasons given for a theoretical linkage, as well as the operational linkage. Similarly, premises and equations, an arrangement of theoretical statements, has the same consequences for definitions and linkages, concepts and statements. Perhaps the best proof of this is a comparison between the author's "Axiomatic Theory of Organizations" (Hage, 1965), which has the first four components of a theory, with the extended example in Chapters 5 and 6. Although the two are similar in nature, most of the axiomatic theory can be reduced to a few equations, and even fewer premises, which are contained in the original theoretical linkages, but these also contained other reasons that are now involved as additional variables, additional premises, and additional equations. The ordering of terms has made some indicators invalid and required the utilization of others not originally conceived of. Formalization has been changed to normative equality, and morale to membership participation with no loss and perhaps some gain in acuity of analysis. These changes would probably have not occurred except as a consequence of continued attempts to order the concepts and their definitions, the connections and their linkages.

Thus, one critical argument for having the six elements of a theory is that each stipulates the boundaries of choice. As there are more elements, this choice becomes more and more narrow; the boundaries are smaller. But from this limitation comes a great creative strength. *First,* it means the choice is less likely to be wrong. *Second,* the choice becomes easier to make because there are fewer alternatives.

The first point is hard to prove, given the present stage of theory development in sociology, and yet it seems plausible. When Newton constructed his laws of motion, he used geometry as a model of theory construction. There are great similarities between the ordering of concepts and definitions into primitive and derived terms and statements and linkages into premises and equations, and geometric models of thinking. In geometry, primitive terms are used to derive other concepts; statements are arranged into axioms or postulates and theorems and corollaries. The great advantage of reasoning, à la geometry, is that one is less likely to make an error by moving in two directions. Proofs require reasoning, forwards and backwards. Geometry is not an empirical system, however. It lacks indicators and operational linkages. In the social sciences, these are essential. As we move up and down in levels of abstraction from primitive terms to indicators and back to premises, we increase the probability that the theory is a good one, a contribution to knowledge.

The second point is somewhat easier to demonstrate. As we add parts, the choice becomes much more restricted, and therefore easier to make. If one chooses distribution as a primitive term, then one is limited as to how to define social structure, and in turn one eliminates a large number of possible choices of indicators for complexity, centralization, stratification, and normative equality. In fact, many of our techniques of theory construction are based on this simple observation.

Thus, the parts lead to a critical and creative dialectic in theory construction. We are forced toward solutions, but solutions that seem to work better. And this is all that we can ask.

CRITERIA FOR EVALUATING THEORIES

What is important about our definition is that it provides a yardstick by which theoretical fragments can be measured. We can now say—and quite objectively—whether such and such a work is a theory as well as how much of a theory it is. For, as is clear from our discussion, we have a variable—closeness to a complete theory—upon which all theoretical work can be evaluated. Thus, if a theory fragment does not contain theoretical definitions, we can say that the meaning of the terms has not been specified. Or, if there are no operational linkages, we do not have testability, something different from measureability; this difference can be easily overlooked, as we have noted in Chapter 4. Empirical indicators allow us to measure the concepts but unless we have some statements about basic form, direction, coefficients, and limits, there is an infinite number of possible combinations to test.

If this standard is used, then it is apparent that sociology really does not have any theories. Most theories fail for lack of operational and theoretical linkages—especially the operational. This should not discourage anyone, nor should it be construed as a negative criticism. It is meant to be constructive criticism, to indicate what needs to be done. The first four chapters provide a series of remedies for the various missing parts. What is missing can be added, and in the process, sociological theory becomes the richer for the effort. Nor should this evaluation be interpreted to mean that there are no theorists even if there are no theories. We are asking *how much* of a theory it is. Complete theories are the culmination of the work of many men, even if the final result is sometimes associated with the name of only one. One great advantage of our definition of a theory is to call attention to what each person does contribute to the final objective.

There are several general standards that can be applied in evaluating a theory. These standards provide some other criteria used implicitly in judging theory. Suppose we have two competing theories available for the same behavioral association; for example, Homans' exchange theory and Heider's balance theory as formalized by Davis (see Table 6.1). There are formal criteria for choosing among the two theory fragments. The four basic standards are: scope, parsimony, precision of prediction, and accuracy of explanation. This evaluation, and understandably so, has been of more interest to philosophers of science.

The idea of the scope of a theory is a simple one. It is a measure of how many of the basic problems in the discipline or specialty are handled by the same theory. When Merton (1968) discussed theories of the middle range, he really had in mind theories of medium scope, such as a theory of role conflict or a theory of status disequilibrium or a theory of differential association. These are theories designed to speak to one or two problems and not to others. It is unlikely that we will have for some time in sociology a very general theory that speaks to most, if not all, issues.

One way of measuring relatively precisely the scope of a theory is to note the number of derived terms relative to the number of primitive ones. The higher the ratio of derived to primitive terms, the wider the scope of the theory. Another term for scope is simply the generality of the theory.

Why should scope or generality be so important? The answer is that usually as theories become more general, they tend to last longer, a point observed by Kuhn (1962). This does not mean that they are never replaced but only that they seem to work better. Theories of the middle range have a shorter intellectual life span. This does not mean that one should not construct them. As we have already suggested, Merton's intellectual strategy is a good one. But, as theories become more general, incorporating more of the discipline's major problems, we find that they seem to stand without revision for longer periods. It is an observation and not a statement that one can prove. But it is for this reason that scope seems so important. Interestingly enough, when evaluating two theories with different scope and assuming equivalence in other matters, we will prefer the one with greater scope. Perhaps it is the same need that leads us to order our concepts into primitive and derived terms in the first place.

Parsimony is a property of the theoretical statements. We are interested in explaining as much as we can with as little as possible. This is sometimes called the power of the theory. A powerful theory is one that makes few assumptions. Parsimony then becomes a ratio of equations to premises. This property is much like scope and has parallel advantages. Scope and parsimony can vary, as is clear from the extended examples in Chapters 5 and 6. This theory has reasonably wide scope but is not very parsimonious. There are a number of premises and not that many more equations; thus, the ratio is a low one and we would say that the theory is not very powerful.

The precision of a prediction is, of course, a standard that can be applied to a single equation. Therefore, it might be rejected by some as a standard for a theory. In sociology, it seems worthwhile to consider the probability that no single equation, even one with 50 variables, is likely to provide precise prediction. We will need sets of equations, especially if we are not sure of the operational linkages between all of the variables. In that instance, we use sets of simultaneous equations. Suppose we want to predict the likelihood of a revolution. It seems unlikely that a single equation, such as the rising-expectations thesis, is sufficient. At a bare minimum, one needs to know how much control is being exerted in the society, how capable the society is of producing its outputs, how able it is to adapt to changing circumstances both internal or external, and whether there are various structural factors causing discontent. That is a large number of equations! Yet, even all these potential candidates for predicting revolution do not include all the possibilities listed by Eckstein (1964) in his review of the etiology of internal wars.

It is important to recognize that even a simple statement, such as there will always be a revolution somewhere in the world, provides some prediction. For those who are concerned about the development of the discipline, this may be some measure of comfort! We may not know how many, when, or where, but at least we can state with reasonable accuracy that there will always be some revolutions. The *precision* of prediction, which is a variable of considerable range, can be increased by being able to predict how many. For example, we can make a reasonably accurate estimate, with only a few variables, of the number of automobile deaths there will be during a long weekend. A more precise prediction would specify how much within a specified period of time, say a year, and at what timepoints within the year. As we attempt to add this precision, we find that we need more equations. Thus, precision of prediction is a property of a theory.

Unfortunately, the number of prediction studies in sociology is relatively few. The work in diffusion research stands out as one of the major exceptions (Rogers, 1962). The result of this lack is that we do not have as yet much experience with measuring the precision of prediction, a problem that the economists have lived with for some time now.

The last criterion of accurate explanation is probably the most difficult to explain and yet, it strikes us as correct that one wants a theory that is somehow right or true or valid. But this involves a number of knotty problems: what is right or truth or validity? Some of these fundamental issues are touched upon in the next section. For now, we can say that when we accept theories, we do so not only because they have broad scope and are parsimonious and because they predict relatively well, but because we are persuaded that the explanation is an accurate one. This is more than just a question of evidence and yet, it is a place where research does play a vital role.

The explanation of any theory lies in its set of premises. These, when amplified, provide a story, if you will, about some chain of events. Although we might predict the outcome of these events quite precisely, it does not mean that the story behind the events, the set of premises or theoretical linkages, is explaining the phenomenon accurately. It could be due to other reasons than those that are stipulated. A simple example is a theory of societal conflict. The equations might precisely predict revolution, but the question remains whether the premises are accurate ones. We have suggested that one explanation lies in the lack of rank consistency for particular social groups and positions. Another explanation is Davis' (1961) rising-expectations thesis. Here, we have two explanations for the same event. Which is more accurate? One must make a judgment about any theory however difficult it may be.

In practice, research plays a critical role in helping us to make these judgments in the following ways. Typically, we search for what are called strategic tests of a theory (Stinchcombe, 1968). These are where several alternative explanations can be held constant. To continue with the same illustration, even though rising expectations may be usually associated with some rank discrepancy, we might find an instance where they are not. This would provide a strategic test of the theories, that is, their explanatory acuity. This is one reason why the experimental research design is considered so fundamental. It frequently affords us the opportunity to eliminate equally plausible sets of premises.

Another way of thinking about the problem of accurate explanation is to think in terms of spuriousness. Simply put, A can be used to predict B precisely because both A and B are caused by C. The explanation that A caused B would not be accurate, that is, we have a case of spuriousness. Although here we are talking about the equations, it is much akin to the problem of explanation. Unfortunately, seldom in our research do we test alternative explanations involving different premises and equations relative to some dependent variable. If more of this kind of research were done, we could make more critical judgments about the adequacy of the explanation in particular theories. But, perhaps that is a stage of research that must wait until we have developed more elegant theories with ordered sets of statements and linkages. Development in one area is frequently linked with development in another.

THE RELATIONSHIP BETWEEN THEORY AND KNOWLEDGE

The most difficult metatheoretical problem—the delineation of what is knowledge and what is truth—has been saved for the last. The problem of what is sociological knowledge and how does sociological theory articulate with it is one that philosophers have been concerned with for some time. Their interest has not been so much the specific question of sociological theory and knowledge, but the more general one of the relationships between science and knowledge. As a consequence, we cannot hope to provide an adequate solution in just a few pages. Instead, our objective is to make explicit a model that we have used throughout this book. In other words, we are articulating a perspective more than we are arguing a position. At the same time, if we did not explicate the implicit definition of knowledge and its relationship to sociological theory, our discussion of theory construction would remain incomplete. The epistemological model lies as an underpinning to everything that has been said. We need to at least expose it for attack and criticism. This is particularly important in this instance because there is just that possibility that many readers might disagree (see Friedrichs, 1970).

The Definition of Sociological Knowledge

The major difficulty in discussing whether there is any sociological knowledge is that many individuals think about this issue in either-or terms. Just as we do not want either-or concepts and either-or connections between them, we do not want an either-or conception of what is knowledge. Because we are used to reasoning in this way, we are prevented from perceiving that perhaps there is some knowledge in sociology, albeit not very much.

Our definition is that *sociological theories are models of social reality.* Some theories approach closer to this reality, but they are never an entirely accurate picture of it. Knowledge is a set of true laws that describe this picture. Thus, theories approach knowledge but they are never quite there. What is essential to this conception is that theories are never true or false, right or wrong, but always more or less true or false.

One way of thinking about the definition of knowledge and how sociological theories may relate to it, is to imagine theories as an attempt to construct a picture with a set of pieces from a jigsaw puzzle. We are aware that we probably do not have all the pieces, one reason why one writes the disclaimer "all other things being equal" but we do not know, of course, what pieces might be absent. We work with what we have. We attempt to fit the pieces together as best we can. Some of the pieces do not fit, so we leave them to the side; these are isolated theoretical concepts that appear to be valuable but are never employed in theoretical statements. We will also have many isolated pairs of pieces—the theoretical statements. Finally, there will be larger combinations: they are our theories. As we continue the task of synthesis, bringing together ever larger and larger numbers of the puzzle pieces, we sometimes find it necessary to rearrange our previous formulations. This represents what Kuhn (1962) has called a revolution. But it might be better to say reformulation because most of the pieces remain the same. Only some are added and subtracted as we obtain a more complete picture by way of the reformulation. The necessity for the rearrangement arises precisely out of our attempt to obtain more of the picture implied by the various isolated pieces and pairs of pieces, the theoretical concepts and statements that we have and that are not as yet integrated with our theories. But as this process continues, although we are able to make better and better estimates of what the final picture may be, we never know all of its details because we never have and never can have all of the pieces.

Our definition of knowledge is the final picture. Theories are the larger combinations of jig-saw puzzles that are estimates of what part of the picture may be like. Thus, *theories are best seen as approximations to knowledge*. The word approximation is quite deliberate and essential to the conception of how theory and knowledge articulate. Theories are models of reality, *not* reality itself. This model of knowledge is frequently overlooked in the various debates about the existence of sociological knowledge. Perhaps if it were acknowledged, much of the heat of the debate would be gone.

Criteria of Evaluation and Knowledge

For those readers who know calculus, we can say that knowledge is a limit towards which theories move. They get closer and closer, but they never reach the limit. This is diagramed in Figure 7.2. What is important to note in the diagram is that as theories do get closer, they increase

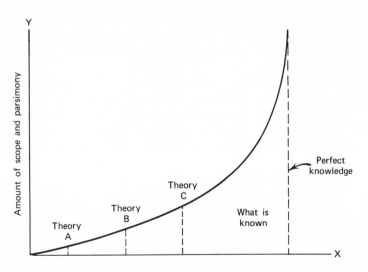

Figure 7.2 The Relationship Between Sociological Theory and Sociological Knowledge.

in scope and parsimony and increase in precision of prediction and accuracy of explanation.

Thus, the justification for our criteria is that they seem to help us make better choices from the standpoint of being closer to our limit of knowledge. If both Theory A and Theory B explain the same behavior, we will accept Theory B as the better one if it has more scope, parsimony, and accuracy of prediction, because it is considered a better approximation to knowledge. Thus, our first three criteria are really the standards in many cases for the fourth, the acuity of explanation. However, there is still room for theoretical judgment.

Nor should this process of one theory replacing another be seen as ever onward and upward. Theory C may be a much better reformulation of Theory A. There is a tendency to go back to some old insights as one moves forward to larger syntheses of existing pieces. Theories are much like weddings; something old, something new, something borrowed, and something blue. The latter represents results we would not like to see, predictions that are disturbing to our values. Usually, good sociological theories have this.

One way of thinking about the precision of prediction is that it is a measure of how close we are to the limit. There is a certain paradox here that we can know this, but not know what the final limit is. We can never eliminate all error just because we can never have all the facts even within the discipline of sociology.

Perhaps some illustrations of how this works can make the point clearer. We might start with a simple example from the attempt to predict weather. A very simple theoretical statement is as follows: the weather will be approximately the same today (tomorrow) as it was yesterday (today). Now, this assertion does predict and with some accuracy. In the midwestern part of the United States, one could predict the weather about three out of every four days with a reasonable degree of accuracy. That is not a bad prediction, all things considered. And while it is not a very elegant theory, it is a first approximation to knowledge. One could make plans at least on a day to day basis. It is clear that it is quite limited in scope; many aspects of the weather are not included unless they are implied. The theory does not have much precision; it does not handle small changes in temperature, wind velocity, barometric pressure, or wind direction. Perhaps most critical is that it does not handle the major changes that are occurring every three or four days as one air mass replaces another. Nor does it say anything about, indeed it ignores, the great meteorological upheavals like hurricanes, tornados, waterspouts, etc. Worse, its only theoretical statement would not work in all places.

It is fine for the center of a large land mass, but along the coast line and in regions with a lot of lakes, it works less well. But it does tell us something.

Of course, the science of meteorology has moved beyond this with a theory of hot and cold air masses that replace each other. As they do, there are predictable sequences of wind directions, movements of clouds and kinds of clouds, changes in air and temperature, etc. The adding of more variables, the improvement of their operational linkages to include polynomic functions, and better premises about the dynamics of weather have allowed meteorologists to start making more accurate predictions and for longer periods of time. There are now five-day forecasts. But, it is still clear that the weathermen are not always right nor can they yet predict for very long periods of time. They have a better approximation of meteorological knowledge, but complete knowledge itself yet eludes them. Nor does it seem likely that they ever will reach the limit.

The same can be said for sociology. We can make reasonable predictions about social collectives with the following statement: social collectives continue to do the same things they have always done. It has all the strengths and all the weaknesses of its meteorological counterpart. But, it is a first approximation to knowledge. It does allow us to make some predictions. Naturally, we want more precision than this. But the price is more theory construction: add more variables, improve the quality of measurement, develop more complicated linkages. Hopefully, the techniques that we have discussed plus others can aid us in moving towards better approximations of the sociological jigsaw puzzle.

This definition of knowledge does not imply that it contains all of reality. The limit in Figure 7.2 is called, perhaps more correctly, scientific knowledge. One needs artistic creations to complete the picture of social reality. Furthermore, there are a variety of puzzles. General variables, as we have argued, are appropriate for the social sciences, such as sociology, political science, and economics; they are not the only kinds of theoretical concepts. Reality can be described with specific nonvariables, the language of history. To argue for the existence of a sociological jigsaw puzzle is not intended to diminish the importance of other puzzles.

We need to rephrase our question of whether sociology has any theories which approximate knowledge. To say that we do not have an equation substantiated by empirical evidence, such as, force equals mass times acceleration (F = MA), is not to say that we do not have any sociological knowledge. Knowledge, like many other things, comes in degrees. Some disciplines have more of it and others have less of it. Psychology and economics have better approximations to their limits than does sociology.

The awarding of a Nobel Prize in economics is indicative of how far that discipline has developed. Physics and chemistry have better approximations to their limits than do psychology and economics. Each discipline is at a different stage of development. The stage of development is influenced by the number of years in which the discipline has been working with general variables, the number of individuals who are members of the discipline, and a number of other factors. Sociology is a relatively new discipline. Our approximations are quite crude but they are a start.

Implications of the Definition for Theory Construction

One of the more critical implications of these definitions of knowledge and theory, suggested in Figure 7.2, is that theories are never true or false. They are partly true, part of the time. Just as a theory is an approximation, it remains something that is never completely right or wrong. Thus, we must strive *continuously* to improve our theories. The task of theory construction never ends. We need constant evaluation, one of the reasons for specifying the contributions of each part, and general criteria for evaluating theories.

Another important implication is that there is a definite direction towards which we are aiming in the construction of theories. Our task is to move beyond the statements to theories of ever more scope and parsimony, striving for greater precision in our predictions and, of course, accuracy in our explanation. Our problem in sociology is that we have remained on the level of theory fragments—an abundance of theoretical concepts, some theoretical statements, and very few sets of theoretical statements. As a consequence, the potential of better approximations to sociological knowledge has not been tapped. Unfortunately, this potential is frequently lost to view in the various debates about sociology.

Another major prescription of theory construction, one that flows from the above, is the need to construct syntheses. We need to combine theories of process with theories of structure; we want to combine Marx's ideas with those of Durkheim; we should explore combining system analysis and value analysis; we need to investigate what happens when, for example, one combines role-set theory with balance theory. As we do these things, our theories will gain in scope and parsimony and probably in the precision of prediction as well.

SUMMARY

Some of the interrelationships between metatheory and theory construction should now be clear. Our definition of a theory tells us why we need six different sets of techniques. Paradoxically, adding more elements creates a dialectic of constructive criticism. As this occurs, we are more likely to move closer to some knowledge. We are more likely to make better choices.

Six components of a theory results in some important emergent properties— greater scope, parsimony, precision of prediction, and acuity of explanation. In turn, these standards tell us how to choose between two theories that can explain the same phenomenon. However, these same standards make apparent that theory construction is a continuous process. They can always have more scope, more parsimony, more precision, and more acuity.

As the process of theory construction continues, we move closer to our limit of perfect knowledge, which is truth, or at least an accurate picture of the sociological component of social reality. But the fact that we can never reach this limit again means that we are always constructing, reconstituting, and reconciling theories. Our work is never finished!

CHAPTER EIGHT

Specifying Theoretical Orientations

When disciplines do not have theories or even what Kuhn (1962) would call a paradigm, then they usually have what might be labeled theoretical orientations. These are loose collections of concepts—an analytical approach—used by one of the schools in the discipline. The presence of a school is itself a sign that the field has not developed much and that theoretical orientations are being employed as an interim analytical device. Since the set of concepts is so loose, it is hard to classify any particular person as representative of a particular orientation. Instead, one finds some of the ideas some of the time in some of the writings of particular individuals and groups who prefer a specific analytical orientation. What is distinctive about theoretical orientations is that they are preached more often than they are practiced. For example, one finds more articles about structural-functionalism and whether or not it can handle change than articles explicitly employing this mode of thinking, at least in sociology in the United States (this is not true for anthropology in the

United Kingdom). This is in sharp contrast to the paradigmatic stage where there is enough consensus about the basic approach so that most of the energy can be concentrated on solving the problems of the paradigm. That sociology does not have a paradigm in this sense is clear (although not everyone would agree; see Friedrichs, 1970) from a random selection of any issue of the major journals.

But, to be in the preparadigmatic stage is not to be lost in the wilderness. We do have some paths—our theoretical orientations. These, or any one of them, may develop into a basic paradigm, such as marginal utility theory has for economics. What is unfortunate about theoretical orientations is their advantage of looseness. This results in a confusion as to what are the essential concepts or ideals defining a particular orientation and thus prevents it from being effectively exploited. In turn, the controversy about the meaning or the definition or who is the true disciple tends to deflect attention away from what should be the concern of all—improving the theoretical orientation so that it can become a paradigm.

The looseness of concepts specifying a theoretical orientation makes the task of explicating particular theoretical orientations a hazardous one. One is always in danger of leaving out someone's pet idea. More importantly, the vagueness results, as we have already noted, in the difficulty of delineating the boundaries of particular orientations. Probably, if one took a random sample of sociologists and asked them what the major theoretical orientations in the discipline were, one would receive a different set of answers from almost everyone.

With these qualifications in mind, my answer to the interviewer would be that there are three theoretical orientations that are central in the discipline and a number of others that are less important. Among the more important are what might be called structural-functionalism, value analysis, and system analysis. Most can agree about the first, many about the second, and probably fewer about the third. But, system analysis, as an approach to sociological problems, seems to be increasing in popularity.

There are several other kinds of theoretical orientations that will not be discussed for specific reasons. Probably, the major omission is Marxian analysis. A number of individuals have found Marx's writings to be insightful. Indeed, they are. The difficulty is that everyone takes what he wants from Marx, and with much to take, it becomes difficult to say the result is a distinctive school of thought. Among other variations on the theme of Marxian analysis are historical-specific analysis, conflict theory, and a social-class analysis. The first I would prefer to avoid discussing because it requires a detailed analysis of how one does historical analysis, which can be specified as a theoretical orientation but requires a whole chapter, if not more, in itself. The other two deal with particular variables or nonvariables as the case may be and thus are more specific than the other three major theoretical orientations tend to be. Marx's theoretical concepts and hypotheses are more like a theory than the three theoretical orientations that we will discuss.

There are also theories of the middle range. They are employed with a particular kind of social collective and frequently with a single major independent or dependent variable. There is the technology school in the study of organizations (Perrow, 1967; Woodward, 1965), the communications school in the study of development (Lerner, 1958; Deutsch, 1966), the coalition theory in small groups (Gamson, 1970; Caplow, 1969), etc. These are not discussed because again they are more like theories than orientations. They could be generalized by using the techniques discussed in Chapter 6.

THE DEFINITION OF A THEORETICAL ORIENTATION

The vagueness of theoretical orientations has resulted in a large number of different ways in which they can be defined. The definitions have been implicit in the works of others who have tried to specify the nature of a theoretical orientation, although they have not always used the term. Sometimes there is a focus on the kind of causal linkage. Much has been made of the difference between structural-functionalism and system analysis on this point (Buckley, 1967; for an interesting variation on this theme see Stinchcombe, 1968). Another approach is to explicate basic premises or very general theoretical statements, such as Merton (1957, Ch. 1) did in his famous discussion of structural-functionalism. Still a third tact is to explicate what might be called working assumptions about the nature of the model of reality that is employed. This is different from theoretical statements as such, because they are not premises in the theory but working assumptions about the nature of the phenomena about which the theory is being written. A simple illustration is the belief in determinism, of which the work of Friedrichs (1970) is a contemporary example. More typically, one finds discussions about the appropriateness or inappropriateness of a biological or a mechanical model of social reality.

Each of these approaches has its merits and perhaps all together they would represent an exhaustive specification of a theoretical orientation.

Yet, one of the critical parts is missing, the specification of the elements of variables involved. There are several reasons as to why one wants to make this the most important part of a definition.

The Advantages of Specifying Elements of Variables

Attempting to define a theoretical orientation by specifying inherent classes of variables would seem to have several distinct advantages. *First,* it avoids the vagueness that has characterized the many discussions of various orientations. Or, at least it seems to make the meaning more concise. *Second,* it encourages the development of a more complete theory or paradigm. As we suggested, the variables are a most important first step. By specifying the element, we have moved in that direction. In other words, we have placed ourselves at the beginning, and, in a position to proceed through the chapters in the process of constructing a theory. *Third,* students should find it easier to apply the approach if various classes of variables are indicated. This tells us what is excluded as well as what is included, a most important piece of information in thinking with any particular orientation. *Fourth,* it avoids the criticisms of Hempel (1959) and others. Many theoretical orientations have been found wanting because they do not contain, or appear to contain, any general variables. The orientation then never moves to the development of theoretical statements and especially ones of a general nature. The metatheoretical diagnosis of the problem of a bad theoretical orientation is usually that it is specific and not general and the proposed remedy is typically to eliminate the school with several seemingly devastating critiques.

The arguments about theoretical orientations are largely resolved once general variables can be specified. Much could be saved and gained by making more explicit the general variables involved in the major concepts and ideas associated with a theoretical orientation. By indicating what are some classes of general variables, we can begin to improve upon what is already contained in the orientation. As we do, we take another step towards finding a paradigm.

The Definition of a Theoretical Orientation

For all of the above reasons, we prefer to define a theoretical orientation as containing an element or several elements of general variables that can be applied to more than one kind of analytical unit. In the case of sociology, of course, we are mainly interested in general theoretical orientations for more than just groups or organizations or societies. In addition to defining inherent elements, our definition of a theoretical orientation includes what might be called the key concepts. These are ideas that usually, if not always, are implied when one is employing a particular analytical approach. They represent the specification of the way of thinking.

What is excluded by the definition are theoretical statements. Typically, the set of ideas is too loose for this. Although, as always, there are exceptions. Merton (1957, Ch. 1) has discussed some of the working assumptions of structural-functionalism of writers associated with that school.

But the heart of any theoretical orientation, as far as we are concerned, is the classes of variables of social phenomena that are its particular focus. This, along with the delineation of the way in which one thinks in the orientation, should make it easy for any reader to use a particular method.

SPECIFYING THREE THEORETICAL ORIENTATIONS

Structural-Functionalism as a Theoretical Orientation

The original imagery of structural-functionalism was a biological analogy. Spencer, one of the first to work with this perspective, went so far as to compare the blood system with the transportation system (Spencer, 1898). While this direct translation of an analogy was readily rejected, Spencer's terms of structure and function have remained. Merton (1957, Ch. 1) helped clarify the meaning of these two concepts. He noted that function meant objective consequences and not subjective motives, and thus he moved the discussion to a more sociological level. Perhaps the most important point that Merton made was that any institutional pattern under scrutiny might have either positive or negative consequences or perhaps no consequences at all. But the problem remains as to which consequences one might want to consider when doing a functional analysis. Davis (1959), interpreting Merton, suggests that structural-functionalism asks what consequences the part has for the whole. Similarly, Nagel (1957, pp. 247–283) has formalized functionalism by stipulating G-states as the special class of consequences or aspects of the whole that need to be considered. But this still leaves unanswered what class of consequences the G-states are, and perhaps more importantly, what are some examples of measurable sociological variables that fall within this class.

The Definition of Function. If we return to the basic imagery of biology, we note that the biologist is usually looking at one or two kinds of variables. Implicit, if not explicit in the concept of function, is a special class of consequences. For example, the biologist might look at the white corpuscle count of the blood, or note the rhythm and number of heartbeats, or measure the body's temperature. In each of these illustrations, the same kinds of variables are involved. Each of them is a measure of either performance or output. The units of analysis vary—blood system, heart, body—but the consequences that are measured are all criteria of physiological performance. Usually the biologist or physiologist examines multiple performance criteria for the same unit of analysis. When examining the adequacy of the functioning of the lungs, he might not only listen to coughing or other noises made during the breathing process but measure the amount of CO_2 expelled, an output and an indicator of the lung's efficiency and effectiveness. Similarly, a cardiologist may examine the heartbeat under a variety of conditions or use an electrocardiogram or listen to particular noises of the heart while estimating the performance level of this organ.

Thus the word function can be defined as a criterion of performance. This idea is implied by Nadel (1957, pp. 7–19), who stated social function was some stipulated measure of effectiveness. This idea is also implied by Merton (1957, p. 82) at various points in his discussion of functionalism when he uses the word effectiveness, although at other times he uses the word consequences in a much broader sense, including other elements of variables as well. While measures of effectiveness are perhaps the most common function, there are other performances besides this one.

The domains of performances and outputs, as defined in Chapter 5, may or may not be goals because as Merton (1957, p. 61) has suggested functions and dysfunctions can be either manifest or latent. The key point is that social functions are measures of adequacy. This seems to be the essential idea involved when a functionalist asks the question how well is the system functioning? This question implied certain measures of performance or outputs even if they are not made explicit in the analysis. The common phrase in the literature, a well-functioning system, now has an empirical referent: it means high effectiveness, high efficiency, high rate of institutional change, high membership participation, and high outputs. Since they have operational indicators, if not complete definitions, hypotheses involving these variables are quite testable. One could add many more examples.

The reader familiar with functionalist writing might indeed ask what happened to integration? This is one of Parsons' four functional prerequisites and has a long history in the structural-functional literature (Parsons, Bales, and Shils, 1953, Ch. 3, 4). The answer is that this variable is not one of social performance but instead either a process variable or a structural variable depending upon its theoretical definition. One must clearly distinguish between variables involving arrangements, their articulations, and their outputs. Said in this way, it is clear that integration cannot be considered an output. If integration is defined in terms of the number of friends or the size of the role-set, then it is a structural variable. If integration is defined in terms of the frequency of interaction or the communication rate or the absence of either deviance or conflict, then it is a process variable. Although process analysis is usually not part of structural-functionalism—a common complaint—it can be included.

Thus, an objective definition is provided for dysfunction, one obviating any subjective evaluation. The definition of social function as a measure of performance or of output is, it is true, in one sense essentially evaluative, as Fallding (1963) has noted. The researcher states that efficiency is high or low, that there is little or much institutional change, or that there is high or low industrial production. But these evaluations are objective ones, when the criteria are clearly stated and easily measured. The relative importance of particular functions and dysfunctions, the ideological question, is a separate problem, as has been noted by Merton (1957, pp. 37–45). Which performances and outputs are most prized varies in groups according to their values. Some people may argue that effectiveness is the most important performance while others may feel membership participation is most critical. But functions or dysfunctions can be measured objectively provided the foregoing definition of social function is accepted.

These above examples of performance measures also allow us to provide a clear definition for Merton's ideas of multiple consequences and the net balance of consequences. A particular institutional pattern may be functional for the volume of production and efficiency, that is, it increases scores on these criteria of social performance, and dysfunctional for satisfaction and institutional change, that is, it decreases scores on these criteria of social performances. Or, some institutional pattern that maximizes the growth of industrial production may minimize some other output. Even the 12 variables suggested in Chapter 5 immediately answer the question of multiple consequences and the net balance of consequences and with actual arithmetic numbers. (For an unusual example, see Bavelas, 1960.) As additional social performances are added, the analysis can be made even richer.

A more complicated issue is the implicit concept of survival and similar ideas. As is well known, the biological analogy carries with it the imagery of death—the relationship between a performance and the continued existence of an organism. How does one measure the survival of a social collective, particularly a society? To make matters worse, while rats and men die fairly quickly, societies frequently endure for centuries. The problem is not an artificial one. Of the three to four thousand societies known to mankind almost all have failed to survive. Presumably, the word survival has some empirical referent and is not just excess baggage in an analogy borrowed from biology.

It is important to recognize that survival is an either-or category along some dimension or general variable, an arbitrary cutting point chosen for analysis. One hint for finding the definition of survival is to look at the definition of a society or social collective. If the unit of analysis no longer exists, then one or more of its properties has ceased to exist. We have suggested that the definition of society includes eight institutional outputs as well as other collective properties. If one of these disappears, presumably we no longer have a society, at least by the logic of the definition. Thus, survival becomes:

> survival, df = the maintenance of the eight outputs
> above some minimum amount.

The operational definition for this is not easy to specify because this approach has not been taken in research. But the definition does focus our attention clearly on the problem at hand and thus eventually we should be able to determine the precise level.

A set of premises about survival and how this is related to the social structure of a society have been given in the extended example in Chapter 6. What has been suggested is that as societies become quite centralized, they are likely to become vulnerable and disappear.

Theoretically, there are great advantages to this line of reasoning. The heart of social engineering requires the assessment of the advantages and disadvantages of particular approaches, structures, programs, etc. It is the Robert S. McNamara cost-effectiveness reasoning. And while what is good for the Defense Department may not be good for the Nation, it can still be true that the analytical approaches can be borrowed with much intellectual gain for the discipline. Unfortunately, this potential as yet has not been realized in sociology.

The Definition of Social Structure. The other essential concept of structural-functionalism has been the idea of social structure. Merton (1957, pp. 50, 55–60) observed that there were statuses or social positions included in a functional analysis. Nadel (1957, p. 16) has explored the different meanings of structure and noted its essential emphasis on re-lationships and arrangements, the idea of a network or pattern among individuals or social positions.

Again the intellectual problem is to identify variables, especially general ones, that can be used to describe these social arrangements. Merton's (1957, Ch. 9) list of group properties contains many variables that can be employed for this purpose. The extent of social interaction can be measured, as it has been in many studies. Some groups or organiza-tions have high average rates of interaction while others have low ones. Similarly, the degree of integration and cohesion can be used to contrast different structures being studied.

Again, the four variables suggested earlier, complexity, centralization, stratification, and normative equality, include some of the critical ones. But it is obvious from the above that these are not the only ones that might be measured. The variables of role-relationships are also examples for those more interested in microsociology.

The Definition of Internal Processes. Usually, structural-functional analysis is limited to just the three elements, structural, performance, and output, but sometimes, albeit rarely, another class of variables is implicit. In fact, one of the major criticisms made of this mode of analysis is the failure to include variables like conflict or deviance. Radcliffe-Brown noted the importance of process and Merton (1957) implies it in his famous paradigm when he speaks of the mechanism by which structure and function are connected. Perhaps, more importantly, this class of variable is needed to include some of the concepts associated with structural-func-tional analysis.

In particular, if one wants to add the basic idea of the need for control, a concept associated with structural-functionalism, not only because of the work of Durkheim (1951) but because of the work of Parsons (1951), then we need to add another element of variables, the ones that we have labeled integration processes. As we do, we are indeed adding conflict and deviance, which are nothing more than the obverse side of the variables of consensus and conformity. This is not to deny that various individuals associated with structural-functionalism have been more concerned with consensus than with conflict. It might be noted in their defense that if one chooses empirically what occurs most often, then the accent should be more on consensus than on conflict. The latter, and especially the more extreme forms of conflict, is the exception and not the rule.

The Thinking of Structural-Functionalism. Structural-functional analysis, in sociology, can be defined as relating structural variables with performance and output variables. This is the logical intent of much of biological analyses. A collapsed lung (physiological structural arrangement) is related to the amount of CO_2 expelled (physiological performance) or a sticky heart valve (arrangement) is related to the heartbeat rate (performance). Physiology has developed many measures of structure and criteria of performance. This thinking permeates other disciplines as well. The structure of a motor in an automobile, that is, the number of cylinders and their arrangement, are related to a variety of performance and output measures, such as R.P.M.'s or gas mileage. While this seems almost trivial because of its simplicity, it has much significance for the understanding of society.

It is insightful to view social collectives as constructed like a motor, at least for the purposes of codifying structural-functional analysis. The crucial question of this mode of thinking is, if we arrange society in a particular way, what performances, whether functions or dysfunctions, are obtained? Is centralization functional for efficiency? Is stratification dysfunctional for membership participation? Is integration functional for effectiveness? Furthermore, these questions can be viewed as causative in nature and are not teleological, as some have argued (Davis, 1959, p. 767; Dore, 1961). The logic of structural-functional analysis is simple, albeit the answer to these questions may not be as easily obtained.

If one wants to include process variables, then the number of theoretical inquiries is considerably broadened. Is conflict functional for the amount of institutional change? Does a higher deviance rate mean a lower rate of attrition? Is coercion dysfunctional for membership participation, that is, does it decrease it? The method of thinking becomes simple once one can define the elements of variables that are typically involved or implied.

We can now define some additional kinds of intellectual analyses. This is done in Table 8.1. Once the elements of general variables are made clear, it becomes obvious that each can represent a separate analytical approach. This is not to say that they represent a tradition within structural-functionalism. Some have been more popular than others. Structuralism relates variables like complexity and centralization or stratification, process analysis relates variables like communication and conflict or deviance, functionalism relates variables, such as institutional change and efficiency or membership participation. A number of examples have been given in Part One. Once said, it should be easy for others to perform any or all these kinds of thinking.

Have we adequately handled all of the criticisms? An examination

Table 8.1 Varieties of Structural-Functional Analyses

Analysis	Definition
Structural-functional	The interrelation of structural variables with performance or output variables.
Functional	The interrelation of performance and output variables.
Structural	The interrelation of structural variables.
Processural-functional	The interrelation of internal process variables with performance or output variables.
Structural-processural	The interrelation of structural variables with internal process variables.
Processural	The interrelation of internal process variables.

of our definition in terms of variables, general ones, suggests that we have. There is no conflict between a structural-functional form of thinking and an evolutionary one if the variables are general ones. The theoretical statement, borrowed from Durkheim, that increasing complexity leads to increasing adaptiveness, is both a structural-functional one and an evolutionary one. It describes what may be the important sociological process in societies, the increasing division of labor or what more recently has been called the process of structural differentiation. This is not to say that all theoretical statements in structural-functionalism are evolutionary ones. Because structural-functionalism does not include all elements of variables, there are evolutionary statements that are not structural-functional ones. For example, the hypothesis that increasing investment leads to increasing stratification, borrowed from Marx, is an evolutionary statement but not a structural-functional one as we have defined it.

As we have noted, the use of general variables and mathematical connections obviates the usual criticisms about historical specificity and the lack of laws of a general nature that have been made by Hempel (1959) and others. Each general variable is a change variable and a statement of X = Y is a change hypothesis. Unfortunately, many have assumed that the deficiencies lie in the analytical approach of structural-functionalism. The real problem has been the lack of general variables and mathematical statements and not in a deficiency of structural-functionalism. We must make a distinction between what people do with an orientation and what can be done with it.

Does this mean that all the specific studies of various cultures and societies are now invalid? The answer would seem to be no, and for several reasons. First, these separate studies provide clues as to additional general structural and functional variables that one might want to consider. Second, any specific institutional pattern can be interpreted, at least partially, by general structural and functional variables. For example, the charismatic, traditional, and rational-legal patterns of authority discussed by Weber (1947, pp. 324–406) can be compared for the degree of centralization involved and then the resulting social performances can be analyzed. In this way, it becomes possible to define precisely the idea of structural equivalents and alternatives (Merton, 1957, p. 57). If each of these has the same degree of centralization, then we can say that they are structural equivalents, at least for this variable. If they have the same scores on particular performances, we can say that they are functional equivalents, at least for the social performances that are measured.

Similarly, we might compare the same institutional pattern, the usual focus of a structural-functional analysis, in two different societies and discover that while the name is the same, they may differ in terms of some general structural variables. This is exactly what Elkins (1968) suggests in his comparison of the institutional pattern of slavery in the United States and in societies of Latin America; he contends that in the United States there was a greater degree of coercive control. Elkins suggests that the coercive control of the concentration camp in Germany was the same as it was for the Negro slave in the United States, and that, correspondingly, the psychological consequences were the same. The *logic of the analysis* is to compare institutional patterns with the same and different names and then to note differences or similarities in terms of certain general structural, process, and/or functional variables.

Another example of how a variety of institutional patterns can be contrasted and compared in terms of a particular structural or functional variable is Stinchcombe's (1961) provocative analysis comparing several agricultural institutional patterns along several dimensions: differences in legal privileges and in style of life. He suggests that the manorial and plantation systems are most alike in terms of these variables. In addition, he notes that the family size tendency was most likely to lead to high class conflict unlike any of the other institutional patterns of agriculture. The importance of this analysis is that specific historical and cultural patterns can be contrasted and compared. The key is to have general structural and functional variables. These variables allow us to handle the specific patterns that heretofore have been the main focus of structural-functionalism.

This approach will allow us to answer several of Merton's queries in his paradigm. General structural and functional variables locate similarities and differences in any number of specific institutional patterns.

Thus, we can validate hypotheses in a wide variety of societies or other kinds of sociological collectives. The pattern is always named and can thus be easily located. The task is then to translate or interpret the specific pattern into one or more general process variables using the techniques of Chapter 1. This procedure allows the sociologist to systematically generalize historical studies, a great advantage.

However, the definition of the variable domains, while perhaps the hardest or most difficult aspect in the specification of a theoretical orientation, is not the only component in an intellectual tradition. Frequently, there are hidden assumptions or premises that are also part of an approach. This is especially true of structural-functional analysis. Merton (1957, Ch. 1) has discussed three of the hidden assumptions inherent in the work of the British social anthropologists, who did much to advance this mode of thinking. But there still remain some implicit kinds of assumptions.

The most common assumption is that there is some need. An example of this has been given in Table 6.2, where integration is used as an illustration. This need may be met by one or more mechanisms, as Merton has noted. Thus the first two kinds of premises are implicitly involved in most analyses of structural-functionalism. What is frequently missing is the stipulation of when one or an alternative mechanism occurs, the action premise. Communication and coercion may both be mechanisms of integration or control, but when is one or the other used? Once this is discovered, then the other premises become more compelling. A number of testable consequences can then follow, and we have the beginning of an interesting theory. Without the third kind of premise, structural-functionalism remains an orientation and not a theory.

Value Analysis as a Theoretical Orientation

Many readers might prefer to lump together value analysis with structural-functionalism since some men, such as Parsons have been associated with both traditions. But value analysis is a fundamentally different way of thinking. Simply put, structural-functionalism puts the emphasis on certain classes of collective behavior. Values are as we have seen in Chapter 5, a kind of collective attitude. This difference is basic and goes to the heart of the question of what are major causes of events, and in particular, what is the relationship between structure and values. Value analysis, although criticized and discussed less, is employed more frequently. For example, in the analysis of development we usually find some form of values being employed (see Hagen, 1962; McClelland,

1961; Lipset, 1967, Ch. 1, 2). Some societies have rapid development because their citizens have achieving needs or value hard work or prefer to save money, and some societies have slow development because they have traditional values. Or, in the area of organizations, we find Crozier believing that the reason why French bureaucracies are different from others is because the French have different values. A typical example of the use of values as an organizing device is found in March's *Handbook of Organizations* (1965); schools, prisons, hospitals, armies, businesses, etc. are seen as different kinds of organizations because they presumably have different values, that is, goals. Parsons' (1951) analysis of the pattern variables is another example of this method of thinking.

If there is something that does come close to being a paradigm, in the sense of being widely accepted, implicit if not explicit, it is value analysis. It has intuitive appeal to large numbers of sociologists. It makes sense to say that the reason people are different is because they have different values. One frequently hears that the remedy for social change is one of changing values. Despite its widespread appeal, it is more difficult to think with this method of analysis than it appears. The problems of how to measure collective attitudes and how to define values are complex and not easily solved. Furthermore, there are some inherent difficulties in using collective values as a causative variable which need to be explicated if not resolved.

The Definition of Collective Values. Specifying collective values as a theoretical orientation is difficult for two reasons. The term value is hardly unambiguous. The term collective seems simple but the distinction between the individual and the collective is confusing. Since values operate on both levels, Parsons (1951) was attracted by the concept. He advocated values as an explanatory concept that united the various social sciences and as the organizing principle of action, whether economic, political, social, or psychological. While this is true, it is also misleading. Collective values can exist quite independently of individual values, and the average of all the individual values is neither a necessary nor a desirable measure for values on the collective level.

The separation of analytical levels has even more meaning (and perhaps fewer measurement difficulties) when we speak about collective values that have no counterpart on the individual level. The values implied in the discussions in the Vietnam war are an excellent illustration. War is a collective act; individuals cannot wage war. Similarly, it is hard to imagine societies making love! Individuals can kill, but murder and war exist on clearly different levels and in different disciplines. This is why we have distinct words for them. It is this difference that goes to the heart of the matter of defining what is the individual and the collective.

This is not to say that all collective values have no counterpart on the individual level. In fact, probably most of those that might interest us have parallels in the collective. But it would be wrong to assume that the best way of describing the values of the collective is by some averaging procedure for the values of its members.

A simple illustration is an attempt to measure collective values in the Catholic Church. The Pope has issued an encyclical on birth control that certainly does not represent majority opinion among members of the church at least within the United States. This, of course, raises a host of measurement problems about when is something a value of the collective. If most of its members disagree, can we speak of a collective value? Hopefully, this example points to the need for considering different levels as well as the role of leadership and of elites in determining what are the collective values. While this might represent an extreme case, it illustrates the problems of finding theoretical and operational definitions. The critical point is that, as sociologists, we should be interested in the problem of collective values and wary of attempts to measure them by public opinion polls.

What is a value? As Dewey has noted, it can be either a means or an end. In practice, we tend to think of values as preferred ends or goals or purposes. The goals toward which the collective works represent their values or what they desire. They may not achieve it—one interesting difference between a value and an output. But as long as the collective is pointed in a particular direction, we label the road sign the collective value.

There are enormous measurement difficulties involved. Zald's work (1963) indicates how many different answers one might obtain about the goals of an organization depending upon the source of the data. He found differences between different levels of the staff and in the charter of an organization. In particular, this points to the issue of choosing between what is said to be the goal and what is actually done as the basis of the measurement. Officials of universities may say that they value education, but they promote faculty on the basis of their research publications and grants. Leaders of societies may say that they value peace and yet they send 500,000 soldiers to wage war. Members of various protest organizations may say that they are in favor of free speech and yet they prevent others from speaking. Which is the goal or value—research or education, war or peace, censorship or free speech? And who speaks for the collective—officials and informal leaders, rank and file, or constitutions and manuals?

Some of these measurement problems can be solved if we go back to our theoretical definition and rephrase it. We are concerned with the actual values and not those necessarily stated as the objectives in some document. This would appear to raise enormous difficulties about how to measure the "real" value. This can be partially solved if we recognize that values are implicit choices among a limited number of objectives. The values of the collective can be determined by measuring which choices are selected from a list of a limited number of general alternatives. In so far as these are consistent over time, then we can speak of value orientations.

Ideally, we would always want a typology of general choices which is mutually exclusive and exhaustive. Then the basis of comparison between nations or communities or groups becomes universal. The eight outputs represent one such attempt to provide a scheme for contrasting social collectives. By observing how the decision-makers in the society allocate their resources, we have a measure of what the society as a collective values, that is, which outputs it is attempting to maximize. Since this is measured relative to all eight outputs, it is a proportion that varies from 0 to 100 percent, a ratio scale. For example, the value or choice of science and the production of knowledge is 3 percent of the G.N.P. in the United States and 1.5 percent of the G.N.P. in Great Britain. The proportion of G.N.P. allocated to education in the U.S.S.R. is 3 percent while it is 6 percent in the U.S.A. This measure is a general one, independent of space and time; it applies to different levels of development as well. The critical factor is to have a list of choices relevant to *all* societies. Presumedly, all societies must allocate some amount of their scarce resources to the production of information, sovereignty, production, rehabilitation, artistic creation, etc. They differ in how they divide the pie. It should also be noted that not only can the total wealth be employed as a measure of relative importance, but so can the proportion of the population working in the different realms, such as the number of scientists and teachers, the number of politicians and civil servants, the number of managers and workers, and so forth. The other resources discussed in Chapter 5 can also be used.

Some work on the problem of measurement has been done by Gendell and Zetterberg (1962). They have suggested a similar way of measuring the relative importance of particular institutional values in their *Sociological Almanac*. For example, they computed the number of artists per 10,000 population and their average annual income as a measure of the value of beauty in the United States. The United States might be contrasted with France where a law requires that of each budget for public-building construction 1 percent must be spent on paintings and sculptures and where, correspondingly, there are a higher proportion of artists.

It can be easily appreciated that this procedure applies to other levels than that of society. The author (1963) measured which goals or purposes were dominant in a hospital—patient care, education, research, or maintenance—by determining which one was chosen whenever there was a manifest conflict between two or more. The other measure of the allocation of resources also helped clarify which values were dominant and at what times. This solution to the measurement problem of values obviously gives weight to those who have the most power in the collective. But this seems justifiable because it is these members who shape the policy of the collective, and thus determine its goals.

One can complicate the analysis of collective values by including the measurement of dissenting groups and opposing preferences for allocation. Once this is done, it leads naturally to the question of whether there is any consensus, or, more realistically, how much there is. It is also a handy device for approaching the problem of value conflict. Thus, we can, with this definition of value and its measurement procedures, determine not only the Pope's values but those of the priests and parishioners, and thereby document the emergence of a schism. It may be somewhat expensive, but it is quite possible with the method.

Our definition places an emphasis on the preferred goal or purpose as manifested in collective choice among a definite list of alternatives. It is also true, however, that values can mean ideals. The output may be self-maintenance of the hospital but the goal, in the sense of ideal, is quality of patient care. The maximized output of the United States would appear to be power although the expressed goal is rehabilitation or welfare. One can study these ideals by doing content analyses of speeches and documents. Although they are easily measured, there is the danger of accepting collective myths. One has only to think about the Russian and American arguments over which country is the true democracy and which values freedom to realize that ideas are tossed around with reckless abandon, and not always necessarily with duplicity or cynicism. Everyone values peace and prosperity as ideals, but they are not the outputs that are being maximized in either society. All nations are surrounded by others but only some respond with large military budgets.

Implied in this attack on the problem of value analysis is that collectives are making the choices. The elites allocate 20 percent of the budget in one year to the investment in the economy with the hope that industrial production will increase some 5 percent. It may not be achieved, but it is the objective. Also implied in this definition of collective values is that societies are limited in their range of choice. The economic institutional realm probably always will receive at least 10 percent of G.N.P. as investment in capital formation and never more than 30 percent. Within this range of about 20 percent, societies differ from each other and oscillate over time.

It is even more difficult to specify ways of discussing values about means without using historically specific content labels such as capitalism, socialism, democracy, dictatorship, or without using the same general variables, such as centralization, complexity, or stratification. If one wants to include values as means, one is forced to take one of these two approaches, that is to say, there is a value for democracy or for decentralization. Any of the variables in the example of Chapter 5 can be translated into this reasoning but there seems to be little advantage in this procedure.

The Thinking of Value Analysis. Implied in value analysis is a kind of thinking that can be self-defeating. One tends to use value analysis as a form of explanation that explains everything and yet nothing. This helps account for its broad appeal. Thus, one says prisons are different or the same as mental hospitals because they have different or the same goals; much of the work on treatment versus custodial goals has been of this nature. A few minutes reflection about it makes it apparent that we have not explained much, or at least the explanation is not very general and therefore interesting. The more extreme form of this is the explanation of X behavior because of X values.

It seems better to focus on two major problems in the orientation. The first is the basic issue of the interrelationship between structure and values, the second is the general assumption that collective values remain relatively constant, which raises the issue of how they do change. The classic example is Weber's *Protestant Ethic and the Spirit of Capitalism* (1930), where he suggests that the rise of industrialization was facilitated by the development of a new set of collective religious values (Weber, by the way, clearly distinguishes between the individual and the collective in this regard) which gave rise to a new set of economic values. In contrast, we find Engels suggesting that Calvinism, the religion that perhaps best exemplified Weber's Protestant Ethic, emerged because a new set of values was needed to justify the emergence of the increasing stratification associated with the rise of the bourgeoisie and to help control those individuals who did not share in the new wealth being created and distributed. Who is right? Where does change begin?

Many sociologists prefer to believe that values affect structure and structure affects values. But I wonder if this middle of the road point of view is the best way of thinking about the problem. If one accepts the above definition of collective value analysis as correct, then it may very well be that value analysis and structural-functional analysis are asking different questions that require different solutions. The causes of a higher degree of complexity in the United States and the cause of a high value on science might be associated, but this does not appear to be at all certain. It might be better to think of two different levels of analysis, collective behavior and collective attitudes. If so, then the answers to causes or the search for consequences might best be made on the same level of analysis without moving to another level. The causes of a value of science might and probably do lie in other collective attitudes, which is the basic insight of Weber, while the causes of a higher complexity might and probably do lie in other collective behaviors. This is not to say that there might not be implications for one or the other level. This remains a major intellectual problem. I am suggesting that values, as they have been defined here, and the structural-functional variables, are attacking separate if related issues. Structure might determine how fast growth occurs but values determine where growth is taking place. For example, high centralization leads to high rates of growth but one society may be maximizing sovereignty or the production of power and another society may be maximizing wealth or the production of rewards.

There are potentially many ways in which the collective values and structural-functional variables could articulate. The conflict over priorities in society, whether there should be more knowledge or more artistic creation, is different from the degree of conflict as an internal process variable, albeit the former may be the content of the latter. The same level of consensus can exist in two societies but their general values can be different. Of course, longitudinal research, which has tended to be rare in sociology except for several case studies, will help to determine the time ordering of changes in structure, values, and their various consequences. In the interim, there may be much gained by keeping the two levels of analysis distinct and not assume that one determines the other or even—the seemingly safe position—that there is an interrelationship between them. If we search for different problems for each analytical approach, we may find them.

Paradoxically, by not too quickly accepting the idea that structure determines values and vice versa, we may more quickly find out how the two are associated. It is for this reason that I advocate keeping the two as distinct theoretical orientations; it encourages the dialectical thinking that eventually might lead to a more satisfying synthesis than the ones that presently exist.

One of the more interesting working assumptions in value analysis is that collective values remain relatively constant across time. There does seem to be some empirical evidence to support this. Education proportionately has been favored in the United States relatively speaking for several centuries. Similarly, the U.S.S.R. was emphasizing rapid development with centralized planning some twenty years before the revolution of 1917. Japan has been fairly consistent in its societal priorities over the past century. One interesting question is why there should be this consistency over time. Socialization is an obvious answer but perhaps one that comes too quickly to the mind. Again, searching for other kinds of answers might be to the advantage of the discipline.

A more fundamental problem is what causes a change. One possible answer is the emergence of a countervailing subculture with a charismatic leader, the intellectual strategy that Weber used. But then, how does the subculture get started? Perhaps the answer lies in the development of crises and the breakdown of normal regulative processes. If so, we need to turn to another analytical orientation, system analysis.

System Analysis as a Theoretical Orientation

Ever since the publication of Parsons' *The Social System* (1951), the word system has become popular in sociology. Indeed, frequently the words system and society are used interchangeably. Although Parsons advocated that the pattern variables, or basic role values, be a major analytical approach, the term system has remained (Friedrichs, 1970) even if the pattern variables are largely forgotten. Recently, a textbook in organizational analysis (Katz and Kahn, 1967) appeared with a variety of different implicit meanings for system analysis, but the authors never explain how to do a system analysis. Buckley (1967) has published a book advocating system analysis as a replacement for structural-functionalism, but unfortunately he does not really provide much of a definition except to suggest that system analysis is superior because it includes the idea of information feedback, and more particularly, adaptiveness. More and more frequently, one sees references to systems analysis and discussions of it. It would seem to represent a wave of the analytical future.

The Conceptions of System Analysis. The popularity of the word system has resulted in its being attached to a number of things. First, some individuals consider system analysis to be a number of mathematical tools, such as matrix algebra, calculus, or set theory. These tools are helpful in solving equations, but they should not be confused with a theoretical orientation as we have defined it, even if they are compatible with it, which they are. Second, some people conceive system analysis as a set of logical categories that are then used to analyze a particular problem. But this definition, which is perhaps the most popular one, is too general; every theoretical orientation is a system analysis. Presumably, there is something distinctive about system analysis that separates it from other ways of thinking. Third, some individuals think that system analysis involves the study of any kind of social collective, for example, societal analysis is system analysis because society is a system. While society is indeed a system, the identity must be demonstrated because the heart of our task is to define what a social system really means. We may in fact be examining one and yet not be doing a system analysis. This error is frequently made.

Just as there is a certain amount of overlap between structural-functionalism and value analysis, there is some overlap between system analysis and structural-functionalism. They tend to include some of the same elements or variables. Yet, the different accents are critical. System analysis is more concerned with input, through-put, and output than it is with structure and performance per se. The addition of input is clearly a different element of variables than what one normally finds in structural-functional analysis. The accent on through-put is an emphasis on a production process, an idea perhaps buried in institutional analysis. More importantly, system analysis adds the idea of feedback and the concept of regulatory processes. Feedback is more than just two directional causality because it involves the idea of an information signal. Regulation, while seemingly akin to the problem of control or integration, is still different.

Perhaps the most popular conception of system analysis is McNamara's cost-effectiveness techniques. This approach is basically quite simple. Several methods, choices, or products are evaluated on the basis of at least two criteria of performance, and as one might guess from the name, usually their relative cost and effectiveness. The latter, in particular, can be understood to include many different kinds of measures, not just one, while cost is measured not only in terms of money but men, machines, space, and time. What is being evaluated may be any kind of thing, as we have already noted. It does not even need to be a variable, because the point of the analysis is not to discover basic hypotheses, but to make choices among alternatives. While this form of analysis is called system analysis, it is more akin to value analysis. For example, we might evaluate a new education program for its costs and its effectiveness. These represent the objectives or goals of the researchers; the values of the collective as well. Indeed, in education and in sociology there is a special branch of research called evaluative research which is exactly like this and like the McNamara method. While it is an offshoot of system analysis, it lacks a number of the key concepts, such as feedback or regulation, or production processes.

The Definition of System Analysis. The definition of system analysis is a set of variables that articulate together in such a way that via feedback of information the set of variables changes such that either one or more variables is maintained within narrow limits, a homeostatic process, or the entire set of variables moves to a new set of scores, a moving equilibrium process. Both kinds of processes are regulatory and represent responses to changes of either an internal or external nature that cause disturbances. The moving equilibrium process can be further divided into adjustment and adaptiveness. The homeostatic process is the more familiar control process.

An illustration of these ideas is in order. First, we need to define a production process. Taking societies as a simple example, we can suggest that there are eight production processes or through-puts for each of the eight outputs. Thus, societies produce information, independence, rehabilitation, just as much as they produce industrial goods. This is quite distinct from the concept of feedback. There is a difference between production processes, that is, a value-added process, and feedback processes, that is, where information about what is occurring in some variable is relayed back resulting in a change in another variable. Naturally, production processes can also be feedback processes—one of the complications of any discussion—but the analytical distinction between building a car and monitoring whether or not the car is being built properly is critical. The former is the production process, and the latter is a control feedback process. This distinction, while quite simple, can be confused.

A process parallel to the production one is the conversion process. This is defined as the transformation of outputs into inputs. Societies take what they produce at the end of the year and then allocate it to particular resources, which gradually accumulate. Simply put, men graduate with degrees and then find jobs in different sectors of society. Industrial production in the form of machines is bought by schools, governmental agencies, and hospitals, as well as business concerns. The decisions are truly societal because they are made by a large number of people frequently acting in concert, such as in organizations or groups, that is, as smaller social collectives within the larger society. Just as production does not involve information feedback as such, neither does the conversion process.

Essential in a feedback process are two kinds of variables that are connected by information. We might call these variables action variables and signal variables. The former alters as a consequence of the message from the latter. Thus, an increase in the variable of conflict is a "message" to the action variable, coercion resulting in an increase in this variable, which generally, but not always, results in a reduction of conflict. This is an example of a regulatory process, and conflict is the homeostatic variable or signal. This means that some attempts are made to keep it within certain limits. Protest marches are allowed but not sniper bullets. Signal variables are monitored and action variables change as a consequence of this monitoring. The difficult task is to determine which variables are action and which are signals in a system. This must be done if we are indeed to argue that we have a system as defined above. This then becomes the first analytical task in specifying system analysis.

Kinds of Feedback Processes. To make system analysis particularly useful we need to define the three kinds of general regulatory processes, indicating their action and signal variables. For the control process, the action variables would appear to be the communication rate and the control rate, while the messages or signal variables that trigger action are conflict and deviance. Thus, conflict increases and the societal response is either heightened communication, as in arbitration during a labor strike, or heightened coercion, as in the calling of the National Guard or police. Durkheim (1938) noted long ago that when crime rates got too high, society tended to increase punishment (coercion). A simple illustration in the United States was the increase in punishment for kidnapping after the famous Lindberg case.

The essential components of the control process is that there are several variables that normally are kept within particular ranges; these can also be called homeostatic variables. For society, these two key variables are the conflict rate and the deviance rate. Some conflict and deviance is desirable, but when the rate gets too high, it is met by an attempt to reduce its occurrence. What is being suggested here is that the typical societal reply is either *communication* or *coercion*. These are not new ideas and have been suggested by others. For societies Parsons (1951) has called this self-control and negative sanctions. March and Simon (1958) have noted the mechanisms of feedback and programming in organizations.

This is not the only way in which conflict or deviance rates can be lowered; the society could change its distribution of rewards or rights or powers, but this is qualitatively a different kind of response, namely, adaptive, which is discussed below. Similarly, this does not mean that control is necessarily effective. This is one difference between social systems and mechanical systems; the control feedback is usually not as quick or effective as it is with a thermostat, the favorite example in discussions of cybernetics.

Perhaps it is this that causes the greatest controversy about the applicability of general systems theory to societal analysis. Some readers find it hard to conceive of homeostatic variables, yet most would agree that conflict and deviance are usually kept within bounds. Even more readers find it difficult to conceive of control feedback when they think of mass revolutions (1776, 1789, or 1917), where control was clearly unsuccessful. We tend to lose sight of the fact that these are the exceptions and not the rule. Furthermore, if we recognize that a society or its elite *attempts* to exert control, then perhaps there would be less argument about the appropriateness of the regulation or feedback model. It is a separate and intriguing theoretical problem as to why control is sometimes effective and sometimes not.

The *adjustment* feedback process relates the outputs back to the inputs. In this instance, the outputs are signal variables, and the inputs are action variables. Unusual changes, whether up or down, in outputs will result in changes in the input variables. Just as society monitors its conflict and deviance, it also watches its production of the eight outputs, some more closely than others. If society does not have enough industrial production, it alters its resource allocation, that is, more investment for industrial production, or perhaps more correctly, the government makes it easier to invest by deficit spending, lower interest rates, and other attempts to manipulate economic investment. This is perhaps easier to see in a planned economy, such as the U.S.S.R., but a reading of Nixon's budget message makes this point quite clear. Our current societal concern over the rapid increase in population is another illustration of adjustment feedback. This should not be confused with the conversion of outputs into inputs. *Adjustment is a change in the conversion process* or, if you will, societal values. All other things being equal, we would expect societies to allocate their outputs somewhat consistently, as we have suggested above but they can and do alter this distribution of outputs to inputs. This then becomes a change in collective values. System analysis thus provides an analytical way of proceeding with the problem of value change.

The dramatic examples of adjustment occur during wartime and depressions. In wartime, the society spends many lives and much more money to maintain or increase independence. In depressions, attempts are made to allocate more to welfare. Likewise, in time of crisis, the first remedy proposed will frequently be a reallocation of inputs. It is important to recognize that what triggers the crisis is usually too much or too little of some output. This is why it is called a feedback process of information. Perhaps the most interesting example of this process in the United States is the present discussion about the amount of money being spent on the war in Vietnam as opposed to the war on poverty, and particularly the problems of the blacks in our ghettos. This argument over priorities in the allocation of scarce resources reflects how societies do adjust. It also indicates how slow this process can be. Although it might appear to be strange to see it as a feedback process, this is what is occurring.

Another illustration of the adjustment process is the changing collective priorities in France. In the middle fifties, 1 percent of France's total revenue was spent on science and education. By the early sixties, this had grown to 2.5 percent, and in the midsixties, it had reached 4.5 percent. Note that we are discussing increases in proportions and not increases in amount, which obviously are much larger. During the same period of time, the proportion spent on the military declined from about 10 percent to less than 7 percent, with some fluctuation for the Algerian crisis. These represent changing values and an attempt upon the part of France's elite to adjust to new internal and external demands. This reflects, in part, a concern with the technological gap—that is, a lower production of information or, more specifically, scientific production. Thus research budgets have grown enormously, accounting for much of the increase in science and education.

The reader should not jump to the conclusion that the elites or members of society see society as though it were a machine with a rational design. Quite the contrary! The adjustments made are frequently not the right ones and are therefore unsuccessful. What is involved, however, is an attempt to regulate the eight outputs. This is done by altering the mixture of inputs.

Again, we are left with the theoretical problem: how much change is required in an output before it is defined as too much or too little— that is, at what point does it become a crisis. Although as yet there are no clear answers, at least the theoretical orientation of system analysis helps us to perceive this problem.

The most difficult feedback process to define is the *adaptive* process. There are as many usages of the term adaptiveness as there are writers about system analysis. Yet there does seem to be one central theme running through much of the literature: the idea that there are fundamental changes in the system of variables itself, the concept of moving equilibrium. Here, the signal variables are the performances, such as institutional change, growth, efficiency, or participation, while the action variables are in the structural domain—centralization, complexity, stratification, and normative equality. Thus, an increase in *conflict* might be reduced by a decrease in stratification, as, for example, the settlement of the May 1968 strike in France. In this instance, coercion was tried and it failed. Only generous wage settlements ended the crisis. This is quite different from regulation of conflict and deviance, the control process as defined above. For this reason, adaptiveness and control need to be separated, even though their consequences might be the same.

Suppose an increased growth, especially in the G.N.P. or national revenue, occurs as a result of increased centralization during wartime, as happened in the United States during the Second World War. Along with this change were a number of other changes in the entire system of variables, again indicating why adaptiveness is different from either the adjustment or the control processes. It is called a feedback process because the performance variable's level or score is inadequate for either the new internal or external conditions. In the example above, war is an environmental condition that requires a society to change its social structure so that it can maximize growth and efficiency.

The three processes are diagrammed in Figure 8.1. What is important is to observe that each feedback process relates different action and signal variables. Control feedback is covered by just the four variables in the integration processes column of Table 5.4. Adjustment relates inputs and outputs together. Adaptiveness relates structures and performances together. Thus, which is a signal and which is an action variable is specified. In the future, we may discover that it is not quite this simple. But here these processes and their suggested definitions provide a model of thinking and that is what is important.

Each of the three information feedback processes can be ranked on the basis of how fundamental is the social change implied in the process. Control is the smallest social change and of the shortest duration. Once the strike is over in the post office, the National Guard is sent back home. Integration variables such as conflict or coercion alter in just a few months

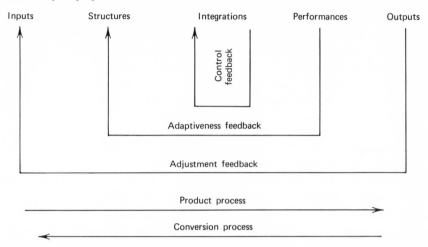

Figure 8.1   The Three Major Regulation Processes in System Analysis: Control, Adjustment, and Adaptiveness.

or even days, as riot reports demonstrate. Adjustment suggests a more permanent alteration in the allocation of resources to various inputs and thus a more permanent alteration in the priorities among the eight production processes that constitute society. In part, this is because the lead-lag time is much greater. To produce more doctors one must build more medical schools and teaching hospitals, offer higher salaries, lower educational requirements, and then wait some six to eight years. Increasing production in any output usually means more men, money, and mental qualifications—a change in a number of inputs. But this requires more time. Thus there is a slower response to signals of the more fundamental output problems, and the response represents a change in collective values.

Adaptive feedback is the most fundamental social change; a change of the entire variable system and not a change within the system (Parsons, 1951, Ch. 12). Alterations in any of the structural and performance variables imply alterations in most of the others as well. Increasing complexity of structural differentiation, the most frequently discussed adaptation, is likely as a consequence of increased institutional change. Increased structural differentiation probably changes and affects communication rates (Hage, Marrett, and Aiken, 1971), and thus the system of control. Increases in structural differentiation are usually nonreversible and permanent. Societies do not normally become less complex, but move more or less continuously towards a more complex division of labor. Similarly, changes in the distribution of power are infrequent and likely to have long-term consequences. Once a group has obtained some power, it is unlikely to give it up.

As we have noted several times, there is no assumption that the particular information signal results in an effective response, that is, that the appropriate variables are altered as a consequence. One might imagine that riots (an increase in deviance), are first controlled by more police (an increase in coercion), and only later by a redistribution of power. The first is a control response, and the second an adaptive one. (For a suggestion of this in organizations, see Cangelosi and Dill, 1965.) The first response might be ineffective because it does not deal with the causes. Societies are not seen as rational systems, but as systems in which there is continual trial and error. The key point is that this is a way of saying that feedback occurs. But as long as there are responses, it is not necessary to argue that they are effective in order to fruitfully apply concepts from general systems theory.

The Thinking of System Analysis. As is inherent in the definition, the core of system analysis is the idea of the maintenance of an equilibrium. In practice, it might be quite difficult to demonstrate that an equilibrium exists. This is a complex concept. There are states of the system, defined by scores on the general variables composing the system, which represent points of equilibrium. A moving equilibrium is nothing more than a change from one of these points to another.

The classic example is to be found in Durkheim (1933) and in Marx and Engels (1959). If we take *The Division of Labor* as an illustration, we find two stable states are defined—a mechanical one and an organic one (see Table 8.2). The evolution from one state to the other is a moving equilibrium. Indeed, one would usually assume that evolutionary processes are also moving-equilibrium processes. The major point to remember is that the same variables are used to define each of the different points of equilibrium; only the scores are different.

In addition to states of equilibrium, there are states of dissequilibrium. These are defined as other combinations of scores, the exceptions to our hypotheses. Suppose we believe that the higher the complexity, the lower the centralization. Then, one stable state is low complexity and high centralization and another stable state is high complexity and low centralization; we might call the former an organic or industrial society and the latter a mechanical or agricultural society. Considering the extreme scores and recognizing that medium scores on both variables

Table 8.2   States   of   Equilibrium   and   Disequilibrium

Structure	Integration
Mechanical Control	
High complexity	Low communication
High centralization	High coercion
High stratification	Some conflict
Low normative equality	Some deviance
Organic control	
High complexity	High communication
Low centralization	Low coercion
Low stratification	High concensus
High normative equality	High conformity
Overcontrol[a]	
Low complexity	High communication
High centralization	High coercion
High stratification	No conflict
Low normative equality	No deviance
Undercontrol[a]	
High complexity	Low communication
Low centralization	Low coercion
Low stratification	High conflict
High normative equality	High deviance

[a] In practice, one would imagine the relationship of the scores on complexity and centralization to be different in both the cases of overcontrol and undercontrol.

are another stable state, we arrive at the following two combinations, which should be unstable if our theoretical statement is approximately correct. One is the combination of high complexity with high centralization. This may be revolution, an interesting kind of disequilibrium where control processes are, by definition, not working! Another is the combination of low complexity and low centralization. These may represent presocietal and therefore unstable social structures. One can find empirical descriptions of this phenomenon in Gluckman (1965).

System analysis allows us to better appreciate not only the meaning of stability but perhaps of instability as well. The idea of moving equilibrium updates evolutionary analysis considerably.

Some of the problems with this mode of thinking are perhaps inherent in what has already been said. When does the message from the signal variable get through and when does it not? Why do some societies respond quicker to crises than others? Can we predict which kind of regulatory process will be used?

The fact that system analysis, regardless of the discipline, contains the same concepts of control, does not mean that societies work like machines. There is a fundamental difference between a machine (mechanistic model), a body (organic model), and a group (purposive model). Perhaps the most obvious differences are mankind's self-awareness and the development of cultural products. Again, there is no inherent epistemological assumption implied here just because system analysis can be employed in the physical sciences. The content of the variables is different and so are the philosophical assumptions. This confusion results from not clearly separating theoretical orientations from mathematical and philosophical models. The one does not necessarily imply the others although they are frequently found together.

SUMMARY

Starting with the definition of a theoretical orientation as one or more elements of general variables combined with several key theoretical concepts, we have attempted to specify three major theoretical orientations in sociology. Structural-functionalism is defined as the study of the interrelationships of structural variables with performance and output variables; collective value analysis is the interrelationships of desired outcomes among a predetermined list of possibilities; and system analysis is the study of a set of variables which operates with regulatory processes by way of information feedback.

Although structural-functionalism, and even more, system analysis, are used in other disciplines, it does not mean that we have borrowed either mechanical or biological models of social reality. One can borrow theoretical concepts without necessarily adopting a particular image of social phenomena.

We have consistently used examples building upon the terms and premises used in Chapters 5 and 6. One could use other variables just as well. With some modifications, these ideas can be translated into words more appropriate for other kinds of social collectives than societies, our main focal point. The main advantage of building upon Chapter 5, other than consistency, is that we have used variables that have measures.

Structural-functionalism requires the definition of survival, collective value analysis requires the definition of who speaks for the collective, and system analysis requires the definition of the different action and signal variables involved in the processes of control, adjustment, and adaptiveness. We have attempted to suggest some simple solutions to these very complex problems only for the sake of discussion and development of these orientations. As is explicit in this entire book, it is better to take a stand, even if it be a simple one so that it can be corrected in the light of criticism and communication with others who have a genuine interest in the problem. And thus our attempt in this chapter was to build some theoretical orientations to the point where they might become paradigms and theories.

Bibliography

Adler, Franz (1947), "Operational Definitions in Sociology," *American Journal of Sociology* **52** (March): 438–444.

Aiken, Michael and Jerald Hage (1966), "Organizational Alienation: A Comparative Analysis," *American Sociological Review* **31** (August): 497–507.

—— (1968), "Organizational Interdependence and Intraorganizational Structure," *American Sociological Review* **33** (December): 912–931.

—— (1971), "The Organic Model and Innovation," *Sociology* **5** (1) (January): 63–81.

Andrews, Frank (1964), "Scientific Performance as Related to Time Spent on Technical Work, Teaching or Administration," *Administrative Science Quarterly* **9** (September): 182–193.

Ashby, W. Ross (1956), *An Introduction to Cybernetics*. New York: Wiley.

Atchley, Robert C. and M. Patrick McCabe (1968), "Socialization in Correctional Communities: A Replication," *American Sociological Review* (October): 774–785.

Bales, Robert (1950), *Interaction Process Analysis*. Cambridge, Mass.: Addison-Wesley.

Barton, Allen (1955), "On the Concept of Property-Space in Social Research" in Lazarsfeld and Rosenberg (Eds.), *Language of Social Research*. Glencoe, Ill.: Free Press.

—— (1961), *Organizational Measurement and Its Bearing on the Study of College Environments*. New York: College Entrance Examination Board.

Barton, Allen and Bo Anderson (1969), "Change in an Organizational System: Formalization of a Qualitative Study" in Etzioni (2nd ed.), *A Sociological Reader on Complex Organizations*, New York: Holt, Rinehart & Winston: 540–558.

Bavelas, Alex (1948), "A Mathematical Model for Group Structures," *Applied Anthropology* (Summer): 16–30.

Berger, Joseph, Morris Zelditch, and Bo Anderson (Eds.) (1966), *Sociological Theories in Progress*. Boston: Houghton Mifflin.

Bergmann, Gustav (1957), *Philosophy of Science*. Madison: University of Wisconsin Press.

Berrien, F. Kenneth (1968), *General and Social Systems*. New Brunswick, N.J.: Rutgers University Press.

Biddle, Bruce and Edwin Thomas (Eds.) (1966), *Role Theory: Concepts and Research*. New York: Wiley.

Bierstedt, Robert (1959), "Nominal and Real Definitions in Sociological Theory," in Gross (Ed.) *Symposium on Sociological Theory*. New York: Harper & Row: 121–144.

Blalock, Hubert M., Jr. (1964), *Causal Inferences in Nonexperimental Research*. Chapel Hill: University of North Carolina Press.

—— (1968), "The Measurement Problem: A Gap Between the Languages of Theory and Research" in Blalock and Blalock (Eds.), *Methodology in Social Research*. New York: McGraw-Hill: 5–27.

—— (1969), *Theory Construction: From Verbal to Mathematical Formulations*. Englewood Cliffs, N.J.: Prentice-Hall.

—— (1971), *Causal Models in the Social Sciences*. Chicago: Aldine.

Blau, Peter M. (1964), *Exchange and Power in Social Life*. New York: Wiley.

—— (1968), "The Hierarchy of Authority in Organizations," *American Journal of Sociology* 73 (January): 453–457.

—— (1970), "A Formal Theory of Differentiation in Organizations," *American Sociological Review* 35 (April): 201–218.

Blau, Peter and Richard Schoenherr (1970), *The Structure of Organizations*. New York: Basic Books.

Blau, Peter M. and W. Richard Scott (1962), *Formal Organizations: A Comparative Approach*. San Francisco: Chandler.

Blauner, Robert (1964), *Alienation and Freedom: The Factory Worker and His Industry*. Chicago: University of Chicago Press.

Blumer, Hubert (1954), "What is Wrong with Social Theory?" *American Sociological Review* 19 (February): 3–10.

Bredemeier, Harry and Richard Stephenson (1962), *The Analysis of Social Systems*. New York: Holt, Rinehart & Winston.

Bridgman, Percy W. (1936), *The Nature of Physical Theory*. New York: Dover.

Brinton, Crane (1965), *The Anatomy of Revolution* (rev. ed.). New York: Random House.

Broom, Leonard and Philip Selznick (1963), *Sociology*, (3rd ed.). New York: Harper & Row.

Buckley, Walter (1967), *Sociology and Modern Systems Theory*. Englewood Cliffs, N.J.: Prentice-Hall.

Bunge, Mario (1967), *Scientific Research*, Vol. 1: *The Search for System*. New York: Springer-Verlag.

Burgess, Robert L. and Ronald L. Akers (1966), "A Differential Association-Reinforcement Theory of Criminal Behavior," *Social Problems* 14 (Fall): 128–147.

Burns, Tom and G. M. Stalker (1961), *The Management of Innovation*. London: Tavistock.

Cadwallader, Mervyn (1959), "The Cybernetic Analysis of Change in Social Organizations," *American Journal of Sociology* 65 (September): 154–157.

Cangelosi, Vincent and William R. Dill (1965), "Organizational Learning: Observations Towards A Theory," *Administrative Science Quarterly* 10 (September): 175–203.

Caplow, Theodore (1964), *Principles of Organization*. New York: Harcourt, Brace & World.

——— (1969), *Two Against One*, Englewood Cliffs, N.J.: Prentice-Hall.

Cassirer, Ernst (1953), *Substance and Function* (trans. by W. Swabey and M. Swabey). New York: Dover.

Cloward, Richard and Lloyd Ohlin (1960), *Delinquency and Opportunity: The Theory of Delinquent Gangs*. Glencoe, Ill.: Free Press.

Cohen, Albert K. (1955), *Delinquent Boys: The Culture of the Gang*. Glencoe, Ill.: Free Press.

Cohen, Morris R. and Ernst Nagel (1934), *An Introduction to Logic and Scientific Method*. New York: Harcourt, Brace & World.

Coleman, James S. (1964), *Introduction to Mathematical Sociology*. New York: Free Press.

Coser, Lewis (1964), *The Functions of Social Conflict*. New York: Free Press.

Costner, Herbert L. and Robert K. Leik (1971), "Deductions from 'Axiomatic Theory' " in Blalock, Jr. (Ed.), *Causal Models in the Social Sciences*. Chicago: Aldine: 49–72.

Cressey, Donald R. (1966), "The Language of Set Theory and Differential Association," *Journal of Research in Crime and Delinquency* 3 (1) (January): 22–26.

Cutright, Phillips (1963), "National Political Development: Measurement and Analysis," *American Sociological Review* 28 (April): 253–264.

——— (1965), "Political Structure, Economic Development, and National Social Security Programs," *American Journal of Sociology* 70 (March): 537–550.

Dalton, Melville (1950), "Conflicts Between Staff and Line Managerial Officers," *American Sociological Review* 15 (June): 342–351.

Davies, James C. (1969), "The J-Curve of Rising and Declining Satisfactions as a Cause of Some Great Revolutions and a Contained Rebellion," in Graham and Gurr (Eds.), *History of Violence in America: Historical and Comparative Perspectives*. New York: Bantam: 690–730.

Davis, James A. (1963), "Structural Balance, Mechanical Solidarity and Interpersonal Relations," *American Journal of Sociology* (March): 444–462; also in Berger, Zelditch, and Anderson (Eds.), *Sociological Theories in Progress*. Boston: Houghton Mifflin.

Davis, Kingsley (1959), "The Myth of Functional Analysis as a Special Method in Sociology and Anthropology," *American Sociological Review* 24 (December): 757–772.

De Fleur, Melvin L. and Richard Quinney (1966), "A Reformulation of Sutherland's Differential Association Theory and a Strategy for Empirical Verification," *Journal of Research in Crime and Delinquency* 3 (1) (January): 1–22.

Denzen, Norman K. (1969), "Symbolic Interactionism and Ethnomethodology: A Proposed Synthesis," *American Sociological Review* 34 (December): 922–933.

Deutsch, Karl (1966), *Nationalism and Social Communication*. Cambridge, Mass.: M.I.T. Press.

Dodd, Stuart (1943), "Operational Definitions Operationally Defined," *American Journal of Sociology* **48** (January): 482–489.

Dore, Ronald (1961), "Function and Cause," *American Sociological Review* **26** (December): 843–853.

Dubin, Robert (1969), *Theory Building: A Practical Guide to the Construction and Testing of Theoretical Models*. New York: Free Press.

Dumont, Richard G. and William J. Wilson (1967), "Aspects of Concept Formation, Explication, and Theory Construction in Sociology," *American Sociological Review* **32** (December): 985–995.

Duncan, Otis Dudley (1966), "Path Analysis: Sociological Examples," *American Journal of Sociology* (July): 1–16.

Durkheim, Emile (1933), *The Division of Labor in Society* (trans. by George Simpson). Glencoe, Ill.: Free Press.

—— (1938), *The Rules of Sociological Method* (trans. by S. Solovay and J. Mueller and ed. by G. Catlin). New York: Free Press.

—— (1951), *Suicide* (trans. by J. Spaulding and George Simpson). Glencoe, Ill.: Free Press.

Eckstein, Harry (1965), "The Etiology of Internal Wars," in George H. Nadel (Ed.), *Studies in the Philosophy of History*. New York: Harper & Row.

Elkins, Stanley (1968), *Slavery,* 2nd ed. Chicago: University of Chicago Press.

Empey, Le Mar T. and Steven G. Lubeck (1968), "Conformity and Deviance in the 'Situation of Company,'" *American Sociological Review* **33** (October): 760–774.

Etzioni, Amitai (1961), *A Comparative Analysis of Complex Organizations: On Power, Involvement, and Their Correlates*. New York: Free Press. (a)

—— (1961), *Complex Organizations: A Sociological Reader*. New York: Holt, Rinehart & Winston. (b)

—— (1968), *The Active Society: A Theory of Societal and Political Processes*. New York: Free Press.

Fallding, Harold (1963), "Functional Analysis in Sociology," *American Sociological Review* **28** (February): 5–13.

Flanigan, William H. and Edwin Fogelman (1968), "Patterns of Democratic Development," paper read at the National Meeting of the American Political Science Association.

Forrester, Jay W. (1969), *Urban Dynamics*. Cambridge, Mass.: M.I.T. Press.

Friedrichs, Robert W. (1970), *A Sociology of Sociology*. New York: Free Press.

Galtung, Johan (1966), "Rank and Social Integration: A Multidimensional Approach," in Berger, Zelditch, and Anderson (Eds.), *Sociological Theories in Progress*. Boston: Houghton Mifflin: 145–198.

—— (1967), *Theory and Methods of Social Research*. London: Allen and Unwin.

Gamson, William A. (1968), *Power and Discontent*. Homewood, Ill.: Dorsey Press.

Glaser, Barney and Anselm Strauss (1967), *Discovery of Grounded Theory: Strategies for Qualitative Research*. Chicago: Aldine.

Gluckman, Max (1965), *Politics, Law and Ritual in Tribal Society*. Chicago: Aldine.

Goffman, Erving (1961), *Asylums: Essays on the Social Situation of Mental Patients and Other Inmates*. Garden City, N.Y.: Doubleday.

Goode, William J. (1960), "Encroachment, Charlatanism, and the Emerging Profession: Psychology, Sociology, and Medicine," *American Sociological Review* **25** (December): 902–914.

Goss, Mary E. W. (1959), "Professionals in Bureaucracy," unpublished Ph.D. dissertation, Columbia University.

Gouldner, Alvin Ward (1954), *Patterns of Industrial Bureaucracy*. Glencoe, Ill.: Free Press.

———— (1959), "Reciprocity and Autonomy in Functional Theory," in Llewellyn Gross (Ed.), *Symposium in Sociological Theory*. New York: Harper & Row.

Graham, Hugh Davis and Ted Robert Gurr (Eds.) (1969), *History of Violence in America: Historical and Comparative Perspectives*. New York: Bantam.

Graham, James Q., Jr. and Don Karl Rowney (Eds.) (1969), *Quantitative History*. Homewood, Ill.: Dorsey Press.

Gross, Llewellyn (Ed.) (1959), *Symposium on Sociological Theory*. New York: Harper & Row.

———— (1959), "Theory Construction in Sociology; a Methodological Inquiry," in Llewellyn Gross (Ed.), *Symposium in Sociological Theory*. New York: Harper & Row: 531–563.

———— (1960), "An Epistemological View of Sociological Theory," *American Journal of Sociology* **65** (March): 441–448.

———— (1967), *Sociological Theory: Inquiries and Paradigms*. New York: Harper & Row.

Gross, Neal C., Ward S. Mason, and Alexander W. McEachern (1958), *Explorations in Role Analysis*. New York: Wiley.

Gurr, Ted Robert (1969), "A Comparative Study of Civil Strife," in Graham and Gurr (Eds.), *History of Violence in America: Historical and Comparative Perspectives*. New York: Bantam: 572–626.

Hage, Jerald (1963), "Organizational Response to Innovation," unpublished Ph.D. dissertation, Columbia University.

———— (1965), "An Axiomatic Theory of Organizations," *Administrative Science Quarterly* **10** (December): 289–319.

———— and Michael Aiken (1967), "Program Change and Organizational Properties: A Comparative Analysis," *American Journal of Sociology* **72** (March): 503–519. (a)

———— (1967), "The Relationship of Centralization to Other Structural Properties," *Administrative Science Quarterly* **12** (June): 72–92. (b)

———— (1970), *Social Change in Complex Organizations*. New York: Random House.

———— and Cora Bagley Marrett (1971), "Organization Structure and Communications," *American Sociological Review* **36** (October): 860–871.

Hage, Jerald and Gerald Marwell (1968), "Toward the Development of an Empirically Based Theory of Role Relationships," *Sociometry* **31** (June): 200–212.

Hagen, Everett C. (1962), *On The Theory of Social Change*. Homewood, Ill.: Dorsey Press.

Hall, Richard (1962), "Intraorganizational Structural Variation: Application of the Bureaucratic Model," *Administrative Science Quarterly* **7** (December): 295–308.

———— (1963), "The Concept of Bureaucracy: An Empirical Assessment," *American Journal of Sociology* **69** (July): 32–40.

—— (1968), "Professionalization and Bureaucratization," *American Sociological Review* 33 (February): 92–105.

—— (1969), *Occupations and the Social Structure.* Englewood Cliffs, N.J.: Prentice-Hall.

Hempel, Carl G. (1952), "Fundamentals of Concept Formation in Empirical Science," *International Encyclopedia of Unified Science* 2 (7). Chicago: University of Chicago Press.

—— (1959), "The Logic of Functional Analysis," in Llewellyn Gross (Ed.), *Symposium on Sociological Theory.* New York: Harper & Row: 271–310.

Hickson, D. J. (1966), "A Convergence in Organization Theory," *Administrative Science Quarterly* 11 (September): 224–237.

Homans, George C. (1950), *The Human Group.* New York: Harcourt, Brace & World.

—— (1961), *Social Behavior: Elementary Forms.* New York: Harcourt, Brace & World.

—— (1964), "Contemporary Theory in Sociology," in Robert Faris (Ed.), *Handbook of Sociology:* 951–977.

Hopkins, Terence K. (1964), *The Exercise of Influence in Small Groups.* Totowa, N.J.: Bedminster.

Johnson, Harry (1960), *Sociology: A Systematic Introduction.* New York: Harcourt, Brace & World.

Kadane, Joseph B. and Gordon H. Lewis (1969), "The Distribution of Participation in Group Discussions: An Empirical and Theoretical Reappraisal," *American Sociological Review* 34 (October): 710–723.

Katz, Daniel and Robert L. Kahn (1966), *A Social Psychology of Organizations.* New York: Wiley.

Kolko, Gabriel (1962), *Wealth and Power in America.* New York: Praeger.

Kornhauser, William (1959), *The Politics of Mass Society.* New York: Free Press.

Kuhn, Thomas (1962), *The Structure of Scientific Revolutions.* Chicago: University of Chicago Press.

Kuznets, Simon (1963), "Quantitative Aspects of the Economic Growth of Nations: VIII Distribution of Income by Size," *Economic Development and Cultural Change* 11 (January): Part II.

Landsberger, Henry A. (1961), "The Horizontal Dimension in Bureaucracy," *Administrative Science Quarterly* 6 (December): 299–332.

Lazarsfeld, Paul F. (1954), *Mathematical Thinking in the Social Sciences.* New York: Free Press.

—— (1965), "Problems in Methodology," in Broom, Merton, and Cantrell (Eds.), *Sociology Today.* New York: Harper & Row: 39–78.

Lazarsfeld, Paul F. and Herbert Menzel (1969), "On the Relation Between Individual and Collective Properties" in Amitai Etzioni (Ed.), *Reader on Complex Organizations,* 2nd ed. New York: Holt, Rinehart & Winston: 499–516.

Lazarsfeld, Paul F. and Morris Rosenberg (Eds.) (1955), *The Language of Social Research.* Glencoe, Ill.: Free Press.

Lenski, Gerhard (1954), "Status Crystallization: A Non-Vertical Dimension of Social Status," *American Sociological Review* 19 (August): 405–413.

—— (1966), *Power and Privilege.* New York: McGraw-Hill.

——— (1967), "Status Inconsistency and the Vote: A Four Nation Test," *American Sociological Review* 32 (April): 298–301.

Lerner, Daniel (1958), *The Passing of Traditional Society.* New York: Free Press.

Lipset, Seymour (1960), *Political Man.* Garden City, N.Y.: Doubleday.

Lopreato, Joseph and Letitia Alston (1970), "Ideal Types and the Idealization Strategy," *American Sociological Review* 35 (February): 88–96.

Lundberg, George, Clarence Schrag, and Otto Larsen (1963), *Sociology,* 3rd ed. New York: Harper & Row.

Lynes, Russel (1950), *The Tastemakers.* New York: Harper & Row.

MacRae, Duncan, Jr. (1969), "Growth and Decay Curves in Scientific Citations," *American Sociological Review* 34 (October): 631–635.

McCleery, Richard (1957), *Policy Change in Prison Management.* East Lansing: Government Research Bureau, Michigan State University.

McClelland, David C. (1961), *The Achieving Society.* Princeton, N.J.: Van Nostrand.

McFarland, David D. (1970), "Intragenerational Social Mobility as a Markov Process: Including a Time-Stationary Markovian Model that Explains Observed Declines in Mobility Rates," *American Sociological Review* 35 (June): 463–476.

March, James G. (1965), *Handbook of Organizations.* Chicago: Rand McNally.

March, James G. and Herbert A. Simon with Harold Guetzkow (1958), *Organizations.* New York: Wiley.

Maris, Ronald (1970), "The Logical Adequacy of Homans' Social Theory," *American Sociological Review* 35 (December): 1069–1081.

Marsh, Robert (1967), *Comparative Sociology: A Codification of Cross-Societal Analysis.* New York: Harcourt, Brace & World.

Marx, Karl (1936), *Capital: A Critique of Political Economy.* New York: Random House.

Marx, Karl and Frederick Engels (1959), "Manifesto of the Communist Party," in Lewis Feuer (Ed.), *Marx and Engels: Basic Writings on Politics and Philosophy* 1–41. Peter Smith.

Merton, Robert K. (1957), *Social Theory and Social Structure,* rev. ed. Glencoe, Ill.: Free Press.

Merton, Robert K., and Robert Nisbet (1966), *Contemporary Social Problems* 2nd ed. New York: Harcourt, Brace & World.

Miller, Daniel and Guy E. Swanson (1958), *The Changing American Parent.* New York: Wiley.

Mills, C. Wright (1959), *The Sociological Imagination.* New York: Oxford Press.

Moore, Barrington (1966), *Social Origins of Dictatorship and Democracy.* Boston: Beacon Press.

Moore, Wilbert E. (1963), *Social Change.* Englewood Cliffs, N.J.: Prentice-Hall.

Morris, Richard T. (1966), "A Typology of Norms," in Biddle and Thomas (Eds.), *Role Theory: Concepts and Research.* New York: Wiley: 110–112.

Mott, Paul E. (1965), *The Organization of Society.* Englewood Cliffs, N.J.: Prentice-Hall.

Nadel, Siegfried (1957), *The Theory of Social Structure.* Glencoe, Ill.: Free Press.

Nagel, Ernst (1961), *The Structure of Science.* New York: Harcourt, Brace & World.

Nisbet, Robert (1967), *The Sociological Tradition.* New York: Basic Books.

—— (1970), *The Social Bond: An Introduction to the Study of Society*. New York: Knopf.

Parsons, Talcott (1937), *The Structure of Social Action*. New York: McGraw-Hill.

—— (1951), *The Social System*. Glencoe, Ill.: Free Press.

—— (1960), *Structure and Process in Modern Societies*. Glencoe, Ill.: Free Press.

—— (1966), *Societies: Evolutionary and Comparative Perspectives*. Englewood Cliffs, N.J.: Prentice-Hall.

——, Robert F. Bales, and Edward A. Shils (1953), *Working Papers in the Theory of Action*. Glencoe, Ill.: Free Press.

Parsons, Talcott and Neil J. Smelser (1956), *Economy and Society: A Study in the Integration of Economic and Social Theory*. Glencoe, Ill.: Free Press.

Perrow, Charles (1961), "The Analysis of Goals in Complex Organizations," *American Sociological Review* 26 (December): 854–866.

—— (1963), "Goals and Power Structures—A Historical Case Study," in Eliot Freidson (Ed.), *The Hospital in Modern Society*. New York: Free Press: 112–146.

—— (1965), "Hospitals: Technology, Structure and Goals," in James March (Ed.), *Handbook of Organizations*. Chicago: Rand McNally: 190–971.

—— "A Framework for the Comparative Analysis of Organizations," *American Sociological Review* 32 (April): 193–208.

—— (1968), "Organizational Goals," in *International Encyclopedia of the Social Sciences*, Vol. 11. New York: Macmillan: 305–311.

Petersen, William (1969), "The Classification of Subnations in Hawaii: An Essay in the Sociology of Knowledge," *American Sociological Review* 34 (December): 863–877.

Phillips, Derek L. and Bernard F. Segal (1969), "Sexual Status and Psychiatric Symptoms," *American Sociological Review* 34 (February): 58–72.

Pondy, Louis (1967), "Organizational Conflict: Concepts and Models," *Administrative Science Quarterly* 12 (September): 296–320.

—— (1969), "Effects of Size, Complexity, and Ownership on Administrative Intensity," *Administrative Science Quarterly* 14 (March): 47–61.

Popper, Karl R. (1959), *The Logic of Scientific Discovery*. London: Hutchinson.

Price, James (1967), *Organizational Effectiveness: An Inventory of Propositions*. Homewood, Ill.: Irwin.

Pugh, Derek S., David J. Hickson, D. R. Hinings, and C. Turner (1963), "A Conceptual Scheme for Organizational Analysis," *Administrative Science Quarterly* 8 (December): 289–315.

—— (1968), "Dimensions of Organizational Structure," *Administrative Science Quarterly* 13 (June): 65–105.

—— (1969), "The Context of Organizational Structures," *Administrative Science Quarterly* 14 (March): 91–114.

Radcliffe-Brown, Alford Reginald (1935), "On the Concept of Function in Social Science," *American Anthropologist* 37 (July): 395–396.

Redfield, Robert (1941), *The Folk Culture of Yucatan*. Chicago: University of Chicago Press.

Reynolds, Paul Davidson (1971), *A Primer in Theory Construction*. Indianapolis: Bobbs-Merrill.

Rex, John (1961), *Key Problems of Sociological Theory*. London: Routledge and Kegan Paul.

Rogers, Everett (1962), *Diffusion of Innovations*. New York: Free Press.

Russett, Bruce M. (1969), "Inequality and Instability: The Relation of Land Tenure to Politics," in Rowney and Graham (Eds.), *Quantitative History*. Homewood, Ill.: Dorsey Press: 356–367.

Sawyer, Jack (1967), "Dimensions of Nations: Size, Wealth, and Politics," *American Journal of Sociology* 73 (September): 145–172.

Seashore, Stanley and Ephraim Yuchtman (1967), "Factorial Analysis of Organizational Performance," *Administrative Science Quarterly* 12 (December): 377–395.

Seeman, Melvin (1959), "On the Meaning of Alienation," *American Sociological Review* 24 (December): 783–791.

Selvin, Hanan C. and Warren O. Hagstrom (1965), "Two Dimensions of Cohesiveness in Small Groups," *Sociometry* 28 (March): 30–43.

Sewell, William H., Archibald O. Haller, and George W. Ohlendorf (1970), "The Educational and Early Occupational Status Attainment Process: Replication and Revision," *American Sociological Review* 35 (December): 1014–1027.

Sewell, William H., Archibald O. Haller, and Alejandro Portes (1969), "The Educational and Early Occupational Attainment Process," *American Sociological Review* 34 (February): 82–92.

Sheldon, Eleanor and Wilbert Moore (Eds.) (1968), *Indicators of Social Change*. New York: Russell Sage Foundation.

Simmel, Georg (1955), *Conflict and the Web of Group Affiliations* (trans. by Kurt Wolff and Reinhard Bendix). Glencoe, Ill.: Free Press.

Simon, Herbert A. (1957), *Models of Man*. New York: Wiley.

Sjoberg, Gidein (1959), "Operationalism and Social Research," in Llewellyn Gross (Ed.), Symposium in Sociological Theory. New York: Harper & Row: 603–629.

Smelser, Neil J. (1959), *Social Change in the Industrial Revolution: An Application of Theory to the Lancashire Cotton Industry*. Chicago: University of Chicago Press.

—— (1963), *Theory of Collective Behavior*. New York: Free Press.

Smith, Thomas S. (1969), "Structural Crystallization, Status Inconsistency, and Political Partisanship," *American Sociological Review* 34 (December): 907–921.

Spilerman, Seymour (1970), "The Causes of Racial Disturbances: A Comparison of Alternative Explanations," *American Sociological Review* (August): 627–649.

Starbuck, William (1965), "Organizational Growth and Development," in James March (Ed.), *Handbook of Organizations*. Chicago: Rand McNally: 451–534.

Stinchcombe, Arthur L. (1961), "Agricultural Enterprise and Rural Class Relations," *American Journal of Sociology* 72 (September): 165–176.

—— (1968), *Constructing Social Theory*. New York: Harcourt, Brace & World.

Svalastoga, Kaare (1965), *Social Differentiation*. New York: McKay.

Tannenbaum, Arnold S. (Ed.) (1968), *Control in Organizations*. New York: McGraw-Hill: Chapters 1, 2, 3.

Tanter, Raymond and Manus Midlarsky (1967), "A Theory of Revolution," *Journal of Conflict Resolution* 11 (September): 264–280.

Thomas, Edwin and Bruce Biddle (1966), "The Nature and History of Role Theory," in Biddle and Thomas (Eds.), *Role Theory: Concepts and Research*. New York: Wiley: 3–19.

Thompson, James D. (1967), *Organizations in Action*. New York: McGraw-Hill.

Thompson, Victor (1961) "Hierarchy, Specialization, and Organizational Conflict," *Administrative Science Quarterly* **5** (March): 485–521. (a)

—— (1961), *Modern Organizations*. New York: Knopf. (b)

Tilly, Charles (1969), "Collective Violence in European Perspective," in Graham and Gurr (Eds.), *History of Violence in America: Historical and Comparative Perspectives*. New York: Bantam: 4–44.

Tittle, Charles R. (1969), "Inmate Organization: Sex Differentiation and the Influence of Criminal Subcultures," *American Sociological Review* **34** (August): 492–504.

Toennies, Ferdinand (1955), *Community and Association* (trans. by Charles Loomis). London: Routledge and Kegan Paul.

Toynbee, Arnold (1946), *A Study of History*. Vol. I (abridgement by D. C. Somerwall). London: Oxford University Press.

Warren, Donald I. (1968), "Power, Visibility, and Conformity in Formal Organizations," *American Sociological Review* **33** (December): 951–970.

Weber, Max (1930), *The Protestant Ethic and the Spirit of Capitalism* (trans. by Talcott Parsons). New York: Scribner.

—— (1947), *The Theory of Social and Economic Organization* (trans. by Henderson and Parsons). Glencoe, Ill.: Free Press.

—— (1949), *On the Methodology of the Social Sciences* (trans. by Edward Shils). Glencoe, Ill.: Free Press.

—— (1963), The Sociology of Religion (trans. by Ephraine Fischoff). Boston: Beacon Press.

Wilensky, Harold (1964), "The Professionalization of Everyone?" *American Journal of Sociology* **70** (September): 137–158.

Willer, David (1967), *Scientific Sociology: Theory and Method*. Englewood Cliffs, N.J.: Prentice-Hall.

Willer, David and Murray Webster, Jr. (1970), "Theoretical Concepts and Observables," *American Sociological Review* **25** (August): 748–757.

Wilson, Everett K. (1966), *Rules, Roles, and Relationships*. Homewood, Ill.: Dorsey Press.

Wolff, Kurt H. (1950), *The Sociology of Georg Simmel*. Glencoe, Ill.: Free Press.

Woodger, Joseph Henry (1939), "The Technique of Theory Construction," *International Encyclopedia of Unified Science* **2** (5). Chicago: University of Chicago Press.

Woodward, Joan (1965), *Industrial Organization: Theory and Practice*. London: Oxford University Press.

Zald, Mayer (1963), "Comparative Analysis and Measurement of Organizational Goals: The Case of Correctional Institutions for Delinquents," *Sociological Quarterly* **4** (Summer): 206–230.

Zetterberg, Hans L. (1962), *Social Theory and Social Practice*. Totowa, N.J.: Bedminster Press.

—— (1963), *On Theory and Verification in Sociology*. Totowa, N.J.: Bedminster Press.

—— (1966), "On Motivation," in Berger, Zelditch, and Anderson (Eds.), *Sociological Theories in Progress*. Boston: Houghton Mifflin: 124–142.

Zetterberg, Hans and Murray Gendell (1963), *A Sociological Almanac*. Totowa, N.J.: Bedminster Press.

Index

Abstraction, levels of, 4, 118, 148
  and knowledge, development of, 97, 141
  methods for recognizing, 21-22, 118
  as a problem in theory, construction of,
    4, 49-50, 121, 141
  and primitive terms, 112, 118, 124, 141
  as a technique for ordering, concepts, 118-
    121, 141
    theoretical statements, 151
  and theoretical statements, 142, 144, 148
  see also Generalizing, process of
Achievement, need for, 59
Activities, 108, 112, 114
  attractiveness of, 106-107
  as a basic element, 26, 120, 125
  independence of, 112, 114
  integration of, 114
  intensity of, 114
  number of, 26
  rehabilitation, 106-107
  scope of, 114
  value of, 114
Adaptiveness, process of, causes of, 163-165
  and centralization, 53, 163-165, 166
  and complexity, 53, 165
  and coordination, 163-164
  definition of, 213-215
  and efficiency, 53
  as a feedback process, 213-215
  and formalization, 53

  as a function, 70, 131
  and institutional change, 163
  and job satisfaction, 53
  and production, 53, 163-164
  and stratification, 53
  in system analysis, 165, 207, 213-215
  see also Adjustment, process of
Adler, 174
Administrative staff, 10, 11
Adjustment, process of, 163-165, 211-213;
    see also Adaptiveness
Aiken, 70, 77, 79, 81, 83, 95-96, 122, 214
Algebraic reasoning, 35-36, 50, 159-160.
    see also Axiomatic reasoning; Geome-
    try, reasoning in; and Thinking, ways
    of
Analysis, *see* Theoretical orientations; Think-
    ing; and specific kinds of reasoning,
    such as algebraic reasoning
Analytical units, 16, 24, 25, 81
  problems in defining, 81-83
  relative emphasis on, 16
  as a system of interrelated variables, 51
  as a technique for finding, nonvariables,
    general, 30-31
    variables, general, 25, 32
  as a technique for generalizing, definitions,
    80-81
    theoretical statements, 50
Analyzability, of problems, 48; *see also*